# 10 Popular Prophecy Myths Exposed and Answered

# Other Books by Gary DeMar

*God and Government: A Bible and Historical Study*

*God and Government: Issues in Biblical Perspective*

*God and Government: The Restoration of the Republic*

*Last Days Madness: Obsession of the Modern Church*

*Ruler of the Nations*

*America's Christian History: The Untold Story*

*Surviving College Successfully: A Complete Manual for the Rigors of Academic Combat*

*The Reduction of Christianity: A Biblical Response to Dave Hunt*

*The Debate Over Christian Reconstruction*

*Christian Reconstruction: What It Is. What It Isn't*

*To Pledge Allegiance: A New World in View*

*To Pledge Allegiance: Reformation to Colonization*

*To Pledge Allegiance: On the Road to Independence*

*War of the Worldviews*

*Is Jesus Coming Soon?*

*Left Behind: Separating Fact from Fiction*

*Thinking Straight in a Crooked World: A Christian Defense Manual*

*America's Christian Heritage*

*The Christian History of America*

*The Early Church and the End of the World*

*Liberty at Risk: Exposing the Politics of Plunder*

*Whoever Controls the Schools Rules the World*

*Memory Mechanics: How to Memorize Anything*

*Why the End of the World is Not in Your Future*

*The Case for America's Christian Heritage*

*Myths, Lies, & Half-Truths*

# 10 Popular Prophecy Myths Exposed and Answered

THE LAST DAYS MIGHT NOT BE AS NEAR AS YOU THINK

## Gary DeMar

AMERICAN VISION PRESS
POWDER SPRINGS, GEORGIA

## 10 Popular Prophecy Myths Exposed and Answered
*The Last Days Might Not Be as Near as You Think*

Copyright © 2010 Gary DeMar. All rights reserved.
Printed May 2010
Reprinted July 2010

Published by The American Vision, Inc.
    *The American Vision, Inc.*
    3150 Florence Road
    Powder Springs, Georgia 30127-5385
    www.AmericanVision.org
    1-800-628-9460

Written permission must be secured from the publisher to use or reproduce any part of this book, except for brief quotations in critical reviews or articles.

Printed in the United States of America.

*Cover: Luis Lovelace*

*Layout: Michael Minkoff, Jr.*

ISBN13: 978-0-9826105-5-8

# Contents

**Preface** vii

**Introduction:** Detecting a Seismic Shift in Eschatology  1

1. The Myth of an Israel-Church Distinction  11

2. The Myth that the Modern State of Israel is a Sign that the Rapture is Near  25

3. The Myth that Only Dispensationalists Have a Redemptive Future for Israel  49

4. The Myth of the Postponed Abrahamic Covenant  65

5. The Myth of "Replacement Theology"  81

6. The Myth that Animal Sacrifices and Circumcision are Everlasting Rites  95

7. The Myth that the Temple Needs to be Rebuilt  103

8. The Myth that the Gospel Has Yet to be Preached in the "Whole World"  119

9. The Myth that Earthquakes Are Signs of the End Times  151

10. The Myth that Oil in Israel is a Prophetic Sign  161

**Appendix A:** "Church" or "Congregation"? A Choice of Deadly Consequence  167

**Appendix B:** "False Teaching about the Last Days"  173

**Index**  191

# Preface

It's time for theological weather forecasting to be given up entirely. Even TV weathermen predicting ordinary events are more accurate.

–Ben Witherington

In many cases sheer fanaticism has been the result of exclusively dwelling on prophecy, and probably more men have gone mad on that subject than on any other religious question.

–Charles H. Spurgeon

Modern-day prophecy writers who rightfully debunk the 2012 Mayan Calendar prophecy have their own calendar problems. How many of you remember a famous Christian prophecy writer who sold millions of books claiming that the calendar was about to run out for his generation? Israel had become a nation again in 1948. Within a generation—40 years from that date—we were all going to be "raptured" to heaven! As you know—at least I hope you know—it didn't happen.

Then there was the famous prophecy related to the so called Jupiter Effect. This, too, was used by a prominent Evangelical prophecy writer as "evidence" that the rapture was near. Astronomers John Gribben and Setphen Plagemann predicted the Jupiter Effect in 1974 in their book of the same name. Supposedly it was a "scientific exploration of the planets as triggers of major earthquakes." They argued that when various planets were aligned on the same side of the sun in 1982, tidal forces would create solar flares, radio interruptions, rainfall and temperature disturbances, and massive earthquakes. The planets did align, as they do regularly, but nothing unusual happened. While Gribbin wrote that he was sorry he "ever had anything to do with it," the above unnamed prophecy writer just moved on to another set of predictions.

While cleaning up my office (a never-ending task), I came across a cassette tape of a sermon a prominent West Coast Christian prophecy expert preached on December 31, 1979. He told his very accepting and excited audience that the rapture would take place in 1981. The former Soviet Republic going into Afghanistan in August of 1978 was the prelude to what he claimed would be a full-force invasion of the Middle East. It would not be long before "Russia" would invade Israel, he told his audience. All of this was said to have been "predicted" by Ezekiel 2600 years ago.

In the same year-end sermon, he went on to claim that, because of ozone depletion, Revelation 16:8 would be fulfilled during the soon-coming Great Tribulation: "And the fourth angel poured out his bowl upon the sun; and it was given to it to scorch men with fire." He argued that Halley's Comet would pass near the Earth in 1986 and would wreak atmospheric havoc for those left behind as debris from its million-mile tail pummeled the earth. Halley's Comet did appear in 1986, as it does every 70 years or so, with no damage done to our planet.

A lesser known prophecy writer was certain that the end of the world would come in 1985. The title of the book was, *I Predict 1985*. In 1986, he published a new book entitled, *I Predict 2000*. There were other books with similar millennium-ending titles: *A.D. 2000...The End?* and *Planet Earth—2000*.

Jerry Falwell (1933–2007) stated during a December 27, 1992 television broadcast, "I do not believe there will be another millennium … or another century." John F. Walvoord, described as "the world's foremost interpreter of biblical prophecy … [expected] the Rapture to occur in his own lifetime.'" It didn't. Walvoord died in 2002 at the age of 92. Consider these statements of prophetic certainty:

- "Never in the history of the Church has there been a time during which more evidence existed that the Rapture is near."

- "Never before in the history of the Church has there been more evidence that the end of the age is at hand."

Walvoord wrote these nearly identical predictive statements in books that were published 36 years apart. Notice his use of "near" and "at hand." In a 1952 book, Walvoord stated, "The twentieth century has witnessed the most significant array of prophecy being fulfilled in any century since the time of Christ." As

Francis Gumerlock has pointed out in his 2000 years of prophetic predictions, Walvoord was in similar company.

It's easy for Christian prophecy writers to take pot shots at New Age eccentrics, advocates of the end of the world in 2012, secular prognosticators, and environmental doomsayers, but there aren't many who are willing to evaluate the evangelical prediction market, and it's a big market. They have their own calendar problem, and they need to be held accountable. The credibility of the Bible and the gospel message are at stake.

Since the reestablishment of Israel in 1948, prophetic speculation by Christians has been on the rise. Of course, there is a long history of date setting, but the past century has seen an exponential increase in the number of books proclaiming that the end is near. It's time that the "Boy who cried wolf" syndrome be dealt with in a biblical way. Many Christians are beginning to question the prediction business. They are willing to take a second look at the biblical prophetic record. A seismic shift in prophetic beliefs is taking place around the world because Christians, some for the first time, are willing to question their beliefs based on what the Bible actually says. *10 Popular Prophecy Myths Exposed and Answered* will rattle your belief system. I admit it. What you are about to read might shake you to the core, but in the end you will be a better study of God's Word. Isn't that what it's all about?

# Introduction:

# Detecting a Seismic Shift in Eschatology

Similar to the way there is a fundamental shift taking place in the realm of theology by a reconsideration of Calvinism,[1] a seismic shift is taking place in eschatology. Eschatology is the study of the "last things." The more popular terminology is "Bible prophecy." There are numerous schools of thought on the subject. The most popular version—dispensational premillennialism—teaches that certain prophetic events are on the horizon, that a "rapture" of the Church precedes a seven-year period that includes the rise of an antichrist, a rebuilt temple, and a Great Tribulation. One of the distinct features of this view is the belief that there is an Israel-Church distinction, and because of this distinction God has two redemptive programs. Over the years I have been critical of this prophetic view and have written extensively on the subject and have even participated in a number of debates. During this time, I have received numerous questions and not a few criticisms of my views. I have tried to answer all those who have taken the time to write to me. Some have been gracious in their replies, and some have not. Many have abandoned their dispensational belief system after reading my published works, some have not. After being engaged in this type of work for more than 30 years, I find that there are some people who are unwilling to put their prophetic system to the test, even though the system has a recent history and is filled with so many novel interpretations. The following is an example of the prophetic criticisms that come across my desk:

> [Gary DeMar] is a self-labeled non-dispensationalist. While that isn't a crime or even a theological *faux pax*, it IS specious, considering that verse which describes "don't boast against the branches, for they [Israel] support YOU" and not *vice versa*. Included in that

---

1. Josh Burek, "Christian faith: Calvinism is back," *The Christian Science Monitor* (March 27, 2010): http://www.csmonitor.com/USA/Society/2010/0327/Christian-faith-Calvinism-is-back

camp is Hank Hanegraaff, who can only be accused of believing one thing years ago and now believes the exact opposite today. Understanding the debate over Replacement Theology [that the Church has replaced Israel in God's economy] is THE topic today and divides the Body like abortion did 20 yrs. ago.[2]

There is a lot to unpack in this paragraph since it meanders through a number of topics that are irrelevant to the central issue in this discussion. Claiming that a debate over "Replacement Theology" is comparable to abortion is absurd, especially when my critic's own prophetic system envisions "the worst bloodbath in Jewish history."[3] Then again, maybe the topic *is* similar to abortion since dispensationalists teach that after the "rapture" "two-thirds of the Jewish people [living in Israel during the Great Tribulation] will be exterminated."[4]

The idea of an Israel-Church distinction, which is a fundamental doctrine of dispensationalism, is built on an interpretive fiction. There is continuity between the covenants. There were Israelite believers prior to, during, and after Jesus' earthly ministry. They were incorporated into the "great cloud of witnesses" from the Old Covenant age (Heb. 12:1). We are reminded of Zacharias (Luke 1:5–23), Elizabeth (1:24–25), John (1:57–63), Mary (1:39–56), Joseph (Matt. 1:18–25), Simeon (Luke 2:25–35), Anna (2:36–37), and others (Luke 19:8–9; John 2:23; 4:39, 50; 7:31; 8:31; 10:42).[5] Simeon quotes an Old Testament passage that links the believing remnant of Israel and the believing remnant from the nations (Gentiles):

> For my eyes have seen Thy salvation, which Thou hast prepared in the presence of all peoples. "A light of Revelation to the Gentiles, and the glory of Thy people Israel" (Luke 2:31–32; see Isa. 42:6; 49:6).

---

2. I've corrected the author's spelling in various places.

3. Charles C. Ryrie, *The Best is Yet to Come* (Chicago, IL: Moody Press, 1981), 86. Dispensationalist Arnold Fruchtenbaum writes something similar: "Israel will suffer tremendous persecution (Matthew 24:15–28; Revelation 12:1–17). As a result of this persecution of the Jewish people, two-thirds are going to be killed." (Arnold G. Fruchtenbaum, "The Little Apocalypse of Zechariah," *The End Times Controversy: The Second Coming Under Attack,* eds. Tim LaHaye and Thomas Ice [Eugene, OR: Harvest House, 2003], 262).

4. Messianic Jewish spokesman Sid Roth in an interview with Pat Robertson on the September 18, 1991 edition of the "700 Club."

5. Howard A. Hanke, *Christ and the Church in the Old Testament: A Survey of Redemptive Unity in the Testaments* (Grand Rapids, MI: Zondervan, 1957).

God always intended that the promises made to Israel would extend to include the nations (Acts 10; 13:47–48; 26:23). This is not to assume that every Israelite and non-Israelite would be saved; it's about the remnant (Rom. 9:27; 11:5), not natural descent (John 1:12–13). As we will see, there is no *new* body of believers called the Church.

## Dispensationalism's Short and Controversial History

Everybody prior to around 1830 was a non-dispensationalist, so I don't see why being a "non-dispensationalist" today carries with it such negative connotations. Furthermore, until the publication of the *Scofield Reference Bible* in 1909, there was no agreed upon dispensational system among even a minority of Christians.[6] It's rather surprising that notes written by one man who had no real theological training would end up creating a brand new prophetic movement wherein the notes more often than not supplant the text of Scripture.

Since its inception, dispensationalism has been considered biblically aberrant by a number of theological traditions.[7] R. B. Kuiper (1886–1966), who served as a professor at Westminster Theological Seminary and President of Calvin Theological Seminary, wrote in 1936 that two grievous errors were "prevalent among American fundamentalists, Arminianism and the Dispensationalism of the Scofield Bible." The General Assembly of the Orthodox Presbyterian Church went so far as to describe Arminianism and Dispensationalism as "anti-reformed heresies,"[8] that is, heretical in terms of the theology that came out of the Reformation.

Professor John Murray, who taught Systematic Theology at Westminster Theological Seminary and wrote a commentary on Romans for the New International Commentary Series, wrote that the "'Dispensationalism' of which we speak as heterodox from the standpoint of the Reformed Faith is that form of interpretation,

---

6. Dispensationalists like to claim that the mere use of the word "dispensation" makes someone a dispensationalist. This is hardly the case. See Ronald M. Henzel, *Darby, Dualism, and the Decline of Dispensationalism: Reassessing the Nineteenth-Century Roots of a Twentieth-Century Prophetic Movement for the Twenty-First Century* (Tucson: Fenestra Books, 2003), 25–29.

7. Oswald T. Allis, *Prophecy and the Church* (Philadelphia, PA: Presbyterian and Reformed, 1945); John Wick Bowman, "The Bible and Modern Religions: II. Dispensationalism," *Interpretation* 10 (April 1956), 170–172; C. Norman Kraus, *Dispensationalism in America* (Richmond, VA: John Knox Press, 1958); Clarence B. Bass, *Backgrounds to Dispensationalism* (Grand Rapids, MI: Eerdmans, 1960); Curtis I. Crenshaw and Grover E. Gunn, III, *Dispensationalism: Today, Yesterday, and Tomorrow*, rev. ed. (Memphis: Footstool Publications, [1985], 1989. There are too many critiques of dispensationalism to list.

8. R. B. Kuiper, *The Presbyterian Guardian* (September 12, 1936), 225–227. Quoted in Edwin H. Rian, *The Presbyterian Conflict* (Grand Rapids, MI: Eerdmans, 1940), 101.

widely popular at the present time, which discovers in the several dispensations of God's redemptive revelation distinct and even contrary principles of divine procedure and thus destroys the unity of God's dealings with fallen mankind."[9] Premillennialism of the covenantal or classical variety was not under attack by these men.[10] Kuiper again writes:

> It is a matter of common knowledge that there is ever so much more to the dispensationalism of the Scofield Bible than the mere teaching of Premillennialism. Nor do the two stand and fall together. There are premillennarians who have never heard of Scofield's dispensations. More important than that, there are serious students of God's Word who hold to the Premillennial return of Christ and emphatically reject Scofield's system of dispensations as fraught with grave error.[11]

This is not to say that advocates of dispensationalism are not heirs of the Reformation in most respects. Most hold orthodox positions on basic Christian doctrines, but dispensationalism as it was codified by Scofield and is taught and promoted today has not been known in the history of the church until very recently.

Dispensationalism has gone through numerous revisions since the publication of the *New Scofield Reference Bible* in 1967. Signs of a more radical change, however, are sweeping the system into oblivion. Thomas Ice, a graduate of Dallas Theological Seminary (DTS), predicted, "By the year 2000 Dallas Theological Seminary will no longer be dispensational. [Professional] priorities are elsewhere than the defense of systematic dispensationalism from external criticism."[12] It seems that the fulfillment of Ice's prophecy has already come to pass. In an interview with Charles Swindoll, who served for a time as president of DTS and is now the school's chancellor, we learn what lies ahead for DTS: "I'm not sure we're going to make *dispensationalism* a big part of our marquee as we talk about our school."[13]

---

9. *The Presbyterian Guardian* (February 3, 1936), 143. Quoted in Rian, *The Presbyterian Conflict*, 236–237.

10. Craig L. Blomberg and Sung Wook Chung, *A Case for Historic Premillennialism: An Alternative to "Left Behind" Eschatology* (Grand Rapids, MI: Baker Academic, 2009).

11. *The Presbyterian Guardian* (November 14, 1936), 54. Quoted in Rian, *The Presbyterian Conflict*, 31.

12. Thomas Ice interview with Martin Selbrede, *Counsel of Chalcedon* (December 1989). Cited in Gary North, *Rapture Fever: Why Dispensationalism is Paralyzed* (Tyler, TX: Institute for Christian Economics, 1993), 145.

13. Quoted in "Dallas's New Dispensation," *Christianity Today* (October 25, 1993), 14.

Dispensationalism is being questioned by the more orthodox charismatics.[14] Dr. Joseph Kikasola, professor of international studies and Hebrew at CBN University believes that there has been a "'diminishing of dispensationalism,' especially among charismatics, who, he says, are coming to see that 'charismatic dispensationalist' is 'a contradiction in terms.'"[15] Many dispensationalists are losing their fascination with date-setting since the fortieth anniversary of Israel's nationhood (1948–1988) passed without a rapture. Dave Hunt, a proponent of the national regathering of Israel as the time indicator for future prophetic events, writes: "Needless to say, January 1, 1982, saw the defection of large numbers from the pretrib position.... Many who were once excited about the prospects of being caught up to heaven at any moment have become confused and disillusioned by the apparent failure of a generally accepted biblical interpretation they once relied upon."[16] He goes on later to assert: "[Gary] North's reference to specific dates is an attack upon the most persuasive factor supporting Lindsey's rapture scenario: the rebirth of national Israel. This historic event, which is pivotal to dispensationalism's timing of the rapture, as John F. Walvoord has pointed out, was long anticipated and when it at last occurred seemed to validate that prophetic interpretation."[17]

Robert L. Saucy, professor of systematic theology at Talbot School of Theology, remarked, "Over the past several decades the system of theological interpretation commonly known as dispensationalism has undergone considerable development and refinement."[18] Saucy gives a great deal away in his new work, so much so that he calls it "the new dispensationalism" or "progressive [dispensationalism] ... to distinguish the newer interpretations from the older version of dispensationalism."[19]

Nothing even remotely associated with modern-day dispensationalism can be found in the creedal formulations of the church going back to the Council of Nicaea in A.D. 325. Not even non-dispensational (classical) premillennialism was written into the basic Christian creeds.[20] Most of the finest Christian scholars the church

---

14. Traditionally, Pentecostalism has been dispensational.

15. Randy Frame, "The Theonomic Urge," *Christianity Today*, (April 21, 1989), 38.

16. Dave Hunt, *Whatever Happened to Heaven?* (Eugene, OR: Harvest House, 1988), 68.

17. Hunt, *Whatever Happened to Heaven?*, 64.

18. Robert L. Saucy, *The Case for Progressive Dispensationalism: The Interface Between Dispensationalism and Non-Dispensational Theology* (Grand Rapids, MI: Zondervan, 1993), 8. Also see, Craig A. Blaising and Darrell L. Bock, *Progressive Dispensationalism: An Up-to-Date Handbook of Contemporary Dispensational Thought* (Wheaton, IL: Victor Books, 1993).

19. Saucy, *The Case for Progressive Dispensationalism*, 9.

20. Gary DeMar and Francis X. Gumerlock, *The Early Church and the End of the World* (Powder Springs, GA: American Vision, 2005), chap. 4.

has ever produced were not then and are not now dispensationalists. Of course, this does not mean dispensationalism is a false system, but it does mean that an amateur theologian who admits he does not "read OR write Hebrew or Greek" has no place to stand to level such a sweeping criticism against non-dispensationalists.

## "Nothing You Say Can Convince Me"

The author is begging the question by assuming dispensationalism is true, biblically foundational, and has a long and respected historical pedigree. He doesn't argue for these positions; he simply states them as fundamental, self-evident truths. His arguments, such as they are, are similar to those used by evolutionists and global warming enthusiasts: "The debate is over! There's nothing to discuss." If that were true for all arenas of theological debate, then the first Jerusalem Council would never have happened (Acts 15) and Paul never would have rebuked Peter for his wrong-headed theology (Gal. 2:11–21).

My critic's arguments are based on what others have written. There is no indication that he has done any independent research. "I've come to trust some and discount others," he writes, "like everybody else." It's obvious that he has read very little of what I have written and is not aware of the mountain of material covering this subject. There is a great deal of independent research in my work. I have shown at least some ability to determine what's to be trusted and what should be discounted, and I work hard to make a case for both. Moreover, I'm willing to discuss and debate the issue with others.

It is neither an argument for nor against a position that someone (*e.g.*, Hank Hanegraaff) has changed his views. It happens all the time. If a non-dispensationalist becomes a dispensationalist after 25 years of being a non-dispensationalist, would my critic condemn this change? Of course not! Those who do change to a new (for them) prophetic position often tell me that they did not know there was an alternative position. They adopted the *status quo* position because someone told them it was what the Bible taught, and they joined a fellowship where nearly everyone held the same view, and if one didn't hold this view, then, well, he obviously wasn't a real Christian. When these view-changers actually started to read and study the Bible on their own, questions arose and good answers were not forthcoming from those who held the present *status quo* (dispensational) view. This is what happened to me, and it's happened to many others. I have the testimonies to prove it.

As the Apostle Paul writes, "Each person must be fully convinced in his own mind" (Rom. 14:5). The Bereans were described as "noble minded," for while "they received the word with great eagerness," they examined the Scriptures daily to determine whether what Paul was saying was true (Acts 17:11). It's no wonder that Paul accepted the scrutiny since he exhorted the Thessalonians to "examine everything carefully; hold fast to that which is good" (1 Thess. 5:21), something some of their countrymen had refused to do (Acts 17:1–9). While we are not to test God, God's word does tell us to "test the spirits to see whether they are from God, because many false prophets have gone out into the world" (1 John 4:1).

When I suggested to my critic that we engage in an exchange of material, here was his response:

> "I'd rather not speak to him. He is convinced & so am I. I'm not going to accept his position no matter the discussion or debate."

Can you imagine such an attitude? He would not accept my position "no matter the discussion or debate." Unbelievable! I've had people fight me tooth and nail over eschatology. It's amazing how many apologies I've received over the years. I remember a call I got some time ago when I was interviewed on an Orlando, Florida, radio station. This guy chewed me out for my "heretical views." I told him to read my book *Last Days Madness*. He called me about six months later to apologize. *Last Days Madness* had convinced him that what he had believed could not stand the scrutiny of the Bible. I've learned a lot from critics. Their arguments force me to do more study. I'm not arrogant enough to believe that I have it all figured out. I want to be challenged. It's how we grow.

## "Boasting Against the Branches"

I would like to know why it's "boasting against the branches" (Rom. 11:18), as my critic maintains, to question the basic assumptions of dispensationalism. Such a specious argument is typical of some dispensationalists who find it difficult to represent non-dispensational views accurately and have trouble offering a coherent biblical defense of their own dispensational paradigm without numerous interpretive caveats (*e.g.*, gaps) when challenged on basic claims (*e.g.*, that dispensationalists are the only ones who interpret the Bible in a consistently "literal" way). Dispensationalists fail to note what else Paul writes just a few verses later in Romans 11: "And they also, **if they do not continue in their unbelief**, will be grafted in, for God is able to graft them in again" (v. 23). Israelites will be grafted in if and only if they give up their unbelief. The same is true of non-Israelites. I don't know anyone who believes Jews are excluded from the gospel now that non-Jews are included. *That* would be "boasting against the branches."

Paul is not dealing with a Church-Israel distinction in Romans 11. There is nothing in the entire book that indicates that there is a Church-Israel distinction. The word "church" doesn't appear until chapter 16 where it refers in two places to local assemblies of believers (16:1, 5). Nothing is said about a "rapture" of the Church, Israel becoming a nation again, a rebuilt temple, or the return of any Jews to their land as a fulfillment of Bible prophecy. There is a single olive tree, and believing Jews and Gentiles become a part of the same tree in the same way: belief in Jesus as the Christ. "For there is no partiality with God.… For he is not a Jew who is one outwardly, nor is circumcision that which is outward in the flesh. But he is a Jew who is one inwardly; and circumcision is that which is of the heart, by the Spirit, not by the letter; and his praise is not from men, but from God" (Rom. 2:11, 28–29). In Galatians we read something similar: "There is neither Jew nor Greek, there is neither slave nor free man, there is neither male nor female; for you are all one in Christ Jesus. And if you belong to Christ, then you are Abraham's descendants, heirs according to promise" (Gal. 3:28–29). It's not flesh and blood Israelites who are the heirs of the promises first made to Abraham. If a person belongs to Christ, then he or she is an heir of Abraham. The Bible couldn't be any clearer on this point.

In Romans 15, we see that the distinction is, once again, between the "circumcision" (Israel) and the "uncircumcision" (Gentiles), not Israel and the Church.

> For I say that Christ has become a servant to the circumcision on behalf of the truth of God *to confirm the promises given to the fathers*, and for the Gentiles to glorify God for His mercy; as it is written, "Therefore I will give PRAISE TO YOU AMONG THE GENTILES, and I will sing to Your name." Again he says, "Rejoice, O Gentiles, with His people." And again, "Praise the Lord all you Gentiles, and let all the peoples praise Him." Again Isaiah says, "There shall come the root of Jesse, and He who arises to rule over the Gentiles, in Him shall the Gentiles hope" (Rom. 15:8–12).

The promises to "the circumcision" (Israel) were not postponed by way of a parenthesis so God could deal with a new redemptive entity called the Church. Paul states that God had *confirmed* "the promises *given to the fathers*." These Old Testament prophecies were being realized in Paul's day. He asks, "God has not rejected His people, has He? May it never be!" (Rom. 11:1). As evidence, he offers himself as proof: "I too am an Israelite, of the seed of Abraham, of the tribe of

Benjamin" (11:1). By his own example and thousands of other Jews who had come to Christ, he assured his readers that "God **has not** rejected His people" (11:2). He is not describing something that's going to take place in the distant future. It was happening right then and there!

Recalling the story of Elijah who thought he was the only one who had not bowed the knee to Baal, Paul writes, "**In the same way** then, there has come **at the present time** a remnant according to God's gracious choice" (11:5). Notice, it's "at the present time" that God is being faithful to the promises He had made "to the fathers" (15:8). Paul was describing what was going on in his own day: "But I am speaking to you who are Gentiles. Inasmuch then as I am an apostle of Gentiles, I magnify my ministry, if somehow I might move to jealousy my fellow countrymen and save some of them" (11:13–14). Paul does not even hint that there is a parenthesis. He is dealing with his "now," not the future separated by a postponed prophetic period that has now stretched to nearly 2000 years: "For just as you [Gentiles] once were disobedient to God, but **now** have been shown mercy because of their [Israel's] disobedience so these also **now** have been disobedient, that because of the mercy shown to you [Gentiles] they [Israelites] also may **now** be shown mercy" (Rom. 11:30–31).

## There's Only One Tree

Two additional points need to be discussed. First, contrary to J. W. Brooks, Gentiles are grafted into Israel; "Jews or Israelites" are not absorbed "into the Gentile Church."[21] The believing Jews and believing Gentiles make up a single body of believers (Eph. 2:11–22) that draws its sustenance (blessings) from the original Israelite Olive tree. This means that Israelites and Gentiles alike partake of what the original tree represents. The promises made to Israel belong to believing Israelites and believing Gentiles since they are part of the same original Israelite Olive tree. If Gentiles had never been grafted in, then the Olive tree would have continued to grow dispensing its blessings to Israelites only. The tree does not stop dispensing covenant blessings to Israelites now that Gentiles are grafted in, and neither are these blessings withheld from Gentiles because they were first promised to Israelites. Whatever nourishment is fed to the Israelite branches are also fed to the Gentile branches. The Olive tree is the new community of believers in Christ, what the New Testament calls the *ekklēsia*, an assembly of believers.

Second, the Israelite branches were broken off because of their unbelief. These Israelite branches thought it was enough to be Abraham's physical seed. John de-

---

21. J. W. Brooks, *Elements of Prophetical Interpretation* (Philadelphia: Orrin Rogers, 1841), 180.

scribes the mindset: "[Jesus] came to His own, and those who were His own did not receive Him. But as many as received Him, to them He gave the right to become children of God, *even* to those who believe in His name, who were born, not of blood nor of the will of the flesh nor of the will of man, but of God" (John 1:11–13). John Murray comments:

> In unbelief there is no respect of persons (*cf.* [Rom.] 2:11). God did not spare the natural branches and neither will he spare the Gentiles (vs. 21). If they continue not in faith, they also will be cut off (vs. 22).... Christian piety is constantly aware of the perils to faith, of the danger of coming short, and is characterized by the fear and trembling which the high demands of God's calling constrain (*cf.* I Cor. 2:3; Phil. 2:12; Heb. 4:1; I Pet. 1:17). "Let him that thinketh he standeth take heed lest he fall" (I Cor. 10:12).[22]

Questioning the dispensational system of interpretation is not questioning what Paul forcefully argues in Romans 9–11. There is one tree, not two. There is one people of God, not two.

---

22. John Murray, *The Epistle to the Romans* (NICNT), 2 vol. ed. (Grand Rapids, MI: Eerdmans, 1968), 2:87–88

# 1

# The Myth of an Israel-Church Distinction

Dispensationalists have perpetrated the myth of an Israel-Church distinction that they say is based on a straightforward reading of the New Testament where at a particular point in biblical history God's redemptive program changed from Israel to a new entity called "the Church." It's at this point, dispensationalists argue, that Israel's prophetic clock stopped and a "mystery parenthesis"[1] called the Church Age was inserted between the 69th and 70th weeks of Daniel's prophecy (Dan. 9:24–27). The Church Age will end, so the argument goes, when the Church is "raptured." It will be at this time that the prophecy clock will begin ticking again and God will once again deal with Israel during the seven-year Great Tribulation, Daniel's 70th week. Dispensationalist author Charles Ryrie considers the Church-Israel distinction to be "the absolutely indispensable part" of dispensationalism.

> What marks off a person as a dispensationalist? What is the *sine qua non* (the absolutely indispensable part) of the system? ... *A dispensationalist keeps Israel and the church distinct....* This is probably the most basic theological test of whether or not a person is a dispensationalist, and it is undoubtedly the most practical and conclusive. The one who fails to distinguish Israel and the church consistently will inevitably not hold to dispensational distinctions; and one who does will.[2]

So then, without an Israel-Church distinction and a shift in prophetic programs from Israel to the Church, there is no dispensationalism. If it can be shown

---

1. H. A. Ironside, *The Great Parenthesis* (Grand Rapids, MI: Zondervan 1943).

2. Charles C. Ryrie, *Dispensationalism*, rev. and ex. ed. (Chicago: Moody Press, 1995), 38–39. This quotation is an expansion of the definition given in the 1965 edition *Dispensationalism Today* (Chicago: Moody, 1965), 44: "A dispensationalist keeps Israel and the Church distinct."

that this Israel-Church distinction and two-program view is based on a redemptive fiction, then the entire dispensational system collapses.

## An Assembly of God's People

Gaining a proper understanding of the Greek word *ekklēsia*, most often translated "church" in the New Testament,[3] should be our starting point since it is Ryrie's most absolutely indispensable part of the dispensational system. Ryrie considers a "historical-grammatical" interpretive method of the Bible to be "the second aspect of the *sine qua non of dispensationalism*," summarized as that approach to the text of Scripture that considers a word's "*normal* or *plain*" meaning.[4] He states that "the meaning of each word must be studied" so that it "involves etymology [the study of word origin], use, history, and resultant meaning."[5] So what is the "normal or plain" meaning of *ekklēsia*? Ryrie never tells us. Although he spends an entire chapter defining "dispensation," he never defines "church." The following from the *Greek-English Lexicon of the New Testament* will prove helpful in establishing a proper lexical definition of *ekklēsia*:

> Though some persons have tried to see in the term ἐκκλησία a more or less literal meaning of "called-out ones" [*ek* + *kaleō*] this type of etymologizing is not warranted either by the meaning of ἐκκλησία in NT times or even by its earlier usage. The term ἐκκλησία was in common usage for several hundred years before the Christian era and was used to refer to an assembly of persons constituted by well-defined membership. For the NT ... it is important to understand the meaning of ἐκκλησία as "an assembly of God's people."[6]

Take note that the authors of this lexicon say the word was in use "several hundred years before the Christian era." Nothing is said about its "dispensational meaning." None of the standard lexicons know anything about the meaning of *ekklēsia* that would square with how dispensationalists understand the word.

---

3. The Greek word *ekklēsia* is used 115 times in the New Testament, and in most translations it is translated as "church." Exceptions are often found in Acts 7:38, 19:32, 39, 41, and Hebrews 2:12.

4. Ryrie, *Dispensationalism*, 40.

5. Ryrie, *Dispensationalism*, 82.

6. J. P. Louw and E. A. Nida, *Greek-English Lexicon of the New Testament : Based on Semantic Domains*, electronic ed. of the 2nd ed. (New York: United Bible Societies, [1989] 1996). United Bible Societies: New York

There is no doubt that *ekklēsia* takes on greater redemptive significance in the New Testament because of Jesus Christ, but not so much so that it is separated root and branch from its Old Testament meaning. It is here that we will learn its "etymology, use, history, and resultant meaning."

We will see that there is a continuity of the people of God—called the *ekklēsia* in the Greek translation of the Old and New Testament—as well as Old Testament images that were first applied to Israel but in the New Testament are applied to the assembly of Israelite and non-Israelite believers in the New Testament. This is summed up very well in the epistle to the Hebrews: "But you have come to Mount Zion and to the city of the living God, the heavenly Jerusalem, and to myriads of angels, to the general assembly and church [*ekklēsia*] of the firstborn who are enrolled in heaven, and to God, the Judge of all, and to the spirits of *the* righteous made perfect, and to Jesus, the mediator of a new covenant, and to the sprinkled blood, which speaks better than *the blood* of Abel" (12:22–23).

Mount Zion and the heavenly Jerusalem are equated with the *ekklēsia* that is enrolled in heaven, that great "cloud of witnesses" that the author spoke of in the previous chapter (12:1). The author of Hebrews is hardly describing a dispensational Israel-Church distinction with two, one earthly (Israel) and one heavenly (Church), redemptive programs. You can see how, like Paul in Galatians 4:24–31, the author of Hebrews meshes Israel's promise of land and place into elements of a "better covenant" that has no individual limits or geographical boundaries.

> "The city of the living God, the heavenly Jerusalem," is in essence the same city to which Abraham in faith looked forward, that is, "the city which has foundations, whose builder and maker is God" (11:10), as it is "the city which is to come," sought in this age by the people of God, who have no lasting city here (Heb. 13:14), and whose true citizenship is in heaven (Phil. 3:20). It is the "the holy city, new Jerusalem," the capital city of the new heaven and the new earth, in which, in fulfillment of his covenant promise, God dwells with men, and they are eternally his people, and all the former things with their sorrows and imperfections have passed away (Rev. 21:1–4). Indeed, the citizens themselves are the citizens, because, as Peter Lombard suggests, God, who gives them life, dwells in them. The presence of God is what constitutes the new Jerusalem.[7]

---

7. Philip Edgcumbe Hughes, *A Commentary on the Epistle to the Hebrews* (Grand Rapids, MI: Eerdmans, 1977), 546.

These heavenly citizens are Israelites *and* non-Israelites. There is no redemptive dualism. This "assembly" (*ekklēsia*) is a gathering of "the first born," "the counterpart of the congregation or 'church' of the Israelites assembled under the leadership of Moses at Sinai. Thus Stephen says of Moses: 'This is he who was in the congregation (*ecclesia*) in the wilderness with the angel who spoke to him at Mount Sinai' (Acts 7:38)."[8] This gathering of Israel "is referred to in Deuteronomy (4:10; 9:10; 18:16) as 'the day of the *ecclesia*' (Septuagint)."[9] The idea of New Testament believers being in the congregation of the "firstborn" is another indicator that the promises made to Israel are possessed by the New Testament *ekklēsia* made up of Israelites and non-Israelites. Israel is God's "son," His "first born" (Ex. 4:22). The New Testament *ekklēsia* is also treated like God's firstborn (Heb. 12:23) because it has attained membership in the pre-existing *ekklēsia*.

## The "Church" is no New Thing

There is no Church-Israel distinction in the Bible because the Greek word *ekklēsia* is not an invention of the New Testament writers. *Ekklēsia* was a common word used to describe an assembly or congregation. It is used this way in the Greek translation of the Old Testament—the Septuagint (LXX)—and the Greek New Testament. This common word is used by Jesus in Matthew's gospel (the most Jewish of the gospels):

- "I also say to you that you are Peter, and upon this rock I will build My church [*ekklēsia*]; and the gates of Hades will not overpower it" (Matt. 16:18).[10]

---

8. Hughes, *A Commentary on the Epistle to the Hebrews*, 547.

9. Hughes, *A Commentary on the Epistle to the Hebrews*, 547.

10. Fruchtenbaum writes that "when the Church is mentioned for the first time in Matthew 16:18, it is still future, as the use of the future tense clearly shows. Jesus did not say, 'I am building,' which would have been the case if the Church was already in existence. The only possible conclusion is that the Church was formed at Pentecost." (Fruchtenbaum, *Israelology*, 466). What Fruchtenbaum does not tell his readers is that while *ekklēsia* is used for the first time in Matthew's gospel, it's not the first time Jesus' disciples had heard the term. They were very familiar with it since it is used throught the Greek translation of the Hebrew Old Testament. Jesus describes how He will build His assembly of believers on the confession that He is "the Christ, the Son of the living God" (Matt. 16:16) which is foundational to the entire Old Testament (Luke 24:27). Its newness is similar to the way the covenant is new (Heb. 8:8); it's the same covenant but only expanded to include non-Israelites and made sure through Jesus' shed blood (Matt. 26:28). Notice the number of passages in Hebrews 8 that are taken from the Old Testament (8:5, 8, 9, 10, 11, 12) and applied to the *ekklēsia* of the New Testament.

- "If he refuses to listen to them, tell it to the church [*ekklēsia*]; and if he refuses to listen even to the church [*ekklēsia*], let him be to you as a Gentile and a tax collector" (Matt. 18:17).

No one asks Jesus, "What's an *ekklēsia*?" They knew what an *ekklēsia* was since they were intimately familiar with the Greek translation of the Hebrew Old Testament. "This Greek version of the Hebrew Scriptures was the Bible of the early church.… Thus, when the writers of the New Testament, whose Bible was the Septuagint, used *ekklēsia*, they were not inventing a new term.[11] They found the term in common use and simply employed what was at hand."[12]

The Greek word *ekklēsia* was used many times in the Septuagint for the Hebrew word *qāhāl* that means "congregation" or "assembly." (Even modern-day Hebrew translations of the Greek New Testament translate *ekklēsia* as *qāhāl*.[13]) Like *ekklēsia*, the Hebrew *qāhāl* is a general term that can refer to "the assembly of Israel" (Deut. 31:30; Joshua 8:35) or to "the assembly of evil doers" (Ps. 26:5). *Ekklēsia* is used in a similar way in the New Testament. It can refer to local assemblies of Christians (Rev. 2:1, 8, 12, 18; 3:1, 7, 14) or pagan assemblies of non-Christians (Acts 19:32, 39, 41). Of course, it also has the meaning of a redemptive body of believers made up collectively of Israelites and non-Israelites. Paul's use of *ekklēsia* in some of his epistles indicates "that *ekklesia* itself still carried a general meaning of 'assembly'; the particular kind of assembly had to be

---

11. Following the LXX, the sacred assembly of Israel was the "*ekklēsia* of the LORD" (Deut. 23:1). "The people of God" are "in the *ekklēsia*" (Judges 20:2). Solomon took "all the *ekklēsia*" to Gibeon where the ark was (2 Chron. 1:3). There the *ekklēsia* inquired of the Lord (2 Chron. 1:5). When the temple was completed, Solomon blessed "all the *ekklēsia* of Israel" (1 Kings 8:14; cp. 8:22, 55; 2 Chron. 6:3). If this verse were in the NT, it would read "all the church of Israel." When Solomon stands before the altar and prays, he is "before all the *ekklēsia* of Israel" (2 Chron. 6:12). The "*ekklēsia* of the LORD" was the covenantal assembly of Israel (Deut. 4:10).

12. Earl D. Radmacher, *What the Church is All About: A Biblical and Historical Study* (Chicago: Moody Press, [1972] 1978), 121, 132. Radmacher argues that "although the etymological associations of *ekklesia* have their unquestionable bearing upon the significance of the term, the deciding evidence must be drawn from the exhaustive investigation of its actual use in the New Testament. While it is true that historical continuity seems to demand that the early appearance of the word *ekklesia* in any new literature should simply suggest 'assembly,' it is also true that the Holy Spirit frequently lifts words from their current usages to a higher plane of meaning and packs into them such vast new content as their etymologies will scarcely account for. Whitney states: 'Philologists agree that the final authority of any word does not lie in its etymological or historical connotation but *in its actual use*'" (132). That is the question. What is its actual use and meaning in the New Testament?

13. *The Hebrew Bible (Old Testament and New Testament)* (Jerusalem, Israel: The Bible Society in Israel, 1970).

indicated by qualifiers similar to the Septuagint use."[14] Robert Saucy references 1 and 2 Thessalonians as examples where *ekklēsia* has a "general meaning." Second Thessalonians was written around A.D. 50.[15] This means that no dispensational specialized meaning was given to *ekklēsia* for more than 20 years after Pentecost when dispensaionalists claim the church was founded. In fact, there is no specialized definition given to the word "church" in Revelation where it refers to local assemblies of believers, a book that was written a few years before the destruction of Jerusalem which took place in A.D. 70.

> The term *ekklēsia* describes an actual assembly, a gathering of people together. The same is true of the Old Testament term *qāhāl* that is translated by *ekklēsia* in the Septuagint version of the Old Testament. The words themselves do not have the restricted meaning of the word, 'church'. Yet, when Jesus said, 'I will build my church'…, he was not simply saying, 'I will bring together a gathering of people'. Rather, he was using a well-known term that described the people of God. The 'assembly in the desert' (Acts 7:38) was the definitive assembly for Israel, the covenant-making assembly when God claimed his redeemed people as his own' (Dt. 4:10 LXX; 9:10; 10:4; 18:16).[16]

Any Jew able to read the Greek translation of the Hebrew Old Testament would have recognized the word and known what it meant. In speaking to his Jewish countrymen, Stephen describes the believing community in the era of the OT as "the congregation [*ekklēsia*] in the wilderness" (Acts 7:38). In Acts 8:1 and 3 the "*ekklēsia* in Jerusalem" was made up exclusively of Jews—all Israelites! If *ekklēsia* means "congregation" in Acts 7:38,[17] then it certainly carries the same

---

14. Robert L. Saucy, *The Church in God's Program* (Chicago: Moody Press, 1972), 16.

15. Gordon D. Fee, *The First and Second Letters to the Thessalonians* (NICNT) (Grand Rapids, MI: Eerdmans, 2010), 237–241.

16. Edmund P. Clowney, "The Biblical Theology of the Church," *The Church in the Bible and the World: An International Study*, ed. D. A. Carson (Grand Rapids, MI: Baker Book House, 1987), 17.

17. "It should be noted that [the translation of *ekklēsia* as 'church' in Acts 7:38] is found in the King James Version. Most other translations have more correctly translated this verse to read, *the congregation in the wilderness*, or *the assembly in the wilderness*. The Greek term *ekklēsia* is not only used in the technical sense of the New Testament Church, but it is also used in the *Septuagint* as the translation of the Hebrew *kahal*, meaning 'congregation.' That was the obvious intent of Acts 7:38. Furthermore, in the Book of Acts itself, *ekklēsia* is used in the non-technical sense of 'assembly,' for it is used to describe an assembly of townspeople who were neither Jews

## The Myth of an Israel-Church Distinction

meaning just a few verses later in Acts 8:1: "Saul was in hearty agreement with putting [Stephen] to death. And on that day a great persecution began against the *ekklēsia* [church] in Jerusalem,[18] and they were all scattered throughout the regions of Judea and Samaria, except the apostles." In Acts 8:3 we read that "Saul *began* ravaging the *ekklēsia* [church], entering house after house, and dragging off men and women" to "put them in prison." The *ekklēsia* that Saul ravaged was made up of believing Israelites who were a living testimony to the fulfillment of God's promises made to Israel through the fathers and prophets. These Israelites didn't believe that they were some "mystery" parenthesis. At Pentecost Peter told the "men of Israel" (Acts 2:22) who were in Jerusalem "from every nation under heaven" (2:5–11) that what was happening was the fulfillment of what Joel and other prophets had prophesied (2:14–47).

> "Men of Judea and all you who live in Jerusalem, let this be known to you and give heed to my words. For these men are not drunk, as you suppose, for it is *only* the third hour of the day; but this is what was spoken of through the prophet Joel" (Acts 2:14b–16).

Peter quotes an Old Testament passage and applies it to the events of Pentecost, as the prophecy's fulfillment. Dispensationalists teach that the Old Testament did not know anything about a New Testament *ekklēsia* (church). If this is the case, then how could a prophecy from the prophet Joel apply to the beginning of the New Testament *ekklēsia* (church) and include "all flesh" (Acts 2:17) and not just Israel? It couldn't. This is why dispensationalist Thomas Ice has to add the word "like" to Peter's God-inspired words so that the passage will say what *he* thinks it should say to maintain the Israel-Church dualism: "But this is [**like**] that which was spoken of through the prophet Joel." He tries to explain the addition of "like" by claiming, "The unique statement of Peter ('this is that') is in the language of comparison and similarity, not fulfillment."[19] There is no indication that it's "like" what Joel prophesied; it *is* what Joel prophesied. It is strange that someone who claims to interpret the Bible literally would add a word to a

---

nor Christians but Gentile pagans [Acts 19:32–33, 41]" (Fruchtenbaum, *Israelology*, 30–31). Of course, the Hebrew *qāhāl* is also used in a non-technical sense of assembly as well as an assembly of believers.

18. Is Luke comparing the Jerusalem of his day to the wilderness? ("the *ekklēsia* in the wilderness" and "the *ekklēsia* in Jerusalem"). Jesus predicted that Jerusalem would be destroyed (Matt. 22:1–14) and the temple would be left to that generation "desolate" (23:38).

19. Thomas Ice, "Acts," in Tim LaHaye, ed. *Prophecy Study Bible* (Chattanooga, TN: AMG Publishers, 2000), 1187.

passage, not for grammatical clarity as many translations do with other passages, but to make a point of theology. The Jehovah's Witnesses do this with Colossians 1:16–17 to avoid the obvious implication that Jesus is a non-created being. Their *New World Translation* inserts the word "other" in brackets before "things": Because by means of him all [other] things were created in the heavens and upon the earth, the things visible and the things invisible, no matter whether they are thrones or lordships or governments or authorities. All [other] things have been created through him and for him. Also, he is before all [other] things and by means of him all [other] things were made to exist" (NWT). In both cases, theology is driving what the text *should* say in order to justify an interpretive system.

Dispensational author Stanley D. Toussaint contradicts Ice on inserting the word "like" between "this" and "that": "This clause does not mean, 'This is *like* that'; it means Pentecost fulfilled what Joel had described."[20] After saying this, he goes on to argue, contradicting what he just wrote: "However, the prophecies of Joel quoted in Acts 2:19–20 were not fulfilled." So which is it? He says the fulfillment will come "if Israel would repent." But the elect remnant of Israel did repent: "Now having heard this, they were pierced to the heart, and said to Peter and the rest of the apostles, 'Brethren, what shall we do?' And Peter said to them, 'Repent…'" (Acts 2:37–38). The result? "So then, those who had received his word were baptized; and there were added that day about three thousand souls" (2:41). While Toussaint dismisses the argument put forth by Ice that Peter was saying "this is *like* that," his claim that "the prophecies of Joel quoted in Acts 2:19–20 were not fulfilled" has Peter saying "this is *not* that," a clear contradiction and even worse than what Ice does with the verse.

Zane C. Hodges agrees that the insertion of "like" "is unlikely on linguistic grounds." He comments further:

> Some dispensational thinkers have urged that the phrase "this is that" is not intended to announce the *fulfillment* of Joel's prophecy on this occasion. Rather, it signifies something analogous to the phenomenon described by Joel. According to this view, the phrase "this is that" means something similar to "this is like that," or "this is that sort of thing."
>
> Such an interpretation is unlikely on linguistic grounds.[21]

---

20. Stanley D. Toussaint, "Acts," *The Bible Knowledge Commentary: New Testament*, John F. Walvoord and Roy B. Zuck (Wheaton, IL: Victor Books, 1983), 358.

21. Zane C. Hodges, "A Dispensational Understanding of Acts 2," *Issues In Dispensationalism*, 168.

Hodges equivocates, but doesn't go as far as Ice and Toussaint. He does imply that Peter's use of "this is that" is not as literal as it seems after the first reading. "We may conclude that Peter meant to say that the outpouring of the Spirit fulfilled Joel's prophecy. But this in no way clashes with fundamental dispensational convictions.... The hidden reality of the church remains hidden reality even when Joel's prophecy is seen to be fulfilled at Pentecost."[22] What Peter "*meant* to say"? What does this mean? The text tells us what Peter *did* say. If, as dispensationalists argue, the church had its beginning at Pentecost, and "Joel's prophecy is seen to be fulfilled at Pentecost," it seems reasonable to conclude that Joel's prophecy applies to the "church," therefore it is not a "hidden reality."

## One New Man in Christ

This original Jewish assembly of believers post-Pentecost is the "*ekklēsia* of God," the congregation and assembly of God's people (Acts 8:1; Gal. 1:13; Acts 20:28; 1 Cor. 1:2; 10:32; 15:9; 2 Cor. 1:1; 1 Tim. 3:5), a continuation of the believing community found throughout the Old Testament. Later in Acts we learn that Gentiles were grafted into an already growing post-Pentecost Israelite *ekklēsia* (Acts 10).[23] There is no discussion among the circumcised about a postponed covenant with Israel. They were "amazed because the gift of the Holy Spirit had been poured out on the Gentiles **also**" (10:45). Note the "also": "To the Jew first and **also** to the Greek" (Rom. 1:16; 2:9–10). The Israelite promises were extended to the Gentiles.

Peter addressed the crowd at Pentecost as the "men of Israel" (Acts 2:22) and "all the house of Israel" (2:36). The "brethren"—Israelite brethren—want to know what they, as Israelites, must do to be saved. Peter tells them, "For the promise is for *you* and *your* children…" (2:39). There is nothing in this chapter

---

22. Hodges, "A Dispensational Understanding of Acts 2," 168–169.

23. As Marten H. Woudstra observes, "The question whether it is more proper to speak of a replacement of the Jews by the Christian church or of an extension (continuation) of the OT people of God into that of the NT church is variously answered." Marten H. Woudstra, "Israel and the Church," in *Continuity and Discontinuity: Perspectives on the Relationship Between the Testaments*, ed. John S. Feinberg (Wheaton, IL: Crossway, 1987), 237. Clarence Bass takes a similar position: "It is not that exegetes prior to his time did not see a covenant between God and Israel, or a future relation of Israel to the millennial reign, but they always viewed the church as a continuation of God's single program of redemption begun in Israel. It is dispensationalism's rigid insistence on a distinct cleavage between Israel and the church, and its belief in a later unconditional fulfilment of the Abrahamic covenant, that sets it off from the historic faith of the church. (Clarence Bass, *Backgrounds to Dispensationalism* [Grand Rapids, Eerdmans, 1960], 27).

that indicates that the promises first made to Israel were not being fulfilled right then and there. Peter continues to preach to his countrymen by informing them that "Jesus the Christ" was "appointed for *you*" (3:20). The "restoration of all things" (3:21) is the pre-ordained redemptive work of Jesus to fulfill what all the prophets had written. Peter tells them that the prophets "announced *these days*" (3:24). "It is *you* who are the sons of the prophets, and of the covenant which God made with your fathers, saying to Abraham, 'And in your seed all the families of the earth shall be blessed'" (3:25).

We read further about the fulfillment of the promise made to Israel, "sons of Abraham's family." The promises are fulfilled, not postponed.

> "From the descendants of this man, according to promise, God has brought to Israel a Savior, Jesus, after John had proclaimed before His coming a baptism of repentance to all the people of Israel. And while John was completing his course, he kept saying, 'What do you suppose that I am? I am not *He*. But behold, one is coming after me the sandals of whose feet I am not worthy to untie.' Brethren, sons of Abraham's family, and those among you who fear God, to us the message of this salvation has been sent. For those who live in Jerusalem, and their rulers, recognizing neither Him nor the utterances of the prophets which are read every Sabbath, fulfilled *these* by condemning *Him*" (Acts 13:23; cf. 13:32–33; 26:6).

Notice how Paul in Romans argues "that the promise will be guaranteed to all the descendants, not only to those who are of the Law, but also to those who are of the faith of Abraham, who is the father of us all" (Rom. 4:16; cf. 9:8; Gal. 3:29; 4:28). Non-Israelite believers, the "uncircumcision" (Eph. 2:11) who are "in Christ," are made a part of the commonwealth of Israel and are extended the promises originally given to Israel:

> Remember that you were at that time separate from Christ, excluded from the commonwealth of Israel, and strangers to the covenants of promise, having no hope and without God in the world. But now in Christ Jesus you who formerly were far off have been brought near by the blood of Christ. For He Himself is our peace, who made both groups into one and broke down the barrier of the dividing wall (2:12–14).

As a result, believing non-Israelites in Christ share in the (1) "**commonwealth of Israel**," as they are (2) no longer "strangers to the **covenants of promise**" (2:12), (3) "no longer strangers and aliens" but (4) "**fellow citizens** with the saints, and (5) are of **God's household**, having been (6) built on the **foundation of the apostles and prophets**, Christ Jesus Himself being the corner stone, in whom the whole building, being fitted together, is growing into (7) a **holy temple** in the Lord, in whom you also are being built together into a dwelling of God in the Spirit" (2:20–22). You can't get much more Israelite than these designations. They drip with Old Testament descriptions for Israel: commonwealth, citizenship, household, foundation of apostles and prophets, holy temple, and covenants. It's through Jesus that "we **both** have our access in one Spirit to the Father" (2:18).

Promises made to Old Testament Israel are said to be fulfilled by Paul in the so-called church age, something a dispensationalist would never acknowledge: "For **we are the temple** of the living God; just as God said, 'I will dwell in them and walk among them; and I will be their God, and **they shall be My people**.… And I will be a father to you, and you shall be sons and daughters to Me,' says the Lord Almighty" (2 Cor. 6:16, 18). How can this be when Paul is citing a verse that originally applied to Israel? How can the church be the temple? The temple is strictly Jewish. Second Corinthians 6:18 is a direct citation of Exodus 29:45: "And I will dwell among the sons of Israel and will be their God." Then there is the statement to the Corinthian *ekklēsia* to "come out from their midst and be separate." This, too, is an Old Testament reference to Israel, as is the reference not to touch "what is unclean" (2 Cor. 6:17b; Isa. 52:11). Finally, Paul tells the Corinthians that God will be a Father to them, and they will be "sons and daughters" to Him (2 Cor. 6:18). Once again, Paul draws on passages that were first applied to Israel (Isa. 43:6; Hosea 1:10).

Notice how 2 Corinthians 7 begins: "Therefore, having **these promises**, beloved, let us cleanse ourselves from all defilement of flesh and spirit, perfecting holiness in the fear of God" (v. 1). "These promises" were made to Israel, and yet Paul applies them to the church at Corinth (1:1).

There is no mention of a postponement of the promises, "an intercalary [inserted into the calendar] period of history,"[24] first made to Abraham. These Jewish believers, the recipients of the promises spoken by the prophets (Acts 3:24), made up "the church" (5:11). So then, when Gentiles were grafted into the existing all-

---

24. E. Schuyler English, *A Companion to the New Scofield Reference Bible* (New York: Oxford University Press, 1972), 135.

Israelite *ekklēsia*, they took part in the same Israelite promises. Dispensationalists have to maintain that this was never God's plan. Citing Isaiah 57:19, Paul assures Israelites and non-Israelites who are in Christ, "and He came and preached peace to you who were far away, and peace to those who were near" (Eph. 2:17). The New Testament *ekklēsia* was always God's plan!

Dispensationalists will still maintain that there are unfulfilled promises for Israel. Where in the New Testament does it say this? Not a single New Testament writer offers a caveat to their claim that the promises have been fulfilled. We have to ask the dispensationalist when these unfulfilled promises are going to be fulfilled. It can't be during the so-called church age since, as dispensationalist Thomas Ice states, "We dispensationalists believe that the church has superseded Israel during the current church age, but God has a future time in which He will restore national Israel 'as the institution for the administration of divine blessings to the world.'"[25] When will this divine blessing to the world take place? It can't take place "during the current church age" since God, according to Ice, has replaced Israel with the church. It's not going to take place during the dispensationalist's version of the Great Tribulation since there will be a mass slaughter of Jews and even greater destruction to the world. Will it be during the "millennium"? Revelation 20 certainly doesn't have anything to say about the promises being finally fulfilled since there is no mention of Israel or the land of Israel.

## Conclusion

Dispensationalists vehemently maintain that the *ekklēsia* (church) was unknown to the Old Testament writers. The so-called church age is said to be a "mystery," a parenthesis, a gap in prophetic time, until the pre-tribulational "rapture" when the church will be removed from the earth and God will deal with Israel again. Then why does the writer to the Hebrews quote Psalm 22:22 and use the Greek word *ekklēsia*, translated accurately in most modern translations as "congregation," as it should be translated elsewhere (see below)?:

> "I will proclaim Your name to my brethren,
> In the midst of the congregation [*ekklēsia*] I will sing Your praise"
> (Heb. 2:12).

---

25. Thomas Ice, "The Israel of God," The Thomas Ice Collection: www.raptureready.com/featured/TheIsraelOfGod.html#_edn3

Philip E. Hughes writes, "The proclamation of the Good News and the praise of God which accompanies it take place, moreover, *in the midst of the congregation,* or more literally (as in the KJV) 'in the midst of the church' ['*ekklēsia* here is the LXX rendering of the Hebrew *qāhāl*'], which in the perspective of the New Testament is God's new temple being built up of those 'living stones' who are brethren with and in Christ (1 Pet. 2:5; Eph. 2:19–22)."[26] If the dispensationalists are correct, then the New Testament writers were awfully confused, in spite of the fact that they, like their Old Testament counterparts, were under the direct inspiration of the infallible Holy Spirit (2 Tim. 3:16–17). Of course, we know they weren't confused in the least. If they had wanted to make such a distinction between Israel and the "church" they certainly would have used a word other than *ekklēsia*, which possessed a *continuity of meaning* spanning both the Old and New Testaments of the Greek Bible.

---

26. Hughes, *A Commentary on the Epistle to the Hebrews*, 108.

# 2

# The Myth that the Modern State of Israel Is a Sign that the Rapture is Near

In addition to dispensationalism's insistence that the application of God's redemptive program changed in the New Testament from Israel to a new entity called "the Church" (see chapter 1), another fundamental principle of dispensationalism is that there are no prophetic signs prior to the rapture. Not one. Zilch. Nada. None. This is because, according to dispensationalists, the Church had its beginning at Pentecost. At that point, the prophetic clock as it relates to Israel stopped (the end of Daniel's 69th week: 483 years). It will not start again until the "rapture" (the start of the 70th week) which they argue is still a future event (Jesus coming *for* His Church) that is different from the Second Coming (Jesus coming *with* His Church).[1] Again, following the dispensational hermeneutic, the so-called Church Age has no prophetic history in the Old Testament. This means that no Old Testament prophecy can find *any* fulfillment from the time of Pentecost when the Church Age had its start and the "rapture" when the Church Age is said to end.

The "rapture" is said to end the Church Age and begin God's dealings with Israel again after a nearly 2000-year (and counting) postponement. Dispensationalists believe the "rapture" is always "imminent," that it can take place at any time during the Church Age. Gerald B. Stanton puts it this way: "*The rapture is signless … and is so presented in the Scripture that every generation may enjoy the hope, challenge, and other blessings of His appearing.*"[2] Take note of the phrase "every generation," because it will serve as an important piece to the "rapture" puzzle that is often missed by those who hold to the any-moment rapture theory. According to Stanton and every other dispensationalist, it means the "rapture" could have taken

---

1. Mark Hitchcock, *Could the Rapture Happen Today?* (Sisters, OR: Multnomah Publishers, 205), chap. 7.

2. Gerald B. Stanton, "The Doctrine of Imminency: Is It Biblical?," *When the Trumpet Sounds: Today's Foremost Authorities Speak Out on End-Time Controversies*, ed. Thomas Ice and Timothy Demy (Eugene, OR: Harvest House, 1995), 223.

place in Paul's generation (1 Thess. 4:17) and any subsequent generation thereafter.[3] Jesse Forest Silver wrote that the apostolic fathers "expected the return of the Lord in their day."[4] Was the stage being set in the post-apostolic era? How could that be when all the major players that dispensationalists say are in place today didn't even exist, including what Tim LaHaye says is the "Super Sign," the return of the Jews to their land?

If the doctrine of imminency[5] is true to itself, the rapture could have taken place prior to the destruction of Jerusalem when the city was sacked by the Romans in A.D. 70, or it could have happened in 1000, 1066, 1492, 1517, 1776, 2001, or today. In theory, the "rapture" could have happened any time after Pentecost. Here's how dispensationalist John MacArthur, who is a representative of the signless, any-moment rapture view, explains the position:

> It could happen at any moment. It is a signless, imminent event, it is the next thing, no signs necessary ... [There are] signs before the Second Coming, [but there are] no signs before the Rapture. We live

---

3. Stanton writes: "Paul seemed to include himself among those who looked for Christ's return (1 Thess. 4:15, 17; 2 Thess. 2:1).... Many have concluded that the expectation of some was so strong they had stopped work and had to be exhorted to return to their jobs (2 Thess. 3:10–12)." ("The Doctrine of Imminency: Is It Biblical?," 224.

4. Jesse Forest Lee, *The Lord's Return* (New York: Fleming H. Revell Co., 1914), 62–63. Quoted in Stanton, "The Doctrine of Imminency: Is It Biblical?," 225.

5. As dispensationalist and promoter of the imminency ("any moment") "rapture" doctrine Earl D. Radmacher states, "The words *imminent* and *impending* are not found in Scripture." (Earl D. Radmacher, "The Imminent Return of the Lord," *Issues in Dispensationalism*, eds. Wesley R. Willis and John R. Master [Chicago: Moody Press, 1994], 248.) It's not so much that the words are not used, but that the concept itself is not found in Scripture because of the specific way words are used to identify when events are to take place. Radmacher acknowledges that it is difficult to develop the doctrine of imminency based on specific words: "With respect to the word *engus*, when it is used in Matthew 26:45–46) ... the thing spoken of as being 'at hand' took place while the speaker was yet speaking: '"Behold the hour is at hand, and the Son of Man is being betrayed into the hands of sinners. Rise, let us going. See, he who betrays Me is at hand." And while He was still speaking, behold, Judas, one of the twelve, ... came.'" (251). Radmacher then compares the Matthew passage with 1 Peter 4:7 which states, "the end of all things is at hand [*engus*]," literally, "has come near." Radmacher concludes that *engus* ("at hand" or "near") means that an event "may happen in a few minutes (Matt. 26:45–47) or in a few thousand years (1 Peter 4:7)" (251). This can hardly be true, especially when a full study of *engus* is made. It's never used in such a way that the reader is left with the impression that an event could happen at any moment, either in a week or two thousand years, but that the event is on the immediate horizon. Similar language is used in Zephaniah 1:14–18 which is a description of what was going to happen to Judah and "all the inhabitants of Jerusalem" (1:4) when "the Lord gave Jehoiakim king of Judah into [Nebuchadnezzar's] hand" (Dan. 1:2). Similar "end of the world" language is found in Psalm 18 for what are obviously local events.

in the light that at any moment in any fraction of a moment, trumps sounds [sic], the angel calls and we go. This is the next event in God's plan. It's only for those who know and love Christ. We're here to serve you and help you."6

MacArthur is not the only dispensationalist to make the any-moment, signless argument. James F. Stitzinger argues in a similar way: "The coming of Christ at the rapture is imminent, in the sense of an any-moment coming. Though there are no signs for the rapture, there are signs of the Second Coming to follow and these may appear before the rapture. Note Phil 3:20–21; 1 Thess 1:10; 4:16; Titus 2:13; Jas 5:7–9."7 Paul Feinberg agrees: "There is no mention of any signs or events that precede the Rapture of the church in *any* of the Rapture passages. The point seems to be that the believer prior to this event is to look, not for some sign, but the Lord from heaven. If the Rapture was a part of the complex of events that make up the Second Advent, and not distinct from it, then we would expect that there would be a mention of signs or events in at least one passage."8 The key phrase is, "there are *no signs* that precede the 'rapture.'" You're going to read a lot of prophecy writers who claim this as the fundamental doctrine of their prophetic system. Without it, there would be no modern-day prophecy movement.

## No and Yes

No, there are no signs. Yes, there are signs. We might restate it something like this, "On the one hand … but on the other hand." Here's a perfect example. Todd Strandberg and Terry James, authors of the book *Are You Rapture Ready?*, write, "The Bible gives no specific signs that will precede the Rapture. It will be unannounced. Instantaneous. World–stunning." Sounds like they are in line with the signless, any-moment "rapture" paradigm. Then *in the following two sentences*, they contradict themselves: "The Bible's prophets, on the other hand, list many prophetic signs that will precede the seven-year period of world trouble known as 'Tribulation,' or 'Apocalypse.' Interestingly enough, prophecy scholars are finding that signs

---

6. John MacArthur, "*The Final Generation of the Future Judgment*," commentary on Luke 21:29–33 (GC 42-264): http://www.biblebb.com/files/MAC/42-264.htm

7. James F. Stitzinger, "The Rapture in Twenty Centuries of Biblical Interpretation," *The Masters Seminary Journal* 13:2 (Fall 2002), 152: http://www.tms.edu/tmsj/tmsj13e.pdf.

8. Paul D. Feinberg, "The Case for the Pretribulation Rapture Position," *The Rapture: Pre-, Mid-, or Post-Tribulational?*, ed. Ben Chapman (Grand Rapids, MI: Academic Books, 1984), 80.

similar to those Bible prophets have for the Tribulation era are all around us."[9] This type of prophetic schizophrenia runs through nearly every popular prophecy book written today, as I will demonstrate below.

The mantra that there are no signs before the "rapture" is an absolutely indispensable part of the dispensational system because imminency "*is* a necessary deduction from pretribulationism."[10] It is the logical extension of the belief in an unforeseen parenthesis that the Old Testament prophets knew nothing about. If the Jews had not rejected Jesus, the dispensationalists claim, the Kingdom as it was promised to Israel would have begun at Jesus' first coming. So "when the Jews rejected Jesus as their Messiah, God suspended the prophetic timetable at the end of Daniel's sixty-ninth week and began building a new and heavenly people: the church."[11] E. Schuyler English, who was chosen in 1954 by Oxford University Press to serve as chairman of a revision committee to edit and update the Scofield Reference Bible, explains it this way:

> An intercalary [inserted into the calendar] period of history, after Christ's death and resurrection and the destruction of Jerusalem in A.D. 70, has intervened. This is the present age, the Church age.... During this time God has not been dealing with Israel nationally, for they have been blinded concerning God's mercy in Christ.... However, God will again deal with Israel as a nation. This will be in Daniel's seventieth week, a seven-year period yet to come.[12]

Scofield had set the pattern for this type of interpretation in his 1909 edition of his *Reference Bible*. Referencing Matthew 4:17b, "Repent for the kingdom of God is at hand," Scofield made these comments on the passage: "'At hand' is never a positive affirmation that the person or thing said to be 'at hand' will immediately appear, but only that no known or predicted event must intervene. When Christ appeared to the Jewish people, the next thing in the order of revelation as it then stood, should have been the setting up of the Davidic kingdom."[13] Of course, a

---

9. Todd Strandberg and Terry James, *Are You Rapture Ready?: Signs, Prophecies, Warnings, Threats, and Suspicions that the Endtime is Now* (New York: Dutton, 2003), xiii–xiv.

10. Richard L. Mayhue, *Snatched Before the Storm!: A Case for Pretribulationism* (Winona Lake, IN: BMH Books, 1980), 4

11. Timothy Weber, "The Dispensationalist Era," *Christian History*, 18:1 (Issue 61), 34.

12. E. Schuyler English, *A Companion to the New Scofield Reference Bible* (New York: Oxford University Press, 1972), 135.

13. Cyrus Ingersoll Scofield, *The Scofield Reference Bible* (New York: Oxford University Press, 1909), 988, note 3. Think through the implications of Scofield's statement. If the nation of Israel

study of "at hand" (*engus*) teaches the opposite.¹⁴ It *always* means something that is proximate, on the horizon of being accomplished, whether referring to people or events (*e.g.*, Mark 14:42; Luke 21:8; John 2:13; 6:4; 7:2, 6; 11:55; Rom. 13:12; James 5:8). Milton Terry, the author of *Biblical Hermeneutics*, a work that is recommended by dispensationalists and non-dispensationalists,¹⁵ offers a good antidote for the claim that time words like "near" and "shortly" mean an extended period of time:

> When a writer says that an event will shortly and speedily come to pass, or is about to take place, it is contrary to all propriety to declare that his statements allow us to believe the event is in the far future. It is a reprehensible abuse of language to say that the words *immediately*, or *near at hand*, mean *ages hence*, or *after a long time*. Such a treatment of the language of Scripture is even worse than the theory of a double sense.¹⁶

Even so, there are those who insist on interpreting the Bible literally who cannot abide by Terry's interpretive explanation. For example, Larry Spar-

---

as a whole had embraced Jesus as the Messiah, then Daniel's 70ᵗʰ week would have commenced immediately. But what happens in this final week? The antichrist makes a covenant with Israel. Russia swoops down and is joined by the Islamic nations (two entities that did not exist in the first century). Then to add insult to injury, after trusting in Jesus, two-thirds of the Jews living in Israel are slaughtered (Zech. 13:8). Can you see how dispensationalism is an impossible interpretive system and why gaps are necessary to make it work? Dispensationalists can keep pushing prophetic events into the future by always claiming that everything will be fulfilled "after the rapture" when no Christian now living will be around to test what they say.

14. "[The Greek word *engus*] is an adverb of time formed from two words: *en* ('in, at') and *guion* ('limb, hand'). Hence the meaning is literally 'at hand.' The Arndt and Gingrich *Lexicon* offers one word, 'near,' as the meaning. [W. F. Arndt and F. W. Gingrich, eds., *A Greek-English Lexicon of the New Testament and Other Early Christian Literature*, 4th ed. (Chicago: University of Chicago, 1957), 213.] Thayer expands on the idea of the word: 'of Time; concerning things imminent and soon to come to pass.' [Joseph Henry Thayer, ed., *Greek English Lexicon of the New Testament* (New York: American Book, 1889), 164.] Some of Thayer's examples are: 'the coming of the Lord is at hand' (James 5:8); 'the time is at hand' (Luke 21:8) 'the day is at hand' (Rom. 13:12); 'the end is at hand' (1 Peter 4:7).] He lists Revelation 1:3 and 22:10 in his series of examples. The word is used frequently of chronologically near events, such as approaching summer (Matt. 24:32), the Passover (Matt. 26:18; John 2:13; 11:55), the Feast of Tabernacles (John 7:2), etc." [Kenneth L. Gentry, Jr., *Before Jerusalem Fell: Dating the Book of Revelation*, 3rd ed. (Powder Springs, GA: American Vision, 1998), 140.]

15. Robert L. Thomas, "The Hermeneutics of Progressive Dispensationalism," *The Master's Perspective on Contemporary Issues* (Grand Rapids, MI: Kregel, 1998), 190.

16. Milton S. Terry, *Biblical Hermeneutics: A Treatise on the Interpretation of the Old and New Testaments* (New York: Phillips & Hunt, 1883), 495–496.

gimino argues that these time words "refer to human affairs. Man has a different sense of time than God."[17] This means, according to Spargimino, that every time you come across words like "near" and "shortly" in a prophetic context, they mean their opposite.

Just to see if anything has changed about the meaning of *engus*, I checked the newly published *Analytical Lexicon of the Greek New Testament*, where two of the three authors served as field linguists and teachers of graduate linguistics in Southeast Asia, and one served in several countries as a Greek consultant for Wycliffe Bible Translators: "[*engus*] adverb (1) of space *near, close to* (JN 3.23); absolutely *close by, near at hand, neighboring* (JN 19.42); (2) of time *near, imminent, close* (MT 26:18); (3) figuratively, of close or intimate relationship *near, close up* (EP 2.17)."[18]

## A Signless Event but with Signs

The essential belief that the "rapture" is a signless event has not stopped dispensationalists from making prophetic announcements or writing books that list signs they claim are evidence that the rapture is near. Jerry Falwell, who stated on a December 27, 1992, television broadcast, that he did "not believe there will be another millennium … or another century," wrote the following on July 23, 2006:

> It is apparent, in light of the rebirth of the state of Israel, that the present-day events in the Holy Land may very well serve as a prelude or forerunner to the future Battle of Armageddon and the glorious return of Jesus Christ.[19]

Mark Hitchcock follows the standard dispensational position that "the Rapture is an imminent, signless event, which, from the human perspective, could occur at any moment,"[20] but then goes on to write other books outlining the signs that he claims are evidence that the "rapture" is near. Here's a description of his book *Seven Signs of the End Times*:[21]

---

17. Larry Spargimino, *The Anti-Prophets: The Challenge of Preterism* (Oklahoma City: Hearthstone Publishing, 2000), 140.

18. Timothy Friberg, Barbara Friberg, and Neva F. Miller, *Analytical Lexicon of the Greek New Testament* (Grand Rapids, MI: Baker Books, 2000), 126.

19. Jerry Falwell, "On the threshold of Armageddon?" (July 23, 2006): www.worldnetdaily.com/news/article.asp?ARTICLE_ID=51180

20. Hitchcock, *Could the Rapture Happen Today?*, 80.

21. Mark Hitchcock, *Seven Signs of the End Times* (Sisters, OR: Multnomah Publishers, 2003).

## The Modern State of Israel and the Imminent Rapture

Since 1948, when the United Nations established a national Israeli homeland, Jews have been returning to the region in massive numbers. Mark Hitchcock says this ingathering, ending centuries of exile, is just one sign of the end times. War in the Middle East, the European Economic Union, globalism, apostasy in the church—all signal that Christ's return is imminent.

After spending more than a hundred pages describing how prophetic events are being fulfilled in our day in his *The Late Great United States*, on page 115 Hitchcock tells his readers, "But the rapture could happen at any time, and after that, all bets are off."[22] If the rapture could happen at any time, and this must have been true before there was a United States, then why is anything that happens to the United States this side of the rapture prophetically *significant*? In another Hitchcock sign-heavy book, *2012: The Bible and the End of the World*, he writes, "Every generation since the first coming of Christ has lived with the hope that it could be the terminal generation and that Christ could return at any moment. No prophetic event must be fulfilled before Christ's coming, so in this sense the end is indeed near."[23] To repeat, if every generation prior to ours could have expected Jesus to return in the "rapture," and if today's signs are unique (atomic weapons, Israel becoming a nation again, implantable microchips, cashless society,[24] etc.), then not a single generation prior to ours could have been "the terminal generation."

Thomas Ice, a co-author of a number of books with Hitchcock, has written an article that admonishes those who argue that there will be prophetic signs before the rapture.

> The thing that bothers me the most about this whole issue is the apparent lack of understanding by the date-setters, who are advocates of pretribulationism, that their very date-setting schemes are inconsistent with the New Testament teaching of the any-moment rapture. They do not seem to realize that by introducing into our futuristic approach to prophecy ideas and conclusions that flow from the logic of the long discredited historicist hermeneutic they are changing and

---

22. Mark Hitchcock, *The Late Great United States: What Bible Prophecy Reveals About America's Last Days* (Colorado Springs, CO: Multnomah Press, 2009), 115.

23. Mark Hitchcock, *2012: The Bible and the End of the World* (Eugene, OR: Harvest House, 2009), 106.

24. Thomas Ice and Timothy Demy, *The Coming Cashless Society* (Eugene, OR: Harvest House, 1996).

misrepresenting the very character of rapture theology. Our friends need to wake up and realize the unintended harm they are doing to the overall teaching on our Blessed Hope—the rapture![25]

On the one hand, Ice, along with two of his co-authors, asserts "the present church age is not a time in which Bible prophecy is being fulfilled," "Bible prophecy relates to a time *after the rapture* (the seven-year tribulation period),"[26] "the Rapture is a signless event," "there are no signs mentioned in the Bible that will indicate the Rapture is near," and "it is impossible for an imminent event to have signs."[27] And then in the next breath, actually the next paragraph, he and LaHaye in their book *Charting the End Times*, states, "we can see that these signs [of the Tribulation period] are drawing nearer to fulfillment during the present church age."[28] This is an interpretive trick. If there are signs for the tribulation period, then there *are* signs for the rapture, but dispensationalists can't admit it since their entire prophetic system is based on the claim that the so-called church age has no prophetic history. If the signs have only appeared in the last 100 years or so, then the "rapture" could not have been imminent before this time.

Notice in the above block quotation that Ice dismisses "the long discredited historicist hermeneutic." What is the historicist hermeneutic? "The historicist approach argues that Revelation supplies a prophetic overview of church history from the first century until the return of Christ,"[29] what dispensationalists call the "Church Age." While Ice dismisses this approach to prophecy, he and Timothy Demy follow it in their *Prophecy Watch* book. The seven churches in Revelation 2–3 are said to be a prophetic overview that "proceeds from Pentecost to the rapture as indicated by the oft-repeated phrase, 'He who has an ear, let him hear what the Spirit says to the churches' (Revelation 2:7, 11, 17, 29; 3:6, 13, 22)."[30] They identify

---

25. Thomas Ice, "Why Date-Setting the Rapture is Wrong": http://www.pre-trib.org/articles/view/why-date-setting-rapture-is-wrong

26. Thomas Ice and Timothy Demy, *Prophecy Watch: What to Expect in the Days to Come* (Eugene, OR: Harvest House, 1998), 10.

27. Tim LaHaye and Thomas Ice, *Charting the End Times: A Visual Guide to Understanding Bible Prophecy* (Eugene, OR: Harvest House, 2001), 118.

28. LaHaye and Ice, *Charting the End Times*, 118.

29. J. Daniel Hays, J. Scott Duvall, and C. Marvin Pate, *Dictionary of Biblical Prophecy and End Times* (Grand Rapids, MI: Zondervan, 2007), 201–202. See Steve Gregg, ed., *Revelation: Four Views—A Parallel Commentary* (Nashville: Thomas Nelson, 1997) and C. Marvin Pate, *Reading Revelation: A Comparison of Four Interpretative Translations of the Apocalypse* (Grand Rapids, MI: Kregel, 2009).

30. Ice and Timothy, *Prophecy Watch*, 45.

the prophetic period of the Laodicean Church Age as starting in 1900. This interpretation is impossible, especially for someone who claims to interpret the Bible literally. Revelation is not describing what the Spirit is saying to the *Church* through the ages, but to seven specific assemblies that were in existence in the first century. It's always "the church in" one of seven locales in Asia Minor (2:1, 8, 12, 18; 3:1, 7, 14). The same language is used in Acts 8:1: "the church in Jerusalem."

Tim LaHaye follows the same discredited historicist method. Like Ice and Hitchcock, he writes that the "first-century church believed in the imminent return of Christ, possibly during their lifetime."[31] He means that first-century Christians believed—because of the dispensational doctrine of "imminency"—that Jesus could come at any moment to "rapture" the church. But later in the same book he writes, "Chapter 1 [of Revelation] is the introduction; chapters 2 and 3 *cover the church age*, using seven historical churches to describe the entire age. (For example, the church in Ephesus is the only one that refers to apostles because the first-century church alone included apostles.)"[32] How could Christians believe that Jesus could come at any moment when dispensationalists like Ice, Demy, and LaHaye argue that the Bible teaches that He would not come until the last of the seven representative churches appears, and that not until 1900? This destroys their doctrine of the any-moment rapture of the church prior to 1900 since the "rapture" could not have taken place until eighteen hundred years later when the Laodicean church age began.[33]

The majority of people who read Tim LaHaye and Jerry Jenkins' multi-volume *Left Behind* series are led to believe that certain prophetic events were lining up for the "rapture" that would probably occur in their lifetime. But dispensational theology says there are no signs to indicate that the "rapture" is near. But this hasn't stopped LaHaye from teaching that there are signs, including what he describes as the "super sign."

LaHaye lists "Twelve Reasons Why This Could be the Terminal Generation." In the "Overview" that introduces LaHaye's article on the twelve reasons, we read: "Are we only a few years away from the second advent of Jesus Christ? Many believe that we are. Without saying that we are, the author [LaHaye] provides 12 reasons

---

31. Tim LaHaye, *No Fear of the Storm: Why Christians Will Escape All the Tribulation* (Sisters, OR: Multnomah, 1992), 65. *No Fear of the Storm* has been republished as *Rapture Under Attack*.

32. LaHaye, *No Fear of the Storm*, 74. See Tim LaHaye, *Revelation Unveiled*, rev. ed. (Grand Rapids, MI: Zondervan, 1999), 51–91.

33. LaHaye, *Revelation Unveiled*, 84.

why he thinks this generation could be living on the verge of Christ's return."[34] According to LaHaye, the "super sign" is related to the renewed national status of Israel in the twentieth century. Depending on which edition of LaHaye's *The Beginning of the End* you read, the key dates are either the advent of World War I and the November 2, 1917 signing of the Balfour Declaration[35] (the 1972 edition)[36] or the world recognition by the United Nations of Israel's statehood in 1948 (the 1991 edition).[37] All the signs that LaHaye lists take place in the so-called Church Age. But according to the any-moment rapture position, there can't be any signs during the Church Age, including Israel becoming a nation again.

As you're beginning to see, while dispensationalists talk a great deal about a signless prophetic parenthesis before the "rapture," what they've named the "Church Age," they also fill their books with what they contend are signs that purportedly confirm that the "rapture" is near. Oswald T. Allis saw this schizophrenia in 1945 when he wrote *Prophecy and the Church*, one of the first full-length critiques of dispensationalism:

> One of the clearest indications that Dispensationalist do not believe that the rapture is really "without a sign, without a time note, and unrelated to other prophetic events"[38] is the fact that they cannot write a book on prophecy without devoting a considerable amount of space to "signs" that this event must be very near at hand. These signs may be wars, famines, pestilences, the political situation—they may even include tanks and airplanes. [William E.] Blackstone listed eight signs. A recent writer gives fifteen.[39] ... Dispensationalists should recognize that the attempt

---

34. Tim LaHaye, "Twelve Reasons Why This Could be the Terminal Generation," *When the Trumpet Sounds*, eds. Thomas Ice and Timothy Demy (Eugene, OR: Harvest House Publishers, 1995), 429.

35. LaHaye calls it the "Balfore Treaty." (LaHaye, "Twelve Reasons Why This Could Be the Terminal Generation," 432).

36. Tim LaHaye, *The Beginning of the End* (Wheaton, IL: Tyndale House Publishers, 1972), 165, 168.

37. Tim LaHaye, *The Beginning of the End*, rev. ed. (Wheaton, IL: Tyndale House Publishers, 1991), 1993. Emphasis added. For a side-by-side analysis of LaHaye's change, see Richard Abanes, *End-Time Visions: The Road to Armageddon?* (New York: Four Walls Eight Windows, 1998), 295.

38. C. I. Scofield, *What Do the Prophets Say?* (Philadelphia, The Sunday School Times Co., 1918), 97.

39. [Louis] Bauman, *Light from Bible Prophecy* (1940). Allis adds: "The discussion of these signs occupies fifty pages or approximately one-third of the book. Some years ago L. S. Chafer

to prove by signs and events that the "signless" and unheralded *any moment* rapture must be near at hand really amounts to a surrender of the *any moment* principle.[40]

But to surrender the any moment "rapture" principle would nullify what Charles C. Ryrie calls the *sine qua non* of dispensationalism, keeping Israel and the church redemptively separate and distinct[41] during the Church Age.

There are dispensationalists who are critical of those who claim to teach a signless "rapture" but also engage in identifying signs they say serve as incontrovertible evidence that the "rapture" is near. Earl D. Radmacher, who is a well known dispensational author, is one of them:

> Equally as unjustified as date-setting for Christ's return are the numerous sermons attempting to find fulfillment of prophecy in this age. Typical of them is a popular author, conference speaker, and television personality who has stated his belief that the "paramount prophetic sign" is that Israel had to be a nation again in the land of its forefathers. This condition was fulfilled, he claims, on May 14, 1948.[42] This pronouncement is simply representative of hundreds, perhaps, thousands, of others who, although eager in their anticipation of Christ's coming, distort the Scripture and cause terrible confusion for God's people.[43]

Radmacher says that using Israel's new national status in 1948 as a prophetic sign is a distortion of Scripture that causes "terrible confusion for God's people." "This conflicting emphasis," he writes, "begets the rather embarrassing plight of

---

published a little book entitled *Seven [Biblical] Signs of the Times* [Philadelphia: Sunday School Times, 1919]. In no respect is the inconsistency of Dispensationalists more glaringly apparent, than in their persistent efforts to discover *signs* of the nearness of an event which they emphatically declare to be *signless*. [John Ashton] Savage appeals to such events, but refuses to call them signs. This shows that he recognized the inconsistency of attempting to prove by *signs* the nearness of an event which is held to be sign*less* (*The Scroll [of Time]*, p. 201)." (Oswald T. Allis, *Prophecy and the Church* [Philadelphia, PA: Presbyterian and Reformed, (1945) 1955], 315, note 10).

40. Allis, *Prophecy and the Church*, 174–175.

41. Charles C. Ryrie, *Dispensationalism*, rev. and ex. ed. (Chicago: Moody Press, 1995), 38–39.

42. "The one event which many Bible students in the past overlooked was this paramount prophetic sign: Israel had to be a nation again in the land of its forefathers." (Hal Lindsey, *The Late Great Planet Earth* [Grand Rapids: Zondervan, 1970], 43).

43. Radmacher, "The Imminent Return of the Lord," 248.

talking about signs of a signless event."[44] And yet, there is a long history of doing just what Radmacher condemns.

Lewis Sperry Chafer did it in his 1919 book *Seven Biblical Signs of the Times*.[45] He begins by telling his readers that the rapture "is imminent, and has been since the first promise regarding it was given."[46] If this is true, and every dispensationalist maintains that it is, then how can Chafer's seven particular signs be "signs of the times"? If they were signs for Chafer's time, then they weren't signs in past generations, especially "since the first promise" was given nearly 2000 years ago. If Israel becoming a nation again is Chafer's first sign, and Jerusalem being freed from Gentile domination is his third sign, then the "rapture" could not have been imminent until the 20th century. Chafer describes a particular "present indication of fulfillment":

> The present indication of fulfillment is found in the fact that Jerusalem and Judea have been wrested from the Turk and are now held by a people who are committed, both by their own desires and by the obligations of a sacred trust, to restore these possessions to the children of Abraham to whom they were given for an everlasting possession.[47]

This line of reasoning means that the rapture could not have been imminent until Jerusalem and Judea had been wrested from the Turk, that is, from Muslim rule. But Islam had no history prior to A.D. 610. So prior to the 7th century, the rapture was never imminent. Of course, none of this really matters since the seventh of the seven church ages in Revelation did not begin until 1900.

Chafer is not the only prominent dispensationalist to claim that the "rapture" is imminent, that is, that no signs precede the event, and then promote the idea that there are signs presently being fulfilled that indicate that

---

44. Radmacher, "The Imminent Return of the Lord," 248.

45. "[1] The Jew arises to national life; [2] Gentile governments turn to democracy; [3] Jerusalem is released from the overlordship of Gentiles; [4] Prophecy is unveiled; [5] Knowledge increases, and men run to and fro, and all creation is to be delivered from the bondage of corruption; [6] An apostasy must appear which retains the outward form of godliness, but denies the power thereof; [7] And treasure must be heaped together for the 'last days.' **These are God's signs and they are being fulfilled at this moment**. The rugged mountains appear; but our blessed haven in the presence of our Lord is even nearer. May this solemn truth lead us to be instant in season and out of season in the work which He has given us to do!" [Lewis Sperry Chafer, *Seven Biblical Signs of the Times* (Chicago: The Bible Institute Colportage Association, [1919], 1928).]

46. Chafer, *Seven Biblical Signs of the Times*, 10.

47. Chafer, *Seven Biblical Signs of the Times*, 10.

the "rapture" is near. John Walvoord, a dispensational author and professor at Dallas Theological Seminary, wrote:

> The hope of the return of Christ to take the saints to heaven is presented in John 14 as an imminent hope. There is no teaching of any intervening event. The prospect of being taken to heaven at the coming of Christ is not qualified by description of any signs or prerequisite events. Here, as in other passages dealing with the coming of Christ for the church, the hope is presented as an imminent event.... Other exhortations in relation to the return of Christ for the church also lose much of their meaning if the doctrine of imminency is destroyed.[48]

In another place, he writes: "the Lord could come at any moment and there are no necessary intervening events."[49] And this was two years after he wrote a book outlining a series of signs that would precede the "rapture."

A belief in imminency and no "intervening event" preceding the "rapture" did not stop Walvoord from making a very good living writing books describing a boat load of intervening events. His 1974 edition of *Armageddon, Oil and the Middle East Crisis* opened with this declaration: "Each day's headlines raise new questions concerning what the future holds."[50] As we now know, Walvoord's book was based on current events and not on sound methods of biblical interpretation, whether dispensational or otherwise. Described as "the world's foremost interpreter of biblical prophecy," in 1991 he expected "'the Rapture to occur in his own lifetime.'"[51] How could he expect it if it was, as he states, "signless"? If he said that the rapture could have happened in his lifetime regardless of anything that was going on in the world, then he would have been consistent with what he had repeatedly taught and refrained from citing any intervening events before the "rapture."

---

48. John F. Walvoord, *The Rapture Question: A Comprehensive Biblical Study of the Translation of the Church* (Findlay, OH: Dunham Publishing Company, 1957), 78–79.

49. John F. Walvoord, *Bibiotheca Sacra*, April-June 1976.

50. John F. Walvoord and John E. Walvoord, *Armageddon, Oil and the Middle East Crisis* (Grand Rapids, MI: Zondervan, 1974), 7.

51. Quoted in Kenneth L. Woodward, "The Final Days are Here Again," *Newsweek* (March 18, 1991), 55.

Walvoord's *Armageddon* book was reprinted in 1976 and then sank without a trace until a revised edition appeared in late 1990. It was decisively predictive based on events transpiring in the first Gulf War:

> The world today is like a stage being set for a great drama. The major actors are already in the wings waiting for their moment in history. The main stage props are already in place. The prophetic play is about to begin.... Our present world is well prepared for the beginning of the prophetic drama that will lead to Armageddon. Since the stage is set for this dramatic climax of the age, it must mean that Christ's coming for his own is very near.[52]

Not many people realized that the basic content of the revised edition was nearly sixteen years old when it was reissued. When the Gulf War ended abruptly, the book was being remaindered for twenty-five cents a copy, if it were bought by the case! But by then the book had sold nearly 1.7 million copies and was "the recipient of the Platinum Book Award from the Evangelical Christian Publishers Association."[53]

Tyndale House Publishers released a third edition in 2007 with a revised title and content to reflect a change in current events—*Armageddon, Oil, and Terror*.[54] There is no mention of what Walvoord wrote in 1957: "There is no teaching of any intervening event." The promotional material assured readers that its content "is as current as today's news … and every prediction rings true." Where have we heard this before? That's right! In 1974, when the first edition of *Armageddon, Oil, and the Middle East Crisis* was published, the same wording was used. With the success of his prediction books, Walvoord went on to write *Major Bible Prophecies: 37 Crucial Prophecies that Affect You Today*.[55] How can this be when Walvoord repeatedly told those who read his prophecy books that a "strict adherence to Scriptural revelation would undoubtedly lead to the conclusion that there are no signs of the rapture of the church revealed in the Scriptures"?[56]

---

52. John W. Walvoord, *Armageddon, Oil and the Middle East Crisis* (Grand Rapids, MI: Zondervan, 1990), 228.

53. As reported in "Zondervan Book on Prophecy Receives Bestselling Award" by Zondervan Publishing House (1991). On file.

54. John F. Walvoord and Mark Hitchcock, *Armageddon, Oil, and Terror: What the Bible Says About the Future of America, the Middle East, and the End of Western Civilization* (Wheaton, IL: Tyndale, 2007).

55. John F. Walvoord, *Major Bible Prophecies: 37 Crucial Prophecies that Affect You Today* (Grand Rapids, MI: Zondervan, 1991).

56. John F. Walvoord, "Is the End of the Age at Hand?," Focus on Prophecy, ed. Charles L.

# The Modern State of Israel and the Imminent Rapture

Walvoord has plenty of company in claiming imminency and then writing books that nullify the idea of imminency. J. F. Strombeck wrote *First the Rapture* in which he states that Christians should expect Jesus to come "at any moment."[57] The book is misnamed. It should be *First a Whole Bunch of Signs and then the Rapture*. Here is his opening paragraph:

> The present is an age of great anxiety because of the catastrophic events that have been predicted. The late H. G. Wells is quoted as having said, "This world is at the end of its tether. The end of everything we call life is close at hand."[58] A great general has said, "We have had our last chance. Armageddon is at hand," and the governor of a great state has said, "At least 90% of all Americans now living will be killed by atom bombs within five years."
>
> The fulfillment of these predictions can be nothing less than the great tribulation foretold by Jesus in the Olivet discourse.[59]

But if atom bombs are prophetic signs, and atom bombs were not developed until the 20th century, then the "rapture" could not have been imminent until the 20th century.

Wendell G. Johnston wrote "that the coming of Christ for the Church is imminent, that is, it could be at any time. There are no events given to us in the Word of God that must be fulfilled before Christ can come back for His Church. In other words, it is the next prophetic event, as far as Scripture is concerned."[60] Having written this, Johnston then goes on to contradict his claim that there are no events that must be fulfilled before the rapture: "Since 1948 Israel has been gaining in power; she becomes more important each day. The Bible prophesies this will happen."[61] If it does, it doesn't prophesy it will happen before the "rapture" since there are no signs before the rapture. If there are, the "rapture"

---

Feinberg (Westwood, NJ: Fleming H. Revell, 1964), 167.

57. J. F. Strombeck, *First the Rapture* (Moline, IL: Strombeck Agency, Inc., 1950), 11.

58. "The end of everything we call life is close at hand and cannot be evaded.... The writer is convinced that there is no way out or round or through the impasse. It is the end." (H. G. Wells, *Mind at the End of Its Tether and The Happy Turning: A Dream of Life* [New York: Didier, 1946], 1, 4).

59. Strombeck, *First the Rapture*, 7.

60. Wendell G. Johnston, "When Can the Church Expect the Lord's Return?," *Jesus the King is Coming* (ed. Charles Lee Feinberg (Chicago: Moody Press, 1975), 37.

61. Johnston, "When Can the Church Expect the Lord's Return?," 45.

would not be an imminent event. Johnston then goes on to discuss Russia and Egypt,[62] two more "signs" for a supposedly "signless" event.

Tim LaHaye had a list of 12 signs, and Mark Hitchcock, following his theological mentor Chafer, offered a similar list in his book *Seven Signs of the End Times*, leading with "The Return of the Jewish People to Israel."[63] Since the New Testament doesn't say anything about Israel becoming a nation again, Hitchcock must look to the Old Testament. But according to one of dispensationalism's major tenets, the Old Testament does not mention the Church Age in any manner, shape, or form.

Like Radmacher, dispensationalist John R. Rice was highly critical of those who claimed that any signs preceded the "rapture."

> Some Christian writers regard the atomic bomb, the rise of Russia, the founding of the new Israel state, the last world war (as they regarded the first world war), as evidence that we are in the very last days before Jesus comes.[64]

* * *

> All these people, usually faithful Bible believers, earnest Christians, have been influenced and misled by a heresy that has become widespread in recent years. This mistaken teaching holds that we are now, according to what are regarded as definite signs, in the very last few weeks or months or years before Jesus must come; that this period which they call "the last days" is more difficult than ever.[65]

* * *

> The custom has grown up among a lot of premillennial Christians of looking for Christ's return because we have had the first or second world war, or of looking for Christ's return because Zionists and infidel Jews have established the modern nation Israel in Palestine. Some are moved more by newspaper accounts than by the plain command of the Lord Jesus.[66]

---

62. Johnston, "When Can the Church Expect the Lord's Return?," 45–46.

63. Hitchcock, *Seven Signs of the End Times*, chap. 1.

64. John R. Rice, *We Can Have Revival Now* (Wheaton, IL: Sword of the Lord Publishers, 1950), 41.

65. Rice, *We Can Have Revival Now*, 41.

66. Rice, *We Can Have Revival Now*, 43.

\* \* \*

One theory is that Jesus will not come until certain signs have appeared. Some think Jesus cannot come until the gospel is preached again to all the world. Some think Jesus could not come until what they call "the budding of the fig tree," the re-establishment of the nation Israel as it has recently been reestablished in Palestine. Others think that Jesus could not return until the so-called "great apostasy," the wave of modernism in the church which has occurred in America in the last fifty years and is now possibly past its climax. Many would say that the first and second world wars are signs of the soon coming of Christ. If that be true, then Jesus could not have come before these wars. Others believe that certain earthquakes, that famine following the wars, that the present capital-labor controversy encouraged by socialists and communists everywhere are signs of Christ's coming, and that therefore Christ could not have come before these clashes occurred and communism and socialism reached their present popularity.[67]

Rice makes these points over and over again in his book. He contends that signs preceding the "rapture" are contrary to the dispensational "doctrine of the imminency of Christ's return." He wants his readers to "note carefully that this doctrine of the imminency of Christ's return contradicts the doctrine that Jesus could not come until a certain set time in a program and that He must come after a number of specified signs are fulfilled."[68]

## Setting the Stage

The prophecy books that sell hundreds of thousands, even millions of copies are those that (1) tell readers that the rapture could occur at any moment, (2) that there are no signs preceding it, and then (3) go on to list numerous signs that they claim are being fulfilled before our very eyes. Some people see through the charade, most do not. David Jeremiah is a prominent pastor and prophecy writer. He's had a number of prophetic bestsellers over the years, including *Escape the Coming Night* and *The Handwriting on the Wall* written with C.C. Carlson. In 2008, Jeremiah wrote *What in the World is Going On?*, an appropriate title since even a regular

---

67. Rice, *We Can Have Revival Now*, 45.
68. Rice, *We Can Have Revival Now*, 45.

attendee at his church was not able to reconcile a signless rapture with all his talk about signs. Here's how Jeremiah tells it:

> One morning recently I spoke about the Rapture during a series of messages on prophecy. Later I was told that on the way out of church, a girl expressed confusion to her mother about something I had said. "Dr. Jeremiah keeps talking about all the signs that are developing concerning the Lord's return. And then in the next breath he says that nothing needs to happen before Jesus comes back to take us home to be with Him [in the Rapture]. I don't understand!" It seemed to this girl that I had contradicted myself. First, I seemed to say that certain prophesied signs would occur before the coming of Christ; then I seemed to say that nothing needed to occur before Jesus comes to claim His own [in the Rapture]. The girl's honest confusion deserves to be addressed because I believe she speaks for many who are similarly puzzled about events relating to the Rapture.[69]

At least he is honest enough to admit that the "there are no signs but there are signs" interpretive model is confusing and puzzling. He writes that "most of the misunderstanding comes from confusing two events: the Rapture and the Second Coming."[70] While there are no signs for the "rapture," there are signs for the seven-year tribulation period that ends with the Second Coming. But after trying to clear up the confusion, on the very next page he once again states, "There are no events that must take place before the Rapture occurs. It's all a matter of God's perfect timing."[71]

David Jeremiah is not the only one who takes this explanatory approach. In their book *Charting the End Times*, LaHaye and co-author Ice write, "we believe that our generation has more signs to indicate that Christ *could* come in our lifetime than any generation before us."[72] They believe God is "setting the stage"[73] for the "rapture." As we've seen, they propose that there are many signs relating to God's end time program for Israel and at the same time state that "prophetic signs

---

69. David Jeremiah, *What in the World is Going On?: 10 Prophetic Clues You Cannot Afford to Ignore* (Nashville: Thomas Nelson, 2009), 99.

70. Jeremiah, *What in the World is Going On?*, 99.

71. Jeremiah, *What in the World is Going On?*, 100.

72. Tim LaHaye and Thomas Ice, *Charting the End Times: A Visual Guide to Understanding Bible Prophecy* (Eugene, OR: Harvest House, 2001), 119.

73. LaHaye and Ice, *Charting the End Times*, 118.

relating to Israel are not being fulfilled in our day." So how do they reconcile what looks like an obvious contradiction?:

> What God is doing prophetically in our day is preparing the world or "stage-setting" for the time when He will begin His plan relating to Israel which will then involve the fulfillment of signs and times. Thus, when we see events happening in our day, they are not a fulfillment of Bible prophecy, instead, they are likely preparation for a future fulfillment during the tribulation. One major indicator that we are likely near the beginning of the tribulation is the clear fact that national Israel has been reconstituted after almost 2,000 years.
>
> The present church age is not a time in which Bible prophecy is being fulfilled. Bible prophecy relates to a time after the rapture (the seven-year tribulation period). However, this does not mean that God is not preparing the world for that future time during the present church age—in fact, He is. But this is not "fulfillment" of Bible prophecy. So while prophecy is not being fulfilled in our day, it does not follow that we cannot track "general trends" in current preparation for the coming tribulation, especially since it immediately follows the rapture. We call this approach "stage-setting." Just as many people set their clothes out the night before they wear them the following day, so in the same sense is God preparing the world for the certain fulfillment of prophecy in a future time.[74]

According to Ice, God is "setting the stage" for the "rapture." He is lining up events that are not in any way prophetic to prepare the Church for the "rapture." Ice is very clear about this: "prophetic signs relating to Israel are not being fulfilled in our day." As we've seen throughout this chapter, according to dispensationalism there are no prophetic signs prior to the "rapture" since the "Church Age" is a parenthesis in prophetic time about which the Old Testament prophets did not, could not, would not prophesy because there is a break in the prophetic calendar until the Church is "raptured" and once again deals exclusively with Israel.

But if God is "setting the stage" for the "rapture" in our day, then He had not been setting the stage for nearly 2000 years. If that's the case, then the "rapture" could not have been imminent until God began to set the stage. But this destroys the very idea of imminency prior to our day. By definition, the "any-moment

---

74. Thomas Ice, "Signs of the Times and Prophetic Fulfillment": http://www.raptureready.com/featured/ice/SignsoftheTimesandPropheticFulfillment.html

rapture" *requires* that nothing needs to be set. It can happen at "any moment." If not, then it would have been easy to argue any time until our generation that the "rapture" was *not* near *because* certain prophetic events (that really aren't prophetic events) were not in place since the stage was not being set. If Israel's nationhood is the "super prophetic sign," as Tim LaHaye describes it, the "rapture" was impossible until this "super prophetic sign" appeared. It's no wonder that John R. Rice spends so much time criticizing this schizophrenic view of Bible prophecy and that the girl who heard David Jeremiah's prophecy series was confused.

## The Fig Tree

A very popular argument for modern-day Israel being the fulfillment of Bible prophecy uses the fig tree illustration found in Matthew 24:32: "Now learn the parable from the fig tree: when its branch has already become tender and puts forth its leaves, you know that summer is near."

The general consensus is that the fig tree has always represented the nation of Israel. Sometimes Israel is compared to a fig tree (Judges 9:10–11), a vine (Hosea 9:10; Judges 9:12–13), an olive tree (Judges 9:8–9), and the cedars of Lebanon (Judges 9:15). In fact, there is no single tree, bush, or shrub that is exclusively identified with Israel. "The vine dries up and the fig tree fails; the pomegranate, the palm also, and the apple tree, all the trees of the field dry up. Indeed, rejoicing dries up from the sons of men" (Joel 1:12). The vine and fig tree are often used together (1 Kings 4:25), neither one being a distinctive identifier for Israel (Joel 2:22; Micah 4:4; Hab. 3:17, with the olive tree).

The New Testament does identify the olive tree as Israel's representative tree (Rom. 11:17, 24). It seems rather odd that Paul would choose the olive tree when so many claim that "the fig tree has always been representative of the nation of Israel." Notice that in the parallel account in Luke's version of the Olivet Discourse, Jesus says, "Behold the fig tree and ALL THE TREES; as soon as THEY put forth *leaves*, you see it and know for yourselves that summer is now near" (Luke 21:29–30).

If the fig tree represents Israel, then there is the problem of what Jesus says about the fig tree earlier in Matthew's gospel: "Now in the morning, when He was returning to the city, He became hungry. Seeing a lone fig tree [Israel] by the road, He came to it [Israel] and found nothing on it [Israel] except leaves only; and He said to it [Israel], "NO LONGER SHALL THERE EVER BE ANY FRUIT FROM YOU [ISRAEL]'" (Matt. 21:18–22). Notice that Matthew 24:32 does not say anything about fruit; it only mentions leaves. It was a "leaves-only" tree, the same type of tree that Jesus said would never bear fruit. So, if the fig tree represents Israel, then there is a contradiction. You can't have it both ways (*not* Israel in Matthew 21 and Israel in Matthew 24).

Dispensationalists have been making the "fig tree" = Israel claim for some time (see the *Scofield Reference Bible*). This is beginning to change because dispensationalists see a number of exegetical, historical, and logical problems. Dispensational prophecy author John F. Walvoord wrote the following about the fig tree being Israel:

> Actually, while the fig tree could be an apt illustration of Israel IT IS NOT SO USED IN THE BIBLE. In Jeremiah 24:1–8, good and bad figs [not trees] illustrate Israel in the captivity, and there is also mention of figs in 29:17. The reference to the fig tree in Judges 9:10–11 is obviously not Israel. Neither the reference in Matthew 21:18–20 nor that in Mark 11:12–14 with its interpretation in 11:20–26, gives any indication that it is referring to Israel, any more than the mountain referred to in the passage. Accordingly, while this interpretation is held by many, there is no clear scriptural warrant. A better interpretation is that Christ was using a natural illustration. Because the fig tree brings forth new leaves late in the spring, the budding of the leaves is evidence that summer is near.[75]

Mark Hitchcock, like Walvoord, takes issue with the often used argument that the fig tree in Matthew 24:32 describes the reinstitution of the nation of Israel, a point he also made in his book *The Complete Book of Bible Prophecy*.[76] Tim LaHaye and many popular prophecy writers see Matthew 24:32 as the key New Testament prophetic passage: "when a fig tree is used symbolically in Scripture, it usually refers to the nation Israel. If that is a valid assumption (and we believe it is), then when Israel officially became a nation in 1948, that was the 'sign' of Matthew 24:1-8, the beginning 'birth pangs'—it meant that the 'end of the age' is 'near.'"[77] The editors of LaHaye's own *Prophecy Study Bible* (2000) disagree: "the fig tree is not symbolic of the nation of Israel" (1040).

---

75. John F. Walvoord, *Matthew: Thy Kingdom Come* (Chicago, IL: Moody, [1974] 1980), 191-192.

76. Mark Hitchcock, *The Complete Book of Bible Prophecy* (Wheaton, IL: Tyndale House Publishers, 1999), 158.

77. Tim LaHaye and Jerry Jenkins, *Are We Living in the End Times? Current Events Foretold in Scripture ... And What They Mean* (Wheaton, IL: Tyndale House Publishers, 1999), 57.

Other dispensationalists are beginning to reject the popular belief that the fig tree of Matthew 24 refers to modern-day Israel. The following comments[78] are from Larry D. Pettegrew, a theology professor at dispensational-oriented Master's Seminary:

> The fig tree, however, does not illustrate Israel becoming a nation in 1948. The fig tree is simply an illustration from nature. The disciples ask, What will be the sign of your coming and the end of the age? And the answer is, the events of the great tribulation. This is illustrated by the cycle of a tree. When leaves appear on a tree, that is a sign that summer is near. Similarly, when the events of the great tribulation unfold, believers can know the second coming is near. There are two evidences for this interpretation. First, when Jesus makes His point from the fig tree illustration, He says, "When you see *all these things*, know that it is near—at the doors!" (33). The Lord is not talking about a single event such as Israel becoming a nation in 1948. He speaks of all of the events of the tribulation being signs of the second coming.
>
> Second, in the parallel passage in Luke, Luke records Jesus adding the phrase, "and all the trees" (Luke 21:19). If the fig tree blossoming is a reference to the founding of Israel, what would the blossoming of the other trees illustrate? The parable understood in this way does not make sense.

Again, the best understanding of the illustration is that the Lord is simply giving an illustration from nature. John MacArthur writes, "The point of the parable is utterly uncomplicated; even a child can tell by looking at a fig tree that summer is near. Likewise, the generation that sees all these signs come to pass will know with certainty that Christ's return is near."[79]

I find it odd that all the weight of an argument that sets out to convince people that the New Testament predicts that Israel will become a nation again rests on a cryptic analogy when the rest of the Olivet Discourse is so particular with its signs (wars, famines, false Christs, etc.). The New Testament does not say anything about Israel becoming a nation again. You won't even find it in Romans 11.

---

78. Larry D. Pettegrew, "Interpretive Flaws in the Olivet Discourse," *TMSJ* 13/2 (Fall 2002), 173–190: http://www.tms.edu/tmsj/tmsj13f.pdf

79. John MacArthur, *The Second Coming: Signs of Christ's Return and the End of the Age* (Wheaton, IL: Crossway Books, 1999), 134.

## Unbelieving or Believing Israel?

Dr. Paige Patterson, president of Southwestern Baptist Theological Seminary and a *dispensational premillennialist*, said the following in a radio debate with me in 1991:

> The present state of Israel is not the final form. The present state of Israel will be lost, eventually, and Israel will be run out of the land again, only to return when they accept the Messiah as Savior.[80]

Why would he say such a thing? Because he knows that Israel's return had to be in belief. Both the Northern and Southern kingdoms went into captivity because of unbelief. It makes no sense to argue that their return, either from exile or from the post-A.D. 70 Diaspora, would be in unbelief given what we read in Deuteronomy 30:1–3:

> So it shall be when all of these things have come upon you, the blessing and the curse which I have set before you, and you call *them* to mind in all nations where the Lord your God has banished you, **and you return to the Lord your God and obey Him with all your heart and soul according to all that I command you today, you and your sons, then the Lord your God will restore you from captivity**, and have compassion on you, and will gather you again from all the peoples where the Lord your God has scattered you.

God has set the standard. It's no wonder that dispensationalist John R. Rice wrote the following: "Thus the trouble in Jerusalem, and the dispersion of Jews among all the nations of Jerusalem throughout this whole age, is simply a continuation of the punishment of God upon the whole race of Jews."[81]

---

80. Stated on Dallas, Texas, radio program KCBI in a debate with me on May 15, 1991.

81. John R. Rice, *The King of the Jews: A Commentary on the Gospel According to Matthew* (Murfreesboro, TN: Sword of the Lord Publishers, 1955), 369.

# 3

# The Myth that Only Dispensationalists Have a Redemptive Future for Israel

Among some of the Reformers and successors of Calvin, such as Bucer, Francis Lambert, Beza, Peter Martyr, and the editors of the Geneva Bible, appeared a belief that the Jewish people would be converted to Christianity and that through their conversion the Church on earth would experience great blessing. Belief in the future conversion of the Jews became widely diffused in England, Scotland, and New England in the seventeenth century. The Puritans followed Calvin in believing the Gospel would progress throughout the world. This understanding of the future is not explicit in the Westminster Confession of Faith, but it can be seen in the Westminster Larger Catechism (answer to Question 191), the Westminster Directory of Worship ("Of Public Prayer before the Sermon"), and the writings of the Westminster divines. While a few were moderate premillennialists, the great majority expected the propagation of the gospel and the Kingdom of Christ among all nations, the conversion of the Jews, the fullness of the Gentiles, and the fall of Antichrist. The common Augustinian eschatology is affirmed in the Westminster Confession, compatible with either its amillennial or postmillennial forms.[1]

A number of people have asked me to respond to a talk that John MacArthur delivered at the 2007 Shepherds' Conference: "Why Every Self-Respecting Calvinist Is a Premillennialist." It seemed out of character for MacArthur because it had a mean-spirited tone to it. It also sounded desperate, as if he has been hearing the foundation stones of dispensationalism cracking all around him. MacArthur, who believes in "sovereign election" as it relates to individual salvation,

---

1. "What Presbyterians Believe: Eschatology in the Reformed Tradition": www.pcusa.org/today/archive/believe/wpb9901d.htm

is surprised that many of his sovereign grace colleagues who are amillennial and postmillennial do not hold to the sovereign election of Israel. He concludes that only dispensational premillennialists take Israel's national election seriously. His logic goes like this: If you believe in the sovereign election of the individual, then you must be a dispensationalist since only dispensationalists hold to the sovereign election of Israel. Election cuts both ways, MacArthur argues.

As a Calvinist, MacArthur surely knows that the whole nation of Israel never was and never will be elected. It's only the remnant that will be saved. "Isaiah cries out concerning Israel, 'THOUGH THE NUMBER OF THE SONS OF ISRAEL BE LIKE THE SAND OF THE SEA, IT IS THE REMNANT THAT WILL BE SAVED'" (Rom. 9:27). Paul makes the same point later in his epistle to the Romans by referring to Elijah who believed that he was the only one who had not bowed the knee to Baal (11:3). God retorts: "'I have kept for Myself seven thousand men who have not bowed the knee to Baal.' In the same way then, there has also come to be at the present time [Paul's time] a remnant according to *God's* gracious choice" (Rom. 11:4). So MacArthur's view of Israel's election is governed by God's election of a remnant. If this remnant idea is yet future, as MacArthur and other dispensationalists believe, then "all Israel" (Rom 11:26) is not every Israelite throughout time but only the elect of Israel at a certain point of time in history. One does not have to be a premillennialist to believe that God is going to save a remnant of Israel, and there is no need for a reconstituted national Israeli state to save a remnant of Israelites. Jews were being saved throughout the diaspora in Paul's day and continue to be saved even today.

As we will see, long before dispensationalism deformed prophetic thought, Calvinist Bible commentators and their doctrinal confessions made specific reference to the future salvation of Israel. Like a number of MacArthur's books on eschatology (*Because the Time is Near* and *The Second Coming: Signs of Christ's Return and the End of the Age*), his Shepherds' Conference talk is poorly argued. Not only does it misrepresent amillennialism and postmillennialism, it also gets a great deal of history wrong. To claim that only dispensationalism takes the promises made to Israel seriously is an exercise in historical revisionism and exegetical manipulation, especially when Calvinist postmillennial commentators and their Confessions are considered.

Keep in mind that dispenstionalism is a nineteenth-century invention and was not systematized until 1909 with the publication of the *Scofield Reference Bible*. The future place of Israel in prophecy has had a long history among postmillennial Calvinists, something MacArthur surely knows and should have discussed even if it was to refute the claim or qualify it.

## The Church Fathers

Dan Shute writes that "most of the church fathers believed that Paul referred to a mass conversion of the Jews as a prelude to the return of Christ."[2] He references the Christian Jewish work *The Testaments of the Twelve Patriarchs,* Tertullian's treatise *De Pudicitia* ("On Modesty"), Cyril of Alexandria's *Explanatio in Epistolam ad Romanos,* and others. According to Theodore of Mopsuestia's *In Epistolam Pauli ad Romanos,* Paul says that the Jews "will not always remain outsiders to true religion: there will be a time when they will also know the truth, as soon as people everywhere may receive knowledge of true religion."[3] in There were a number of early church fathers who did not believe that Israel held any special status. Dispensationalist Alan Patrick Boyd writes that the "majority of the writers/writings in this period [A.D. 70–165] completely identify Israel with the Church."[4] Boyd references Papias, 1 Clement, 2 Clement, Hermas, the *Didache,* and Justin Martyr's *Dialogue with Trypho, a Jew.* Boyd writes that the author of the Epistle of Barnabas "totally disassociated Israel from the precepts of the Old Testament. In fact he specifically designates the Church to be the heir of the covenantal promises made to Israel." The Shepherd of Hermas (which was written before 150 AD) contains, according to Boyd, "the employment of the phraseology of late Judaism to make the Church the true Israel." Justin Martyr "claims that the Church is the true Israelitic race, thereby blurring the distinction between Israel and the Church."

"To sum up," Dan Shute argues, "the church fathers took as a received Christian teaching that the Jews would eventually be converted to Christ: at the same time, some hesitated to identify 'all Israel' with Jews only." This view continued during the Medieval period. "Thomas Aquinas, for example in his commentary on Romans, interprets both Romans 11:15 ('life from the dead')

---

2. Dan Shute, "*And All Israel Shall be Saved*: Peter Martyr and John Calvin on the Jews According to Romans, Chapters 9, 10 and 11," *Peter Martyr Vermigli and the European Reformations: Semper Reformanda,* ed. Frank A. James III (Leiden, the Netherlands: Koninklijke Brill, 2004), 162.

3. Quoted in Shute, "*And All Israel Shall be Saved,* 162.

4. Alan Patrick Boyd, "A Dispensational Premillennial Analysis of the Eshatology of the Post-Apostolic Fathers (Until the Death of Justin Marlyr)," unpublished master's thesis, Dallas Theological Seminary, 1977, p. 47.

and 11:25–26 ('And so all Israel will be saved') as references to the conversion of the Jews in the latter days."[5]

## The Reformers

Prior to writing his 1542 anti-Semitic pamphlet "On the Jews and their Lies," Martin Luther also affirmed a future for Israel based on Romans 11:25:

> They indeed are enemies of God for your sakes who believe in the gospel: but as regards election, they are those whom God elected from eternity, and he loved them more than others: thus for the sake of the fathers they are elect until now.... The fact that they are indeed the people of God for the sake of the fathers is plain. Nor does God repent of his promise. He called Israel to be his people: therefore that people will not be damned but will return to faith and will be saved, even though they have been rejected for a time.[6]

John Calvin, the one person who is most often identified with the doctrine of election, a position that MacArthur holds, can be read several ways based on what published works are consulted. He contends that the use of "all Israel" in Romans 11:26 includes "all the people of God" and not the Jews exclusively. He implies that that true religion will not be restored to the "again as before." And yet in Calvin's *Institutes of the Christian Religion* we see a different emphasis:

> By virtue of this, [Paul] teaches, the Jews are the first and natural heirs of the gospel, except to the extent that by their ungratefulness they were forsaken as unworthy—yet forsaken in such a way that the heavenly blessing has not departed utterly from their nation. For this reason, despite their stubbornness and covenant-breaking, Paul still calls them holy [Rom. 11:16].... Yet, despite the great obstinacy with which they continue to wage war against the gospel, we must not despise them, while we consider that, for the sake of the promise, God's blessing still rests among them. For the apostle indeed testifies that it will never be completely taken away.[7]

---

5. Shute, "*And All Israel Shall be Saved*, 163.

6. Martin Luther, *In Epostolam ad Romanos Annotationes in Opera ... Latinorum Scriptorum* (Zurich: Schulthess, 1838). Quoted in Shute, "*And All Israel Shall be Saved*, 164.

7. John Calvin, *Institutes of the Christian Religion*, ed. John T. McNeill, 2 vols. (Philadelphia: The Westminster Press, 1960), (IV.XVI.14) 2:1336–1337.

Theodore Beza (1519–1605), John Calvin's successor in Geneva, taught that the world would "be restored from death to life again, at the time when the Jews should also come, and be called to the profession of the Gospel." Martin Bucer (1491–1551), the reformer of Strasbourg and perhaps the continental Reformer who had the most direct influence on English Puritanism, wrote in a 1568 commentary on Romans that Paul prophesied a future conversion of the Jewish people.[8]

In England, the place of the Jews in prophecy was a prominent issue in the seventeenth century and was most true among the generally postmillennial English and Scottish Puritans. The English preacher and theologian Thomas Brightman (1562–1607) developed, according to Peter Toon, "the first important and influential English revision of the Reformed, Augustinian concept of the millennium."[9] In this revision, Brightman emphasized the conversion of the Jews. In his *Apocalypsis Apocalypseos* (*A Revelation of the Revelation*), Brightman argued that the fall of the Turkish Empire would be followed by "the calling of the Jews to be a Christian nation," an event that would lead to "a most happy tranquillity from thence to the end of the world."[10] His commentary on Daniel 11–12 included the subtitle, *The Restoring of the Jews and their Calling to the Faith of Christ after the Utter Overthrow of their Three Last Enemies is set forth in Lively Colors.*[11] Brightman believed the Jews would be restored to Jerusalem and that "the Jewish Christian Church w[ould] become the centre of a Christian world."[12] He found Scriptural support for this conclusion in Daniel 12:2–3 and Revelation 20:11–15, both of which describe "the rebirth of a Christian Israelite nation."[13] Iain Murray summarizes the seventeenth-century concern for Israel in this way:

> The future of the Jews had decisive significance for them because they believed that, though little is clearly revealed of the future purposes of God in history, enough has been given us in Scripture to

---

8. Quotations from J. A. DeJong, *As the Waters Cover the Sea: Millennial Expectations in the Rise of Anglo-America Missions, 1640–1810* (Kampen: J. H. Kok, 1970).

9. Peter Toon, "The Latter-Day Glory," in *Puritans, the Millennium and the Future of Israel: Puritan Eschatology 1600–1660,* ed. Peter Toon (Cambridge: James Clarke, 1970), 26.

10. Toon, "The Latter-Day Glory," 27.

11. Toon, "The Latter-Day Glory," 30.

12. Toon, "The Latter-Day Glory," 30. Toon's words.

13. Toon, "The Latter-Day Glory," 30. Toon's words. Toon notes that "Brightman's eschatological scheme may be described as a form of postmillennialism since, and this is important, he expected Christ to return in glory only at the end of the second millennium and at the end of the age" (31).

> warrant the expectation that with the calling of the Jews there will come far-reaching blessing for the world. Puritan England and Covenanting Scotland knew much of spiritual blessing and it was the prayerful longing for wider blessing, not a mere interest in unfulfilled prophecy, which led them to give such place to Israel.[14]

This emphasis fits neatly into what many modern-day postmillennialists teach: The latter-day glory of the Church will be inaugurated by the conversion of the Jews to Christ; this is what Paul meant when he said that the conversion of the Jews would be "life from the dead" (Rom. 11:15).

Murray's *Puritan Hope* provides abundant documentation of the postmillennial redemption of Israel. This view was advanced in the notes to the 1560 Geneva Bible: "Again, that he may join the Jews and Gentiles together as it were in one body, and especially may teach what duty the Gentiles owe to the Jews, he emphasises, that the nation of the Jews is not utterly cast off without hope of recovery [Rom. 11:28].… The reason or proof: because the covenant made with that nation of everlasting life cannot be frustrated or in vain" [Rom. 11:29]. Peter Martyr (1499–1562), who taught at Cambridge and Oxford (1568), presented a "careful exposition of the eleventh chapter [of Romans that] prepared the way for a general adoption amongst the English Puritans of a belief in the future conversion of the Jews."[15]

> The sum of this chapter's teaching can be briefly reviewed in the following way: the Jews have not so perished without exception that no hope remains for their salvation. To this day remnants are preserved who are saved, now to be sure in a small number (even so they are the salt of the earth), but one day they will become a mighty band in full view.[16]

For Martyr, "one day" means "towards the end of the world."[17]

Scottish theologian Charles Ferme, writing sometime in the late sixteenth century, argued that Paul indicated that "when the fulness of the Gentiles shall have been brought in, the great majority of the Israelitish people are to be called,

---

14. Iain Murray, *The Puritan Hope: Revival and the Interpretation of Prophecy* (London: The Banner of truth Trust, 1971), 59–60.

15. Murray, *The Puritan Hope*, chap. 3.

16. Peter Martyr Virmigli, *In Epistolam S. Pauli Apostoli ad Romanos*, 3rd ed. (Basil, 1568). Quoted in Shute, "*And All Israel Shall be Saved*, 166.

17. Martyr, *In Epistolam S. Pauli Apostoli ad Romanos*, 496. Quoted in Shute, "*And All Israel Shall be Saved*, 167.

through the gospel, to the God of their salvation, and shall profess and own Jesus Christ, whom, formerly, that is, during the time of hardening, they denied."[18]

In a 1635 letter, the Scottish theologian Samuel Rutherford expressed a wish to live to see the conversion of the Jews:

> O to see the sight, next to Christ's Coming in the clouds, the most joyful! Our elder brethren the Jews and Christ fall upon one another's necks and kiss each other! They have been long asunder; they will be kind to one another when they meet. O day! O longed-for and lovely day-dawn! O sweet Jesus, let me see that sight which will be as life from the dead, thee and the ancient people in mutual embraces.[19]

Rutherford, a postmillennialist, found a place for Israel in prophecy, and, just as clearly, it was an important element in his view of prophecy, second only to the Second Coming of Christ.

William Perkins, a leading Puritan teacher and writer, taught that there would be a future national conversion of the Jews. Similarly, Richard Sibbes wrote that "The Jews are not yet come in under Christ's banner; but God, that hath persuaded Japhet to come into the tents of Shem, will persuade Shem to come into the tents of Japhet." Elnathan Parr's 1620 commentary on Romans espoused the view that there would be two "fullnesses" of the Gentiles: one prior to the conversion of the Jews that has been taking place since their grafting into the olive tree (Rom. 11:17–24) in the first century and one following as the fullness of the kingdom demonstrates itself: "The end of this world shall not be till the Jews are called, and how long after that none yet can tell."[20]

Speaking before the House of Commons in 1649, during the Puritan Revolution, John Owen, a postmillennial theologian, spoke about "the bringing home of [God's] ancient people to be one fold with the fulness of the Gentiles … in answer to millions of prayers put up at the throne of grace, for this very glory, in all generations."[21] Giles Fletcher (c. 1549–1611) was a fellow at King's College, Cambridge, served as Queen Elizabeth's ambassador to Russia, and authored *Of the Russian Commonwealth* (1591). A year before his death, Fletcher wrote *The Tartars Or, Ten Tribes* in which he argued that the Tartars of central and northeastern Asia near the Caspian Sea were the ten lost tribes of Israel. Fletcher's work was pub-

---

18. Quoted in Murray, *The Puritan Hope*, 64–65.
19. Quoted in Murray, *The Puritan Hope*, 98.
20. From DeJong, *As the Waters Cover the Sea*, 27–28.
21. Quoted in Murray, *Puritan Hope*, 100.

lished in *Israel Redux* (1677), a book edited by Samuel Lee (1625–1691) who was a member of Owen's congregation.[22]

## The Westminster Larger Catechism

Contrary to MacArthur, the historical record demonstrates that postmillennial Calvinists had developed a prophetic role for the Jews hundreds of years before Scofield without the attendant near destruction of the Jewish people during a period of "Great Tribulation" where two-thirds of the Jews living in Israel will be killed. The books and articles that make this case are not obscure or difficult to find. They are certainly available (or they should be) in the library at MacArthur's Master's Seminary. In fact, Iain Murray, author of *The Puritan Hope*, a book that I'm using to help make my historical case against MacArthur's claims, spoke at an earlier Shepherds' Conference on March 11, 2001. So MacArthur and the seminary faculty know of Murray's work. If students at The Master's Seminary are not being taught these things in their classes dealing with prophecy, then they are being shortchanged, misinformed, and, dare I say, misled.

In the mid-seventeenth century, the Westminster Larger Catechism, in the answer to Question 191, outlined the hope for a future conversion of the Jews. Part of what we pray for in the second petition, "Thy kingdom come," is that "the gospel [be] propagated throughout the world, the Jews called, the fullness of the Gentiles brought in." In his commentary on the Larger Catechism, Thomas Ridgeley (1667–1734) wrote, "Hence, we cannot but suppose that those prophecies which [refer to the conversion of the Jews], in the latter day, together with the fullness of the Gentiles being brought in, shall be more eminently accomplished than they have hitherto been."[23] Ridgeley spends a number of pages refuting "ancient and modern Chiliasts, or Millennarians"[24] and defending what can only be described as postmillennialism over against premillennialism.

> We freely own, as what we think agreeable to scripture, that as Christ has, in all ages, displayed his glory as King of the Church, so we have ground to conclude, from scripture, that the administration

---

22. Samuel Lee, *Israel Redux: The Restauration of Israel, Exhibited in Two Short Treatises* (London : Printed by S. Streater, for John Hancock, 1677). Peter Toon, *God's Statesman: The Life and Work of John Owen* (Grand Rapids, MI: Zondervan, 1971), 152.

23. Thomas Ridgeley, *Commentary on the Larger Catechism*, 2 vols. (Edmonton, AB Canada: Still Waters Revival Books, [1855] 1993), 2:621. Ridgeley's original work was titled *A Body of Divinity: Wherein the Doctrines of the Christian Religion are Explained and Defended, Being the Substance of Several Lectures on the Assembly's Larger Catechism* and was published in 1731.

24. Ridgeley, *Commentary on the Larger Catechism*, 1:558–562.

of his government in this world, before his coming to judgment, will be attended with greater magnificence, more visible marks of glory, and various occurrences of providence, which shall tend to the welfare and happiness of his church, in a greater degree than has been beheld or experienced by it, since it was planted by the ministry of the apostles after his ascension into heaven. This we think to be the sense, in general, of those scriptures, both in the Old and New Testament, which speak of the latter-day glory.[25]

\* \* \*

We have, hence, sufficient ground to conclude, that, when these prophecies shall have their accomplishment, the interest of Christ shall be the prevailing interest in the world, which it has never yet been in all respects; so that godliness shall be as much and as universally valued and esteemed, as it has hitherto been decried, and it shall be reckoned as great an honour to be a Christian, as it has, in the most degenerate age of the church, been a matter of reproach.... In short, there shall be, as it were, a universal spread of religion and holiness to the Lord, throughout the world."[26]

This is postmillennialism at its best. Ridgeley knew his history well enough to know that the majority of theologians in the seventeenth century held to an advancing kingdom through the proclamation of the gospel which includes the future conversion of the Jews. Amillennialist Johannes G. Vos, in his commentary on the Larger Catechism, takes a similar view.[27] So does Joseph Morecraft, III in his multi-volume commentary on the Larger Catechism.[28]

Similarly, the Westminster *Directory for Public Worship* instructed ministers to pray "for the Propagation of the Gospel and Kingdom of Christ to all nations, for the conversion of the Jews, the fullness of the Gentiles, the fall of Antichrist, and the hastening of the second coming of the Lord."[29] In 1652, a group of eighteen Puritan ministers and theologians, including both Presbyterians and Independents,

---

25. Ridgeley, *Commentary on the Larger Catechism*, 1:562.

26. Ridgeley, *Commentary on the Larger Catechism*, 1:563–564.

27. Johannes G. Vos, *The Westminster Larger Catechism: A Commentary*, ed. G. I. Williamson (Phillipsburg, NJ: Presbyterian and Reformed, 2002), 552–553.

28. Joseph Morecraft, III, *Authentic Christianity*, 5 vols. (Powder Springs, GA: American Vision, 2009–2010), 5:xxx.

29. Quoted in DeJong, *As the Waters Cover the Sea*, 37–38.

affirmed that "the Scripture speaks of a *double conversion* of the Gentiles, the first before the conversion of the *Jews*, they being *Branches wild by nature* grafted into the *True Olive Tree* instead of the *natural Branches* which are broken off.... The second, after the conversion of the Jews."[30]

## The Savoy Declaration

The *Savoy Declaration*, drawn up in October 1658 by English Congregationalists meeting at the Savoy Palace, London, included the conversion of the Jews in its summary of the Church's future hope:

> We expect that in the latter days, Antichrist being destroyed, the Jews called, and the adversaries of the kingdom of his dear Son broken, the churches of Christ being enlarged and edified through a free and plentiful communication of light and grace, shall enjoy in this world a more quiet, peaceful, and glorious condition than they have enjoyed.[31]

Because they believed that the Jews would be converted, Puritan and Presbyterian churches earnestly prayed that Paul's prophecies would be fulfilled. Murray notes that "A number of years before [the Larger Catechism and Westminster Directory for Public Worship] were drawn up, the call for prayer for the conversion of the Jews and for the success of the gospel throughout the world was already a feature of Puritan congregations."[32] Also, among Scottish Presbyterian churches during this period, special days of prayer were set aside partly in order that "the promised conversion of [God's] ancient people of the Jews may be hastened."[33] In 1679, Scottish minister Walter Smith drew up some guidelines for prayer meetings:

> As it is the undoubted duty of all to pray for the coming of Christ's kingdom, so all that love our Lord Jesus Christ in sincerity, and know what it is to bow a knee in good earnest, will long and pray for the out-making of the gospel-promises to his Church in the latter days, that King Christ would go out upon the white horse of the gospel, conquering and to conquer, and make a conquest of the

---

30. Quoted in Murray, *The Puritan Hope*, 72.
31. Quoted in DeJong, *As the Waters Cover the Sea*, 38.
32. Murray, *The Puritan Hope*, 99.
33. Quoted in Murray, *The Puritan Hope*, 100.

travail of his soul, that it may be sounded that the kingdoms of the world are become his, and his name called upon from the rising of the sun to its going down. (1) That the old offcasten Israel for unbelief would never be forgotten, especially in these meetings, that the promised day of their ingrafting again by faith may be hastened; and that the dead weight of blood removed off them, that their fathers took upon them and upon their children, that have sunk them down to hell upwards of seventeen hundred years.[34]

Puritan Independent Thomas Goodwin, in his book, *The Return of Prayers*, encouraged people to pray for "the calling of the Jews, the utter downfall of God's enemies, the flourishing of the gospel." Goodwin assured his readers that all these prayers "will have answers."[35]

## Jonathan Edwards

Jonathan Edwards, a noted postmillennialist and someone MacArthur quotes unfavorably in his Shepherds' talk, outlined the future of the Christian Church in his 1774 *History of Redemption*. Edwards believed that the overthrow of Satan's kingdom involved several elements: the abolition of heresies and infidelity, the overthrow of the kingdom of the Antichrist (the Pope), the overthrow of the Muslim nations, and the overthrow of "Jewish infidelity":

> However obstinate [the Jews] have been now for above seventeen hundred years in their rejection of Christ, and however rare have been the instances of individual conversions, ever since the destruction of Jerusalem … yet, when this day comes, the thick veil that blinds their eyes shall be removed [2 Cor. iii.16] and divine grace shall melt and renew their hard hearts … And then shall the house of Israel be saved: the Jews in all their dispersions shall cast away their old infidelity, and shall have their hearts wonderfully changed, and abhor themselves for their past unbelief and obstinacy.

He concluded that "Nothing is more certainly foretold than this national conversion of the Jews in Romans 11."[36]

---

34. Quoted in Murray, *The Puritan Hope*, 101–102.

35. Quoted in Murray, *The Puritan Hope*, 102.

36. Jonathan Edwards, "History of Redemption," *The Works of Jonathan Edwards*, 2 vols. (Edinburgh: The Banner of Truth Trust, [1834] 1974), 1:607.

Edwards was no dispensationalist. He believed, for example, that the Olivet Discourse referred to the destruction of Jerusalem in A.D. 70. In fact, he was a postmillennialist and believed that the "coming" mentioned in Matthew 24 refers to Jesus' coming judgment against Jerusalem in A.D. 70.[37] Edwards takes the same position on the meaning of "coming" in the Olivet Discourse as do modern-day preterists:

> 'Tis evident that when Christ speaks of his coming; his being revealed; his coming in his Kingdom; or his Kingdom's coming; He has respect to his appearing in those great works of his Power, Justice and Grace, which should be in the Destruction of Jerusalem [in A.D. 70] and other extraordinary Providences which should attend it.[38]

* * *

> The degree of their punishment, is the *uttermost* degree. This may respect both a national and personal punishment. If we take it as a *national* punishment, a little after the time when the epistle was written, wrath came upon the nation of the Jews to the uttermost, in their terrible destruction by the Romans; when, as Christ said, "was great tribulation, such as never was since the beginning of the world to that time," Mat. 24:21. That nation had before suffered many of the fruits of divine wrath for their sins; but this was beyond all, this was their highest degree of punishment as a nation.[39]

John MacArthur needs to rethink his understanding of eschatology, for his sake and the sake of the students at The Master's Seminary who are being misinformed on this subject.

## Robert Haldane

Robert Haldane, an early nineteenth-century Swiss Reformed preacher, preached through the book of Romans in Geneva in 1816. On Romans 11:26, he made this comment:

---

37. John H. Gerstner, "The Latter-Day Glory and Second Coming: From Jonathan Edwards—A Mini-Theology" (www.graceonlinelibrary.org/etc/printer-friendly.asp?ID=602).

38. Jonathan Edwards, "Observations on the Facts and Evidences of Christianity, and the Objections of Infidels," *The Works of Jonathan Edwards*, Part 1, Chap. 2, § 17. www.ccel.org/ccel/edwards/works2.x.ii.i.html

39. Jonathan Edwards, "When the Wicked Shall Have Filled Up the Measure of Their Sin, Wrath Will Come Upon Them to the Uttermost" (May 1735): www.biblebb.com/files/edwards/uttermost.htm

The rejection of the Jews has been general, but at no period universal. This rejection is to continue till the fulness of the Gentiles shall come in. Then the people of Israel, as a body, shall be brought to the faith of the Gospel.[40]

## Thomas V. Moore

Thomas V. Moore (1818–1871) was pastor of the First Presbyterian Church, Richmond, Virginia. He is best known for his commentaries on the Minor Prophets. The following is from his comments on Zechariah 10:6–12 in his 1856 *Prophets of the Restoration*: "Henderson follows Grotius in supposing that this restoration took place before the coming of Christ, but the terms in which it is described can hardly be restricted to any return that took place during that period. Calvin refers it entire to a spiritual restoration. But the most natural interpretation seems to be that which predicts a future return to their own land, and a spiritual return to God, which is predicted as a separate and ultimate result in v. 12."[41]

## Charles Hodge

The great Princeton theologian Charles Hodge found in Romans 11 a prophecy that "the Gentiles, as a body, the mass of the Gentile world, will be converted before the restoration of the Jews, as a nation." After the fullness of the Gentiles comes in, the Jewish people will be saved: "The Jews, as a people, are now rejected; as a people, they are to be restored. As their rejection, although national, did not include the rejection of every individual; so their restoration, although in like manner national, need not be assumed to include the salvation of every individual Jew." This will not be the end of history, however; rather, "much will remain to be accomplished after that event; and in the accomplishment of what shall then remain to be done, the Jews are to have a prominent agency."[42]

---

40. Robert Haldane, *The Epistle to the Romans* (London: Banner of Truth Trust, 1958), 541.

41. Thomas V. Moore, *The Prophets of the Restoration* (Carlisle, PA: The Banner of Truth Trust, [1856] 1979), 245.

42. Charles Hodge, *A Commentary on Romans* (London: Banner of Truth Trust, [1864] 1972), 374.

## John Brown

John Brown, a nineteenth-century Scottish theologian, wrote in a similar way in his comments on Romans 11:

> The apostle [Paul] contrasts the former state of the Gentiles with their present state, and the present state of the Jews with their future state. The past state of the Gentiles was a state of disobedience—their present state, is a state of gracious salvation. The present state of the Jews is a state of disobedience—their future state is to be a state of gracious salvation.[43]

The reason for God's rejection of the Jews and for their future restoration is to display both the total depravity of men—both Jew and Gentile—and the pure and sovereign grace of salvation, the very thing that MacArthur claims is an inconsistency among non-dispensationalists regarding Israel.[44]

## Robert L. Dabney

Southern Presbyterian theologian Robert L. Dabney included under the category of "unfulfilled prophecy" the "general and national return of the Jews to the Christian Church. (Rom. ix: 25, 26)."[45]

## John Murray

This same view was taught by some of the leading contemporary Reformed theologians. John Murray of Westminster Theological Seminary, for example, wrote this comment on Romans 11:26:

> If we keep in mind the theme of this chapter and the sustained emphasis on the restoration of Israel, there is no alternative than to conclude that the proposition, "all Israel shall be saved", is to be interpreted in terms of the fulness, the receiving, the ingrafting of Israel as a people, the restoration of Israel to gospel favour and

---

43. John Brown, *Analytical Exposition of the Epistle of Paul the Apostle to the Romans* (Edinburgh: Oliphant, Anderson, & Ferrier, 1883), 417.

44. Brown, *Analytical Exposition of the Epistle of Paul the Apostle to the Romans*, 418–419.

45. Robert L. Dabney, *Lectures on Systematic Theology* (Grand Rapids, MI: Zondervan, [1878] 1972), 838.

blessing and the correlative turning of Israel from unbelief to faith and repentance.... The salvation of Israel must be conceived of on a scale that is commensurate with their trespass, their loss, their casting away, their breaking off, and their hardening, commensurate, of course, in the opposite direction.[46]

Postmillennialist Gary North comments that it was a series of lectures by John Murray on Romans 11 and his own reading of "Revelation 12 in the light of his concept of genetic Israel" that converted him from hyper-ultradispensationalism to postmillennialism.[47]

## Conclusion

Many more examples of the postmillennial concern for the conversion of Israel could be cited, but enough evidence has been supplied to refute John MacArthur's claim that only dispensational premillennialism has the theological system that can account for the fulfillment of these promises. Even preterist postmillennialists like John Owen and Jonathan Edwards, both of whom argued that the Olivet Discourse refers to the destruction of Israel's Temple in A.D. 70, also believed in a future conversion of national Israel.

A study of J. A. DeJong's *As the Waters Cover the Sea* (now back in print) and Iain Murray's *The Puritan Hope* (never out of print since 1971) give ample evidence concerning the historical postmillenialism and preterism of our Protestant forefathers. Given these resources, there is no excuse for John MacArthur's misinformed misrepresentations of postmillennial expectations for the Jews. What MacArthur and his fellow dispensationalists have yet to explain is how their future hope for Israel is more favorable toward Jews than the redemptive expectations of the purportedly Anti-Semitic "Replacement Theologists," since the dispensationalist future for the Jews is that two-thirds of them will be slaughtered before the promises are fulfilled (Zech. 13:8) in what Charles Ryrie has described as "the worst bloodbath in Jewish history."[48]

---

46. John Murray, *The Epistle to the Romans*, 2 vols. (Grand Rapids, MI: Eerdmans, 1968), 2:98.

47. Gary North, "Editor's Introduction," *The Journal of Christian Reconstruction*, Symposium on the Millennium (Winter, 1976–1977), 4.

48. Charles C. Ryrie, *The Best is Yet to Come* (Chicago, IL: Moody Press, 1981), 86.

# 4

# The Myth of the Postponed Abrahamic Covenant

But we were hoping that it was He who was going to redeem Israel. Indeed, besides all this, it is the third day since these things happened (Luke 24:21).

And we preach to you the good news of the promise made to the fathers, that God has fulfilled this promise to us their children in that He raised up Jesus, as it is written in the second Psalm, "Thou art My Son; today I have begotten Thee." *And as for the fact* that He raised Him up from the dead, no more to return to decay, He has spoken this way: "I will give you the holy and sure blessings of David" (Acts 13:32–34).

J. Dwight Pentecost writes that the Abrahamic covenants, "according to the Scriptures, are *eternal*."[1] The Bible describes them as "everlasting." If "everlasting" means "lasting or enduring through all time," then dispensationalists do not believe that the Abrahamic covenants are "everlasting" since they have been postponed for nearly 2000 years! Given that dispensationalists claim that they alone follow a consistently literal method of interpretation, it's surprising that they equivocate on the meaning of "everlasting." Consider Charles Ryrie's standard definition of "literal interpretation" and apply its principles to how dispensationalists propose a postponement theory to explain how the Abrahamic covenant was not realized during Jesus' ministry and the post-ascension period:

> Dispensationalists claim that their principle of hermeneutics is that of literal interpretation. This means interpretation that gives

---

1. J. Dwight Pentecost, *Things to Come: A Study in Biblical Eschatology* (Grand Rapids, MI: Zondervan, [1958] 1964), 69.

to every word the same meaning it would have in normal usage, whether employed in writing, speaking, or thinking.[2]

Another often quoted definition is David L. Cooper's Golden Rule of Interpretation which states, "When the plain sense of Scripture makes common sense, seek no other sense; therefore, take every word at its primary, ordinary, usual, literal meaning unless the facts of the immediate context, studied in the light of related passages, and axiomatic and fundamental truths, indicate clearly otherwise."[3] The problem is, dispensationalists do not always follow these guidelines. This is especially true in the way they interpret "everlasting."[4] By applying the Ryrie/Cooper literal litmus test, "everlasting" should have "the same meaning it would have in normal usage, whether employed in writing, speaking, or thinking." To go further and to be more accurate, "everlasting" should have the same meaning it has elsewhere in the Bible unless there is a specific indication that the meaning is being used in a different way from its more common usage.

All the dispensational writers I have consulted, who have the irritating habit of quoting one another to support their claims, agree that the "Abrahamic covenant is called eternal in the Word of God" (Gen. 17:7, 13b, 19; 1 Chron. 16:16–17; Psalm 105:9–10).[5] Paul Benware, former professor of Bible and theology at Moody Bible Institute, writes, "Those blessings included the guarantee of national existence as well as the greatness of the nation, the land area of Canaan as an everlasting possession, and the continuation of the Abrahamic covenant as an everlasting covenant."[6]

At the same time the Abrahamic covenant is said to be "everlasting," dispensationalists insist that it has been postponed. Mal Couch, an advocate of dispensational theology, writes:

---

2. Charles Caldwell Ryrie, *Dispensationalism Today*, rev. ed. (Chicago, IL: Moody Press, 1995), 80.

3. David L. Cooper, *When Gog's Armies Meet the Almighty in the Land of Israel: An Exposition of Ezekiel Thirty-Eight and Thirty-Nine*, 3rd ed. (Los Angeles, CA: Biblical Research Society, [1940] 1958), [i].

4. Eugene H. Merrill writes that the "everlasting covenant of salt" is "probably … a metaphor to speak of its durability [Num. 18:19]." (Eugene H. Merrill, "Numbers," *The Bible Knowledge Commentary: Old Testament*, eds. John F. Walvoord and Roy B. Zuck [Wheaton, IL: Victor Books, 1985], 236). See the later discussion of how "everlasting" is defined.

5. Charles Caldwell Ryrie, *The Basis of the Premillennial Faith* (Neptune, NJ: Loizeaux Brothers, 1953), 49.

6. Paul N. Benware, *Understanding End Times Prophecy: A Comprehensive Approach* (Chicago: Moody Press, 1995), 33.

Most dispensationalists hold to a kingdom postponement theory.... Dispensationalists believe that the kingdom was set aside, the Jews suffered the final dispersement, and the church, which was not mentioned in the Old Testament, was given to reach the Gentile nations.[7]

Does "everlasting" include the idea of postponement in its dictionary definition or its biblical usage so that it passes as the "primary, ordinary, usual, literal meaning" of the word? Is there anything in "the immediate context" of Genesis 17 or when "studied in the light of related passages, and axiomatic and fundamental truths" that would "indicate clearly" that a definition of "everlasting" can include the idea of postponement? Absolutely not. "Everlasting" and "postponed" are contradictory labels.

## The First Everlasting Covenant

Prior to the establishment of the Abrahamic covenant, God instituted the Noahic covenant. Even though "the intent of man's heart is evil from his youth," God says that He "will never again destroy every living thing" (Gen 8:21). The everlasting nature of this covenantal promise is so secure that the earth itself would have to pass away in order for it to be postponed, put off, or revoked (8:22). Couch insists that the Noahic covenant will remain in effect "as long as earth history remains in its present physical state."[8] He can affirm this because, as the Bible states, it's an "everlasting covenant":

> And I will remember My covenant, which is between Me and you and every living creature of all flesh; and never again shall the water become a flood to destroy all flesh. When the bow is in the cloud, then I will look upon it, to remember the *everlasting covenant* between God and every living creature of all flesh that is on the earth (Gen 9:15–16).

Following dispensational postponement theology, God could send another worldwide flood and claim that He was not abrogating the everlasting nature of

---

7. Mal Couch, "The Postponement Theory," *An Introduction to Classical Evangelical Hermeneutics: A Guide to the History and Practice of Biblical Interpretation* (Grand Rapids, MI: Kregel Publications, 2000), 221. The book is misnamed. Dispensational hermeneutics cannot be described as "classical."

8. Couch, "Hermeneutics and the Covenants of Scripture," 140.

the Noahic covenant. God could claim, following Ryrie and other dispensational advocates, that He was only interjecting a parenthesis, an indeterminate period of time in which the keeping of the promise is delayed (stopping the prophetic clock, so to speak). Would anyone accept such an argument as being legitimate? And yet this is exactly what dispensationalists do with the Abrahamic covenant.

Dispensationalists see no problem in manufacturing gaps, delays, postponements, and parentheses[9] while still claiming that the Abrahamic covenant is eternal. But they would be hard pressed to apply and defend a similar methodology when it came to God's everlasting character (Gen. 21:33; Ps. 93:2; Isa. 40:28; 1 Chron. 16:34, 41; 2 Chron. 5:13; Ps. 136; Ps. 119:142; 135:13; 145:13; Is. 45:17; Jer. 31:3; Hab. 3:6) or the everlasting nature of the Noahic covenant.

## Israel's Disobedience

The Noahic covenant remains in force, according to the dispensationally oriented *Nelson Study Bible*, "no matter how evil Noah's descendants got. Indeed, He promised that until the end of the earth, there would be seasons of planting and harvest and day and night. God unilaterally promised to uphold the rhythms of the earth in order to sustain human life—even though humans had rebelled against Him, their Creator."[10] But to a dispensationalist, this same promise does not apply to the Abrahamic covenant which is also said to be everlasting.

Pentecost writes that when the nation of Israel refused to embrace Jesus as the promised Messiah, the kingdom offer "was withdrawn and its establishment postponed until some future time when the nation would repent and place faith in Jesus Christ."[11] There is no such condition attached to the Abrahamic covenant as dispensationalists continually insist. The maintenance of the covenant is not dependent on the response of those with whom it was made since God deals with a remnant of Israel (Rom. 11:1–5; cf. Matt. 21:43–44; 1 Peter 2:9–10).

---

9. John F. Walvoord writes: "As H. A. Ironside had made clear in his thorough study of this problem, there are more than a dozen instances of parenthetical periods in the divine program." (John F. Walvoord, *The Rapture Question*, rev. ed. [Grand Rapids, MI: Zondervan, 1979], 26). Philip Mauro is correct when he writes, "Never has a specified number of time-units making up a described stretch of time, been taken to mean anything but *continuous* or *consecutive* time-units." (Philip Mauro, *The Seventy Weeks and the Great Tribulation*, rev. ed. [Swengel, PA: Reiner Publications, n.d.], 93). Emphasis in original. Dispensationalists like Walvoord see gaps because their system requires gaps in order to make it work.

10. Earl D. Radmacher, "The Noahic Covenant," *The Nelson Study Bible* (Nashville, TN: Thomas Nelson Publishers, 1997), 20.

11. Pentecost, *Thy Kingdom Come*, 293.

## Adding to the Word of God

Of the Abrahamic covenant, Ryrie writes, "The Scriptures clearly teach that this is an eternal covenant based on the gracious promises of God. There may be delays, postponements, and chastisements, but an eternal covenant cannot, if God cannot deny Himself, be abrogated."[12] As we've seen, the Abrahamic covenant is identical in wording to the Noahic covenant in that both are said to be everlasting. Let's apply Ryrie's qualifier to the Noahic covenant that he applies to the Abrahamic covenant and see if it makes sense: "The Scriptures clearly teach that the Noahic covenant is an eternal covenant based on the gracious promises of God. *There may be delays and postponements*, but an eternal covenant cannot, if God cannot deny Himself, be abrogated." An eternal covenant cannot be abrogated or delayed or postponed and still be described as "eternal."

A fundamental question remains: Does the everlasting Abrahamic covenant mention anything about the possibility of postponements or delays? Dispensationalists are quick to point out that there are no conditions to the Abrahamic covenant,[13] but they seem to ignore the fact that the postponements and delays they propose presuppose a conditional covenant. Where do we find a verse that reads something like this?: "And I will establish My covenant between Me and you and your descendants after you throughout their generations for an everlasting covenant, to be God to you and to your descendants after you *although there may be delays or postponements*"? If conditions cannot be added *ex post facto*, then neither should new definitions of everlasting be invented.

## The Elasticity of "Everlasting" in Dispensationalism

Dispensationalist Arnold G. Fruchtenbaum states that the English words "everlasting" and "perpetual" "do tend to carry concepts of eternity," but "that is not the meaning of the Hebrew words themselves." Simply put, he does not believe "everlasting" means "forever." If this is the case, then dispensationalism does not have a leg to stand on. He continues:

> The Classical Hebrew term "forever" (*olam*) as [the Hebrew lexicon] BDB states, means "long duration," "antiquity," or "futurity." The Hebrew forms mean nothing more than, "until the end

---

12. Ryrie, *The Basis of the Premillennial Faith*, 53.

13. Ryrie writes: "The original promises given to Abraham were given without any conditions whatsoever" (Ryrie, *The Basis of the Premillennial Faith*, 54).

of a period of time." What the period of time is must be determined by the context or determined by related passages. In classical Hebrew, these words never meant or carried the concept of eternity, but had a time limitation. The period of time may have been to the end of a man's life, or an age, or dispensation, but not *for ever* in the sense of eternity.[14]

Fruchtenbaum is not alone in defining *olam* this way. In the *Theological Wordbook of the Old Testament*, published by dispensational publisher Moody Press, Allan MacRae writes "that neither the Hebrew [*olam*] nor the Greek word [*aion*] in itself contains the idea of endlessness.... Both words came to be used to refer to a long age or period...."[15] John H. Walton, former professor of Old Testament and Hebrew at Moody Bible Institute, writes:

> There are many contexts where *olam* [everlasting] clearly has more to do with an open-ended perpetuity than an absolute eternity. In 1 Samuel 1:22, Hannah vows that her son will remain in the house of the Lord *olam*. This clearly does not mean for all eternity, nor does it even mean for his entire life. It merely indicates that her vow is open-ended. It is not just for one year or five, but in perpetuity [see Deut. 15:17; 1 San. 2:30; Jer. 17:4]. There is no designated term. Even today it is not unusual to hear 'May the king live forever,' which is equivalent to 'Long live the king'—indicating that nothing is being done to limit his reign.
>
> What, then, should be understood when the text speaks of a covenant that is *olam*? The implication of the terminology is that these agreements are not temporary, not stopgap, nor are they on a trial basis. *They are permanent in the sense that no other alternative arrangement to serve that purpose is envisioned.* This does not mean that the purpose it serves will never be obsolete. Circumcision, for example, became obsolete even though it is designated here as a covenant *olam*. Likewise the Aaronic covenant for priesthood became obsolete even though it was designated a priesthood *olam* (Num. 25:13).[16]

---

14. Arnold G. Fruchtenbaum, *Israelology: The Missing Link in Systematic Theology* (Tustin, CA: Ariel Ministries, 1994), 655–656.

15. Allan MacRae, "Olam," *Theological Wordbook of the Old Testament*, eds. R. Laird Harris, Gleason L. Archer, Jr., Bruce K. Waltke, 2 vols. (Chicago, IL: Moody Press, 1980), 2:673.

16. John H. Walton, *Genesis: The NIV Application Commentary* (Grand Rapids, MI: Zondervan,

# The Myth of the Postponed Abrahamic Covenant 71

Let's apply the two definitions of "everlasting" ("forever" and "long duration") to the land promise. Ryrie states that Israel is to have "*permanent* possession of the promised land."[17] John Walvoord concurs: "A literal interpretation of the Abrahamic covenant involves the *permanent* existence of Israel as a nation and the fulfillment of the promise that the land should be their everlasting possession."[18] Permanent means "continuing or enduring without fundamental or marked change." If something is permanent, there can't be a postponement, especially one that's been in effect for nearly two millennia. As we stand right now, the Abrahamic covenant has been in its postponement phase longer than its fulfillment phase. This hardly passes for permanent or everlasting.

Then there's Fruchtenbaum's definition of "everlasting" (*olam*). He claims that it means "nothing more than 'until the end of a period of time.'" Who makes the determination of what that period of time is? The dispensationalist will have one opinion and the non-dispensationalist will have another. Since the Bible tells us that Israel did possess the land, contrary to what many dispensationalists claim,[19] then one could make the case that the specified period of time has passed. But contrary to what the Bible actually states, dispensationalists argue that Israel never had full possession of the land, so the "everlasting" nature of the promise (no matter which definition is used) is not effective until the Jews are reestablished as a nation and living in the full borders of their land. But Israel did enter and possess the land thousands of years ago:

> So the LORD gave Israel all the land which He had sworn to give to their fathers, and they possessed it and lived in it. And the LORD gave them rest on every side, according to all that He had sworn to their fathers, and no one of all their enemies stood before them;

---

2001), 450. Emphasis added.

17. Ryrie, *The Basis of the Premillennial Faith*, 48. Emphasis added.

18. John F. Walvoord, *The Millennial Kingdom* (Grand Rapids, MI: Dunham Publishing Co., 1959), 139–140. Emphasis added.

19. One of the most ingenious efforts to make a text say something it does not comes from Elliott E. Johnson. Quoting Joshua 21:43–45, he claims that "Joshua introduces the inaugural or partial fulfillment of the covenant as given to Abraham." The text says no such thing. Johnson continues by claiming that "it is inaugural or partial because of the limited scope. That limitation is indicated in a second summary statement (Josh. 13:1–7)." (Elliott, "Covenants in Traditional Dispensationalism," *Three Central Issues in Contemporary Dispensationalism*, 137). In Joshua 13 the Israelites had not possessed the land, but by the time we get to Joshua 21, we're told that "they possessed it and lived in it" (21:43). This makes perfect chronological sense. In order to make his view work, Johnson must place the events of Joshua 13 after Joshua 21.

the LORD gave all their enemies into their hand. Not one of the good promises which the LORD had made to the house of Israel failed; all came to pass (Joshua 21:43–45).

All the elements necessary for the fulfillment of the Abrahamic covenant as related to the land are present in these verses: God gave the Israelites the land He had promised to give; they possessed and lived in the land; they had rest; their enemies did not stand before them; not one of the promises God made to the house of Israel failed. If these verses do not teach what they seem to teach, then how else could God have put it, said it, or written it if He had *wanted* to inform the Israelites that they had in fact possessed the land as promised? Even after being confronted with these crystal clear words from Joshua, futurists continue to insist that they do not teach what they say. Consider the commentary of Old Testament scholar Walter C. Kaiser, Jr.:

> Oftentimes students of the Bible point to three passages that appear to suggest that the promise of land to Israel has indeed been fulfilled: Joshua 21:43–45; 23:14–15; Nehemiah 9:8. These texts assert that "not one of all the LORD's good promises to the house of Israel failed; every one was fulfilled" (Josh. 21:45; cf. 23:14).
>
> However, the boundaries mentioned in Numbers 34:2–12 are not the ones reached in the accounts of Joshua and Judges. For example, Joshua 13:1–7 and Judges 3:1–4 agree in maintaining that there was much land that remained to be taken.[20]

---

20. Walter C. Kaiser, Jr., *Back Toward the Future: Hints for Interpreting Biblical Prophecy* (Grand Rapids, MI: Baker Books, 1989), 111. Benware references Joshua 23:4–7 to support his contention that "The statement in Joshua reflects an Old Testament concept of fulfillment wherein the promise of God was being fulfilled and that generation was getting their share. But it was not the final or ultimate fulfillment of the promise" (*Understanding End Times Prophecy*, 55). What is "the final or ultimate fulfillment of the promise"? Is it in the physical land of Israel, or does the NT direct us to consider a more permanent possession of which the physical land of Israel was a mere type and shadow similar to the tabernacle, temple, circumcision, priesthood, and animal blood sacrifices? (John 4:21; Rom. 4:13; Gal. 4:25–26; Heb. 11:15–16; 12:22–23). "After depicting the role of the servant in this restoration (52:13–53:12), Isaiah pictured the great expansion Zion will experience (54:1–3). This expansion is expressed in territorial terminology. It says, 'Your descendants [seed] will dispossess nations and settle in their desolate cities' (54:3). This is reminiscent of the territorial connotations noted earlier in Genesis 22:17, where it says Abraham's offspring will possess the gates of their enemies" (Thomas Edward McComiskey, *The Covenants of Promise: A Theology of the Old Testament Covenants* [Grand Rapids, MI: Baker Book House, 1985], 54). Paul makes use of Isaiah 54 by showing how the fulfillment is not in the "children of a bondwoman, but of the free woman" (Gal. 4:31). And who are

So much for a literal interpretation of the Bible. Here's how an emailer explains the use of "all" in Joshua 21:43–45:

> "And of course, what Dr. DeMar again fails to realize is that using a 'literal' interpretive principle does not necessarily mean that the words of a given text or passage will be taken *literally*."

This is a literalist saying this. I'm not interpreting what I *think* he is saying. When literalists are pushed to support their claim that they alone interpret the Bible literally, "literal" apparently takes on a less than literal meaning. He goes on to explain himself by using a contemporary example:

> "I went to a professional basketball game not long ago. The score was extremely close and at one point in the game, it was a definite fight to the finish. After a great deal of effort, the home team won the game by one three-pointer. At that point, everyone was on their feet, shouting at the top of their lungs! Now, is my statement correct as written? Of course it is, because I was there and it happened. I witnessed it. But wait; what if there were a few people who were *not* on their feet, shouting at the top of their lungs? Does my statement then become false? Of course it doesn't. Would someone reading my account or listening to me retell it believe that every single person who attended that game (including the workers at the arena), was on their [sic] feet and shouting at the top of their [sic] lungs? I can't imagine it. Moreover, no one would accuse me of lying even if a decent sized group of people did not join in the revelry. This is called a generalization and quite acceptable. People simply understand the general meaning of what is being stated, including the fact that while not everyone did as I said, my statement is still considered truthful."

Of course, there are times in Scripture where "all" does *not* mean everyone or everything without exception (Matt. 3:5; 24:14, 22; Acts 2:17; Rom. 11:26), but sometimes it does. Let's take another look at Joshua 21 and compare what it says to the description of the crowd at the basketball game.

If we only had "So the LORD gave Israel **all the land** which He had sworn to give to their fathers, and they possessed it and lived in it" (Joshua 21:43), then "all" might have less than an all-inclusive meaning. But we have verse 45: "**Not**

---

the children of the free woman? Those who reside in "the Jerusalem above" which "is free" (4:26).

**one** of the good promises which the Lord had made to the house of Israel failed; **all** came to pass." "Not one … failed" defines "all." If I had asked the emailer, "Did everyone stand up and cheer?," and he said, "Not one failed to stand up and cheer," I would have to assume that everyone stood up.

Since Numbers 34:2–12 and Joshua 13:1–7 precede Joshua 21:43–45, it seems obvious that by the time we get to the end of the book of Joshua the land was in Israel's possession even though there were nations dwelling in Israel's midst (Josh. 23:4–7). Just because other nations resided in the land does not mean that Israel did not have full possession of the land. The nations are said to be "an inheritance for your tribes" (23:4). Notice the conditions of remaining in the land: "Be very firm, then, to keep and do all that is written in the book of the law of Moses, so that you may not turn aside from it to the right hand or to the left" (Josh. 23:6). Failure to follow this specific condition will mean that these nations "shall be a snare and a trap to you, and a whip on your sides and thorns in your eyes, until you perish from off this good land which the LORD your God has given you" (23:13).

What about Judges 3:1–4? While the land was possessed and was in the hands of the Israelites before Joshua died, some nations were left "to test Israel … to find out if they would obey the commandments of the LORD" (Judges 3:1, 4). It was Israel's disobedience that put the land back into the hands of her enemies. God delivers Israel through Othniel, and then we read, "Then the land had rest forty years" (3:11): Not part of the land, but *the land*—the land occupied by Israel—had rest.

In 1 Kings 4:21, 24–25 we read: "Now Solomon ruled over all the kingdoms from the River to the land of the Philistines to the border of Egypt; they brought tribute and served Solomon all the days of his life.… For he had dominion over everything west of the River, from Tiphsah even to Gaza, over all the kings west of the River; and he had peace on all sides around about him.… So Judah and Israel lived in safety, every man under his vine and his fig tree, from Dan even to Beersheba, all the days of Solomon." The "River" is a reference to the Euphrates River which is far north of Israel. The Philistines were to the east and, of course, Egypt was in the south. What is it about this passage that does not confirm the claim that Israel had been given all the land promised to her? Here's how one dispensational writer tries to explain why this passage does not fulfill the Abrahamic Covenant of Genesis 15:18–20: "for not all the territory was incorporated into the geographic boundaries of Israel; many of the subjected kingdoms retained their identity and territory but paid taxes (**tribute**) to Solomon."[21] What does Genesis 15:18 say when compared to 1 Kings 4:21 and 2 Chronicles 9:26: "To your descendants I have given this land, **from the river of Egypt as far as the great river, the river Euphrates**." Genesis 15:19–21 implies that other nations could still be living within Israel's borders. This matches the borders attributed to Solomon's dominion. Notice the statements that "Judah and Israel lived in safety" and "had peace on all sides."

## What Does the New Testament Say?

The New Testament says nothing about there being a need to fulfill the land promises. In fact, we are told, "When [God] had destroyed seven nations in the land of Canaan, He distributed their land as an inheritance—all of which took about four hundred and fifty years" (Acts 13:19). There is no discussion about re-inheriting the land. The physical land of Israel has no role to play in the fulfillment of the Abrahamic covenant since the coming of Christ. The same is true about circumcision, animal sacrifices, the temple, the throne of David, and the need for human priests. These were all to be part of the everlasting covenant. Consider Jeremiah 33:20–22:

> "Thus says the Lord, 'If you can break My covenant for the day and My covenant for the night, so that day and night will not be at their appointed time, then My covenant may also be broken with David My servant so that he will not have a son to reign on his throne, and with the Levitical priests, My ministers. As the host of heaven cannot be counted and the sand of the sea cannot be measured, so I will multiply the descendants of David My servant and the Levites who minister to Me.'"

According to this passage, dispensationalists argue, "The OT promised that Israel would again be restored by God to international prominence in spite of their ancient exiles, Ezek 37:15–28 being the most prominent text. Both Jer 31:35–37 and 33:19–26 guarantee that this promise is as sure as the laws of nature."[22] But Jeremiah 33 states that God "will multiply the descendants of David My servant

---

21. Thomas L. Constable, "1 Kings," *The Bible Knowledge Commentary: Old Testament* (Wheaton, IL: Scripture Press/Victor Books, 1985), 497.

22. Richard Mayhue, "New Covenant Theology and Futuristic Premillennialism," *The Masters Seminary Journal* 18/1 (Fall 2007), 221–232: http://www.tms.edu/tmsj/tmsj18j.pdf

[2 Sam. 7:8–16] and the Levites [Num. 25:12–13] who minister to Me" (Jer. 33:22). Why does God need to multiply the Levites who were involved in the temple and the sacrificial system when Jesus has fulfilled all the requirements of the covenant? Jesus is the greater David (Acts 2:22–36), the final sacrifice (Gen. 22:8; John 1:29, 36), the new temple (John 2:13–22),[23] circumcision,[24] and "a faithful" and "great high priest" (Heb. 2:17; 3:1; 4:14; 10:21). To be "in Christ" is to have all the fullness of the covenant promises. The author of Hebrews consistently calls the new covenant a "better covenant" (Heb. 7:22; 8:6; 12:24). It's not surprising therefore that the Jewish Christians saw nothing covenantally askew when they decided to sell their land:

> For there was not a needy person among them, for *all who were owners of land or houses would sell them* and bring the proceeds of the sales, and lay them at the apostles feet; and they would be distributed to each, as any had need (Acts 4:34–37).

Notice that the Bible does not say that they sold their possessions or "their goods," as the dispensational oriented *Bible Knowledge Commentary* states it. They sold their land and houses. Jesus had told them earlier that the temple would be destroyed and Jerusalem judged within a generation (Matt. 24:1–34). Jesus is the focal point of history not dirt (land), stone (temple) (John 2:19; 3:20–24; Eph. 2:19–22; 1 Peter 2:4–8), or blood (John 1:13). Nothing in the New Testament is said about a return to the land or rebuilding the temple. The New Testament describes the destruction of the temple (Matt. 23:38; 24:2) and indifference to the land (Matt. 28:18–20). At no time do the evangelists in the Acts era make any mention about Jews returning to the land of Israel.

In what way could the Jeremiah promise of descendants of David and Levitical priests be fulfilled? We could follow the dispensationalists and argue that the entire old covenant system of blood sacrifices will be reinstated or we could find the fulfillment in the person and work of Jesus. The dispensational option would nullify the redemptive work of the cross when Jesus declared "it is finished" (John 19:30) and "the veil of the temple was torn in two from top to

---

23. Notice what John 2:22 states: "So when He was raised from the dead, His disciples remembered that He said this; and they believed the Scripture and the word which Jesus had spoken." Believed what? That Jesus was the fulfillment of the temple. In fact, He is the fulfillment of all Scripture (Luke 24:27, 44–45).

24. Seed (semen) had to pass through blood. Once Jesus came, there is no longer any need for blood-washed seed.

bottom" (Matt. 27:51; Mark 15:38; Luke 23:45). A new priesthood would mean the reinstitution of animal sacrifices and a rebuilt temple with a new veil. There is no other option. But under the new covenant, anyone in Christ is a descendant of David in the same way he or she is a descendant of Abraham: "And if you belong to Christ, then you are Abraham's descendants, heirs according to promise" (Gal. 3:29; cf. Acts 3:25; Rom. 4:13, 16; Gal. 3:7–9, 14, 16). A person does not have to be a physical descendant of Abraham to be a true and *bona fide* descendant of Abraham. Mention of David's descendants being multiplied might have something to do with his status as a king. Christians are described as a "kingdom" (Rev. 1:6). We learn from Paul that we have been raised up by God to sit with Jesus in heavenly *places*" (Eph. 2:6). This is a kingly position.

On the priestly side, Peter writes that we are "as living stones … being built up as a spiritual house for a holy priesthood, to offer up spiritual sacrifices acceptable to God through Jesus Christ" (1 Peter 2:5). In verse 9 Christians are said to be "a chosen race, a royal priesthood, a holy nation." For those who argue that I am "spiritualizing the Bible," I suggest that they take up their argument with Peter. Henry Cowles offers a helpful summary of Jeremiah 33:22 and its only possible New Covenant fulfillment:

> Here as in chap 31:35–37 the richest promises are confirmed by the strongest assurances. The Lord's covenant of the day and of the night (see Gen. 1 and Ps. 136: 8, 9); the divine constitution of nature whereby the succession of day and night will continue while the world shall stand is beautifully appropriated as the symbol and the pledge of this never failing promise respecting the eternal kingship and priesthood of the Messiah. To the Messiah this must mainly and ultimately refer and not to the merely human kings of David's line or to the priests of Aaron's. For plainly the promises had no adequate fulfillment in those lines apart from the Messiah. Its spiritual fullness forbids us to think of any thing less or other than the work of Christ.— Note also that the countless multitudes of the seed of David and of the Levites in the priesthood can be fulfilled only as we refer the word David to the Messiah and take his seed in the broad sense which includes all the people of the living God, Gentiles indeed as well as Jews that great multitude which no man can number seen by the revelator (Apoc. 7:9).[25] These are all both

---

25. "Apoc." refers to the book of Revelation (The *Apocalypse* of John).

kings and priests unto God (Apoc. 1:6 and 1 Pet. 2:5). Even Isaiah saw that all the people of God and not least the Gentiles would be priests (chap 61:6 and 66:21).[26]

One final point needs to be made. Dispensationalists will point to Jeremiah 31:35–37 as prime evidence that there is a holdout for the future fulfillment of a national establishment of Israel.

> "Thus says the Lord, Who gives the sun for light by day
> And the fixed order of the moon and the stars for light by night,
> Who stirs up the sea so that its waves roar;
> The Lord of hosts is His name:
> 'If this fixed order departs
> From before Me,' declares the Lord,
> 'Then the offspring of Israel also will cease
> From being a nation before Me forever.
> Thus says the Lord,
> 'If the heavens above can be measured
> And the foundations of the earth searched out below,
> Then I will also cast off all the offspring of Israel
> For all that they have done,' declares the Lord."

Verse 36 is the key: "'If this fixed order departs from before Me,' declares the Lord, 'Then the offspring of Israel also **will cease from being a nation before Me forever.**'" But Israel did cease from being a nation when the Romans sacked the city of Jerusalem, destroyed the temple, and scattered those Jews who stayed to fight the invading armies and survived the slaughter. Dispensationalists have made a point of declaring that Israel becoming a nation again in 1948 was a fulfillment of Bible prophecy. So from A.D. 70 to 1948 Israel was not a nation. How does this square with Jeremiah 31:36?

Dispensationalist Lewis Sperry Chafer contended, since he wrote before 1948, that the Jews were in their "third dispersion" since A.D. 70. This is a direct contradiction to what God says in Jeremiah 31:36! God does not say, "When Israel becomes a nation again for the final time, they will remain a nation forever." Jeremiah is prophesying a restoration after the Babylonian captivity, a point made by Daniel's reading of Jeremiah's prophecy (Dan. 9:1–2; 2 Chron. 36:21; Ezra 1:1; Jer.

---

26. Henry Cowles, *Jeremiah, and His Lamentations; with Notes, Critical, Explanatary and Practical, Designed for Both Pastors and People* (New York: D. Appelton and Co., 1880), 260.

25:11, 12; 29:10–14). Others argue that there will be "one more forced exile from the land in the middle of the Great Tribulation, the one spoken of in Matthew 24:15–28 and Revelation 12:6–14. After the second coming, Israel will experience her final restoration. For some, this would be called the fourth, while for others it would be the completion of the third."[27] Either way, like Chafer's third-restoration interpretation, it's a contradiction of what Jeremiah 31:36 makes very clear. Israel's fortunes were restored after its seventy-year captivity, therefore, the promise that the offspring of Israel will never cease from being a nation should have continued from that point in time and beyond. The forced exile that took place in A.D. 70 and the next one that some dispensationalists claim is going to happen are contrary to what Jeremiah was promised by God.

So either the Bible is in error or the dispensationalists are in error. Could the fulfillment be in what Jesus states in Matt. 21:43?: "Therefore I say to you, the kingdom of God will be taken away from you and given to a nation [*ethnei*], producing the fruit of it" (also see Acts 2:5; 10:22, 35; Rom. 10:19; 1 Pet. 2:4–12; Rev. 5:9; 7:9; 13:7; 14:6). Further evidence of a fulfillment is found in Hebrews 11:

> By faith [Abraham] lived as an alien in the land of promise, as in a foreign *land,* dwelling in tents with Isaac and Jacob, fellow heirs of the same promise; for he was looking for the city which has foundations, whose architect and builder is God.… All these died in faith, without receiving the promises, but having seen them and having welcomed them from a distance, and having confessed that they were strangers and exiles on the earth.… And indeed if they had been thinking of that *country* from which they went out, they would have had opportunity to return. But as it is, they desire a better *country,* that is, a heavenly one. Therefore God is not ashamed to be called their God; for He has prepared a city for them (vv. 9–10, 13, 15–16.

## The Unconditionality of the Covenant

Another major tenet of dispensationalism is that the covenant made with Israel is unconditional. If this is true, then why did God have to suspend the prophetic timetable for Israel? Since modern-day Jews have returned to their homeland in unbelief, and this is said to be a fulfillment of Bible prophecy since, some

---

27. Arnold Fruchtenbaum, *Israelology,* 418.

# 5

# The Myth of "Replacement Theology"

Replacement theology has become dispensationalism's latest prophetic boogeyman. If you want to end a debate over eschatology, just charge your opponent with holding to replacement theology. Here's a typical internet analysis of the topic: "One of the most *dangerous* and *subversive* doctrines held by adherents of Preterism is the view that in A.D. 70, at the destruction of Jerusalem by the Roman armies, God's covenant nation of Israel was *superseded* by the Christian church."[1] Not to be outdone, "There is a *demonic cancer* coursing through the life blood of the Church of Jesus Christ and its name is REPLACEMENT THEOLOGY." Certainly less strident than "demonic," another prophecy pundit describes the position as "a *heresy*."[2] A watchdog website warns, "There is a powerful movement afoot called Replacement Theology which states that the church is Israel and the promises given to Israel were primarily for the church. This movement is incurring the wrath of God...."[3] These types of indictments are not found only on the internet. Noted Old Testament scholar Walter Kaiser wrote, "Replacement theology is just plain *bad news* for both the Church and Israel."[4]

What is "replacement theology," sometimes called "supersessionism," and why do dispensationalists accuse non-dispensationalists of holding the position? Here's a typical dispensational definition:

> **Replacement Theology**: a theological perspective that teaches that the Jews have been rejected by God and are no longer God's Chosen People. Those who hold to this view disavow any ethnic

---

1. Brian Simmons, "Preterism and Replacement Theology": http://tinyurl.com/26pdfvk
2. John E. Young, "Clear View: Replacement Theology": http://tinyurl.com/25plwah
3. Anonymous, "Replacement Theology": http://tinyurl.com/2vk9s8e.
4. Quoted by Thomas Ice in "What is Replacement Theology?": http://tinyurl.com/38ettfe

future for the Jewish people in connection with the biblical covenants, believing that their spiritual destiny is either to perish or become a part of the new religion that superseded Judaism (whether Christianity or Islam).[5]

As anyone who is familiar with the Bible knows, Christianity does not "supersede Judaism." The genealogies found in Matthew and Luke clearly show that Jesus is "the son of David, the son of Abraham" (Matt. 1:1). The first New Covenant believers were from the nation of Israel (Luke 1–2) with hints of a later expanded redemptive role for Samaritans (John 4:7–45), Greeks (John 12:20–22), the nations (Luke 2:32), and the world (John 3:16; 4:42). At Pentecost, we see that "to the Jew first" (Rom. 1:16) predominates—"Now there were Jews living in Jerusalem, devout men, from every nation under heaven" (Acts 2:5)—but later extends "also to the Greek" (Rom. 1:16) as Peter's encounter with Cornelius shows (Acts 10). Notice Peter's evaluation of these events and the response of his fellow Jews:

> "And as I began to speak, the Holy Spirit fell upon them just as *He did* upon us at the beginning. And I remembered the word of the Lord, how He used to say, 'John baptized with water, but you will be baptized with the Holy Spirit.' Therefore if God gave to them the same gift as *He gave* to us also after believing in the Lord Jesus Christ, who was I that I could stand in God's way?" When they heard this, they quieted down and glorified God, saying, "Well then, God has granted to the Gentiles *also* the *repentance that leads to life*" (Acts 11:15–18).

"The Gentiles *also*." Gentile believers were grafted into the Jewish assembly of believers and were given "the same gift," the Holy Spirit (see Acts 1:8; 2:38).

Pentecost was not the beginning of dispensationalism's "parenthesis" since Peter declares that the events of that day were a fulfillment of a prophecy given to Joel, an Old Testament prophet: "this is what was spoken of through the prophet Joel" (Acts 2:17; Joel 2:28–32). Peter's message was to "all the house of Israel" (2:36). When these Israelites asked, "Brethren, what shall we do?" 2:37), Peter made the following reply: "For the promise is for **you** and **your children**, and for **all who are far off**, as many as the Lord God shall call to Himself" (2:39).

Israel's spiritual destiny is the same as it is for non-Israelites: Repent and believe in Jesus! No one said anything about a delay in the promises that had

---

5. Randall Price, *Unholy War: America, Israel and Radical Islam* (Eugene, OR: Harvest House, 2001), 412.

been made to Israel centuries ago. In fact, Peter clearly informed them that the promises were for them and their children (Acts 2:38). There is no mention of the land, a rebuilt temple, the reinstitution of animal sacrifices, or anything else related to the shadows of the Old Covenant. In fact, "for all who were owners of land or houses sold them" (4:34). They possessed something better, the forgiveness of their sins (2:38). Jesus is "the mediator of a better covenant, which has been enacted on better promises" (Heb. 8:6). What would they rather have?: land, stone, the cutting of their flesh, and yearly bloody sacrifices, or forgiveness of sins, the power of the Holy Spirit (Acts 1:8), and Jesus who intercedes as a mediator for them daily? The answer is obvious as the book of Hebrews makes clear in multiple chapters.

The charge of "Replacement theology" obscures the obvious. The charge is a tactical red herring to get people's attention away from what the New Testament shows about the relationship between the promises of the Old Covenant and their fulfillment in the New Covenant with Israel and how Gentiles are grafted in to an Israelite assembly (*ekklēsia*) of believers. How in any way is this even close to a replacement? It's not. The replacement theology epithet is dispensationalism's trump card in any debate over eschatology because it implies anti-semitism. Once the charge is made, all rational discourse ceases.

Dispensationalism has established a false Israel-Church distinction that leads to the claim that anyone who is not a dispensational premillennialist is either anti-Semitic or, to use a less pejorative term, "anti-Judaism." Hal Lindsey pulled the anti-Semitic card with the publication of his poorly researched and poorly argued book *The Road to Holocaust*,[6] essentially claiming that if you aren't a dispensationalist then you are a self-conscious or latent anti-Semite. If you are losing a debate, the simplest and quickest way to recover is to call someone a hater, a racist, an anti-Semite, or an advocate of "Replacement Theology," which, of course, is the same as being a hater, racist, and anti-Semite. A quick read of the New Testament will show that no one makes the charge of "Replacement Theology," and no one holds out for the reinstitution of the shadows of the Old Covenant.

## The Rest of the Untold Story

Barry Horner uses the phrase "anti-Judaism" instead of the more inflammatory "anti-Semitic" in his book *Future Israel*. He means to convey the same idea, however. It carries a similar negative connotation of being "anti-Jew" if you don't follow his

---

6. Hal Lindsey, *The Road to Holocaust (*New York: Bantam Books, 1989).

understanding of national Israel's future role in redemptive history. While I don't fault Dr. Horner for pointing out harsh language used by a "number of those holding to Reformed convictions"[7] regarding present-day unbelieving Israel, I do fault him for leaving so much unsaid. He certainly is aware of the long history of how Reformed/Calvinistic scholars have treated prophecy regarding the Jews since he references Iain Murray's *The Puritan Hope* and Peter Toon's *Puritans, the Millennium and the Future of Israel*, albeit buried in a footnote on page 152 of *Future Israel*. I also question the claim that premillennialism, whether the classic or dispensational variety, is up to challenging what he describes as "Christian anti-Judaism." There is a very dark side to dispensationalism as it relates to the future of Israel.

Horner claims that "quite a few [non-premillennialists], by their derogatory manner have inferred that they would be delighted if the Arabs would push Israel into the Mediterranean Sea, repossess Palestine, and thus vindicate their Eschatology!"[8] He doesn't identify these people or offer supporting documentation, but I'll assume that he can produce the documentation if asked to do so. I can produce the following from Dr. Paige Patterson, president of Southwestern Baptist Theological Seminary and a *premillennialist*:

> The present state of Israel is not the final form. The present state of Israel will be lost, eventually, and Israel will be run out of the land again, only to return when they accept the Messiah as Savior.[9]

These aren't the words of a so-called "Replacement Theologist." Not quite as stark as Patterson's view, David Jeremiah is quick to point out "that Israel's presence in her land today is [not] the fulfillment of God's promise to regather His people. Many assume that it is, but I have to tell them that the answer is no! What is happening in Israel today is primarily the result of a secular Zionist movement, whereas Ezekiel [in chapter 36] wrote about a spiritual return of God's people to Him.…"[10]

What should Christians do if Israel is about to be "run out of the land again" as Patterson claims *will happen* based on his prophetic system? If Christians support the expulsion or do nothing to stop it, will this be "anti-Judaism"? If Christians

---

7. Barry Horner, *Future Israel: Why Christian Anti-Judaism Must be Challenged* (Nashville: Broadman & Holman, 2007), xviii.

8. Horner, *Future Israel*, xviii.

9. Stated on Dallas, Texas, radio program (KCBI) in a debate with me on May 15, 1991.

10. David Jeremiah, *What in the World is Going On?: 10 Prophetic Clues You Cannot Afford to Ignore* (Nashville: Thomas Nelson, 2008), 17.

defend Israel against a forced expulsion, will we be thwarting God's redemptive plan for Israel?

As a premillennialist, Patterson's position makes logical sense because prior to the rapture, Israel has no special status. Israel plays no prophetic role until the period of the Great Tribulation when the "church" is taken off the earth and all hell breaks loose on Israel and the world. If the promises to Israel as a people and nation are postponed until the rapture, as dispensationalism teaches, then the land promise and the promise of "those who bless you, I will bless" also have been set aside until the prophetic clock starts ticking again. One premillennialist explains it this way:

> Today is an in-between age which is commonly called the Age of Grace, the Age of the Holy Spirit, or the Church Age (the Church being the body of believers in Christ, the total and complete group, whosoever that may be, Gentile or Jew). During this period in between the First and Second Coming[s] of Jesus Christ, a Satanic counterfeit—political Zionism—masquerading as the State of 'Israel' will be established.[11]

Premillennialist John R. Rice wrote something similar: "Thus the trouble in Jerusalem, and the dispersion of Jews among all the nations of Jerusalem throughout this whole age, is simply a continuation of the punishment of God upon the whole race of Jews."[12] Did this include Martin Luther's anti-Semitic writings, the pogroms against the Jews, and current Islamic threats to "wipe Israel from the map"? Is the whole race of Israelites still under God's punishment during this time when the Church supersedes Israel until the time of the "rapture"? In 1950, Rice made it clear that Israel becoming a nation again prior to the rapture is prophetically inconsequential and those who take the position that Israel's new national status is a fulfillment of Bible prophecy are teaching "heresy."[13] John F. Walvoord and Lewis Sperry Chafer hold to three dispersions and restorations while "other dispensationalists have refined this system and see four dispersions and restorations."[14] Since the

---

11. Stan Rittenhouse, *"For Fear of the Jews"* (Vienna, VA: The Exhorters, 1982), 7. This was the view of Arno C. Gaebelein in *Hath God Cast Away His People?* (New York: Gospel Publishing Office, 1905), 200–201.

12. John R. Rice, *The King of the Jews: A Commentary on the Gospel According to Matthew* (Murfreesboro, TN: Sword of the Lord Publishers, 1955), 369.

13. John R. Rice, *We Can Have Revival Now* (Greenville, SC: Bob Jones University Press, 1950), chap. 3.

14. Arnold G. Fruchtenbaum, *Israelology: The Missing Link in Systematic Theology*, rev. ed.

New Testament does not mention a future restoration, it's hard to see either a third or fourth one. The second post-exile restoration is the only one that matters since it prepares the way for the ultimate promised Restorer Jesus Christ. Jesus is the "guarantee of a better covenant" (Heb. 7:22) based on "better promises" (8:6). How is a rebuilt temple, limited by the land of Israel, the requirement of animal sacrifices for atonement, and the reinstitution of circumcision better than the freedom that Christians, whether Jew or non-Jew, have in Jesus? An illustration might help to put the better covenant of Jesus in perspective:

> It is as if a wealthy parent, in the "horse and buggy" days, promised his son if he would not smoke until he was twenty one, he would have a horse and buggy of his own on that birthday; but gave him a fine automobile when the time arrived, because in the meantime autos had come into general use. Has the father been faithful to his promise? Most assuredly, and much more to the delight of his son than if the promise had been literally fulfilled.[15]

Dispensationalists have the Jews looking forward to a horse and buggy covenantal age with all the encumbrances of the Levitcal requirements, when the Bible tells us that all things have been made new in Jesus Christ (2 Cor. 5:17).

## Dispensationalism's Holocaust Problem

Dwight Wilson, author of *Armageddon Now!*, "a third-generation premillenarian who has spent his whole life in premillennialist churches,"[16] argues that some noted premillennialists advocated a "hands off" policy regarding Nazi persecutions of the Jews during World War II. Since, according to dispensational views regarding Bible prophecy, "the Gentile nations are permitted to afflict Israel in chastisement for her national sins," there is little that should be done to oppose it. Wilson writes, "It is regrettable that this view allowed premillennialists to expect the phenomenon of 'anti-Semitism' and tolerate it matter-of-factly."[17]

---

(Tustin, CA: Ariel Ministries, [1989] 2001), 418.

15. Albertus Pieters, *The Seed of Abraham: A Biblical Study of Israel, the Church, and the Jews* (Grand Rapids, MI: Eerdmans, 1950), 128.

16. Dwight Wilson, *Armageddon Now!: The Premillenarian Response to Russia and Israel Since 1917* (Grand Rapids, MI: Baker Book House, 1977), 13.

17. Wilson, *Armageddon Now!*, 16.

Wilson describes "premillenarian views" opposing "anti-Semitism" in the mid-thirties and thereafter as "ambivalent."[18] There was little moral outcry "among the premillenarians ... against the persecution, since they had been expecting it."[19] He continues:

> Another comment regarding the general European anti-Semitism depicted these developments as part of the on-going plan of God for the nation; they were "Foregleams of Israel's Tribulation." Premillennialists were anticipating the Great Tribulation, "the time of Jacob's trouble." Therefore, they predicted, "The next scene in Israel's history may be summed up in three words: purification through tribulation." It was clear that although this purification was part of the curse, God did not intend that Christians should participate in it. Clear, also, was the implication that He did intend for the Germans to participate in it (in spite of the fact that it would bring them punishment) ... and that any moral outcry against Germany would have been in opposition to God's will. In such a fatalistic system, to oppose Hitler was to oppose God.[20]

Wilson maintains that it was the view of a predicted Jewish persecution prior to the Second Coming that led to a "hands off" policy when it came to speaking out against virulent "anti-Semitism." "For the premillenarian, the massacre of Jewry expedited his blessed hope. Certainly he did not rejoice over the Nazi holocaust, he just fatalistically observed it as a 'sign of the times.'"[21]

Premillennialist James M. Gray of the Moody Bible Institute believed in the authenticity of the *Protocols of the Elders of Zion*. He defended Henry Ford when Ford published installments of the *Protocols* in his self-funded *Dearborn Independent* newspaper. In a 1927 editorial in the *Moody Bible Institute Monthly*, Gray claimed that Ford "had good grounds for publishing some of the things about the Jews.... Mr. Ford might have found corroborative evidence [of the Jewish conspiracy] had he looked for it."[22] As time went on, Gray was coming under increasing pressure to repudiate the *Protocols* as a forgery. Not only Gray, but *Moody Bible Institute*

---

18. Wilson, *Armageddon Now!*, 94.

19. Wilson, *Armageddon Now!*, 94.

20. Wilson, *Armageddon Now!*, 94. Emphasis added.

21. Wilson, *Armageddon Now!*, 95.

22. Timothy P. Weber, *Living in the Shadow of the Second Coming: American Premillennialism, 1875-1982* (Grand Rapids, MI: Zondervan/Academie, 1983), 189.

*Monthly* was being criticized by the evangelical *Hebrew Christian Alliance* for not condemning the manufactured *Protocols*. Gray grew indignant and once again voiced his belief that the *Protocols* were authentic. He did this in the *Moody Bible Institute Monthly*. Gray, of course, pointed out that "Moody Bible Institute had always worked for the highest interests of Jews by training people to evangelize them."[23]

Even so, Gray went on to assert that "Jews were at least partly to blame for their ill treatment." He supported this contention by referring his readers to an article written by Max Reich, a faculty member at the Moody Bible Institute. Reich wrote: "Without religion, the Jew goes down and becomes worse than others, as a corruption of the best is always the worst corruption."[24]

Charges of "anti-Semitism" were not abated by Gray's attempts at clarification. His views concerning the Jews remained. "By the beginning of 1935, Gray was fending off charges from the *American Hebrew and Jewish Tribune*, the *Bulletin of the Baltimore Branch of the American Jewish Congress*, and even *Time* magazine that persons connected with Moody had been actively distributing the *Protocols*."[25]

Of course, Gray was not the only dispensational premillennialist who vouched for the genuineness of the *Protocols* and had rather negative ("anti-Judaism"?) things to say about the Jews. Arno C. Gaebelein, an editor of the *Scofield Reference Bible*, believed that the *Protocols* were authentic, that they accurately revealed a "Jewish conspiracy." His *Conflict of the Ages*[26] would be viewed today as an "anti-Judaism" work because it fostered the belief that communism had Jewish roots and that the Bolshevik revolution of 1917 had been masterminded by a group of well-trained Jewish agitators. At the same time that Gaebelein was using anti-Semitic rhetoric, he had a thriving evangelistic ministry to Jews in New York City. Why the double-mindedness? Dispensationalism expects both the persecution and salvation of a remnant of Jews.[27] This is why George Marsden could write that "fundamentalists between [World War I and II] could be both pro-Zionist and somewhat anti-Semitic, favoring the return of the Jews to Israel, which would lead eventually to their conversion; yet in the meantime especially distrusting apostate Jews."[28]

---

23. Weber, *Living in the Shadow of the Second Coming*, 189.

24. Quoted in Weber, *Living in the Shadow of the Second Coming*, 190.

25. Weber, *Living in the Shadow of the Second Coming*, 189.

26. Arno Clemens Gaebelein, *The Conflict of the Ages: The Mystery of Lawlessness: Its Origin, Historic Development and Coming Defeat* (New York: Publication Office "Our Hope," 1933).

27. Timothy P. Weber, "A Reply to David Rausch's 'Fundamentalism and the Jew,'" *Journal of the Evangelical Theological Society* (March 1981), 70.

28. George M. Marsden, *Fundamentalism and American Culture: The Shaping of Twentieth*

As Peter Leithart and I point out in *The Legacy of Hatred Continues*,[29] which is a response to *The Road to Holocaust*, that it's dispensationalists who hold to a form of replacement theology since they believe that Israel does not have any prophetic significance *this side of the rapture!* Prior to the rapture, in terms of dispensational logic, the Church has replaced Israel. This is unquestionably true since God's prophetic plan for Israel has been postponed until the prophetic time clock starts ticking again at the beginning of Daniel's 70th week, an event that starts only after the Church is taken to heaven in the so-called rapture.[30] Until then, God is dealing redemptively with the Church. Consider the following by dispensationalist E. Schuyler English:

> An intercalary[31] period of history, after Christ's death and resurrection and the destruction of Jerusalem in A.D. 70, has intervened. This is the present age, the Church age.... During this time God has not been dealing with Israel nationally, for they have been blinded concerning God's mercy in Christ.... However, God will again deal with Israel as a nation. This will be in Daniel's seventieth week, a seven-year period yet to come.[32]

According to English, and every other dispensationalist for that matter, the Church has replaced Israel until the rapture. The supposed unfulfilled promises made to Israel are not fulfilled until after the Church is taken off the earth. Thomas Ice, a co-author with prophecy writers Tim LaHaye and Mark Hitchcock, admits that the Church replaces Israel this side of the rapture: "We dispensationalists believe that the church has superseded Israel during the current church age, but God has a future time in which He will restore national Israel 'as the institution for the administration of divine blessings to the world.'"[33]

---

*Century Evangelicalism: 1870–1925* (New York: Oxford University Press, 1980), 187–188, note 15.

29. Gary DeMar and Peter J. Leithart, *The Legacy of Hatred Continues: A Response to Hal Lindsey's* The Road to Holocaust (Powder Springs, GA: American Vision, 1989).

30. H. A. Ironside, *The Great Parenthesis: Timely Prophetic Messages of the Interval Between the 69th and 70th Weeks of Daniel's Prophecy* (Grand Rapids, MI: Zondervan, 1943).

31. Inserted into the calendar.

32. E. Schuyler English, *A Companion to the New Scofield Reference Bible* (New York: Oxford University Press, 1972), 135.

33. Thomas Ice, "The Israel of God," The Thomas Ice Collection: www.raptureready.com/featured/TheIsraelOfGod.html#_edn3

Non-dispensationalists like me would say that all the promises made to Israel have been fulfilled, and the redemption of Israel according to those promises made it possible for Gentiles to be grafted into an already existing Jewish assembly of believers that the Bible calls the Church. Soon after Jesus' ascension, the gospel is preached to "Jews living in Jerusalem, devout men, *from every nation under heaven*" (Acts 2:5). If this is not God dealing specifically and solely with Israel, then I don't know what is. To say that the Church is a "mystery" unknown to the Old Testament prophets contradicts what Peter states in Acts 2:16: "*this* is what was spoken of through the prophet Joel." "This," a near demonstrative, is a reference to the events of Pentecost. If Joel predicted what was happening, and the dispensationalists claim that Pentecost is the beginning of the Church Age, then the Church is not a mystery; it is the fulfillment of Bible prophecies made first and foremost to Israel.

Ice understands the implications of this logic, so he must add a word to Acts 2:16 to make it fit his parenthesis eschatology. He rewrites the verse to read, "But this is [like] that which was spoken by the prophet Joel." He tries to explain the addition of "like" this way: "The unique statement of Peter ('this is that') is in the language of comparison and similarity, not fulfillment."[34] He's begging the question, assuming what he must first prove. Dispensational author Stanley D. Toussaint writes, contradicting Ice on his point, "This clause does not mean, 'This is *like* that'; it means Pentecost fulfilled what Joel had described."[35] After saying this, he goes on to argue: "However, the prophecies of Joel quoted in Acts 2:19–20 were not fulfilled." So which is it? He says the fulfillment will come "if Israel would repent." But Israel did repent: "Now having heard this, they were pierced to the heart, and said to Peter and the rest of the apostles, 'Brethren, what shall we do?' And Peter said to them, 'Repent…'" (2:37–38). The result? "So then, those who had received his word were baptized; and there were added that day about three thousand souls" (2:41).

Dispensationalists will argue that "all Israel" must be saved (Rom. 11:26). In context, "all Israel" is the believing elect remnant (11:5). Dispensationalists don't interpret "all Israel" to mean every Israelite who has ever lived. They don't even understand "all Israel" to mean every Jew alive during the post-rapture great tribulation period since they believe that two-thirds of them will be slaughtered (cf. Zech. 13:8). They mean by "all Israel" *the remnant*, what's left of Israel after the antichrist

---

34. Tim LaHaye, ed. *Prophecy Study Bible* (Chattanooga, TN: AMG Publishers, 2000), 1187, note on Acts 2:16.

35. Stanley D. Toussaint, "Acts," *The Bible Knowledge Commentary: New Testament*, John F. Walvoord and Roy B. Zuck (Wheaton, IL: Victor Books, 1983), 358.

has his way with the newly constituted nation. If "all Israel" can mean a remnant in a seven-year, post-rapture period of time, then it certainly can mean a remnant in a pre-destruction of Jerusalem period of time.

Peter addresses the crowd at Pentecost as the "men of Israel" (Acts 2:22). He expands his message to include "all the house of Israel" (2:36). The "brethren"—Jewish brethren—want to know what they, as Jews, must do to be saved. Peter tells them, "For the promise is for *you* and *your* children..." (2:39). There is nothing in this chapter that indicates that the promises first made to Israel are not being fulfilled right then and there. Peter continues to preach to his countrymen by informing them that "Jesus the Christ" was "appointed for *you*" (3:20). The "restoration of all things" (3:21) is the pre-ordained redemptive work of Jesus to fulfill what all the prophets have written. Peter tells them that the prophets "announced *these days*" (3:24). "It is *you* who are the sons of the prophets, and of the covenant which God made with your fathers, saying to Abraham, 'And in your seed all the families of the earth shall be blessed'" (3:25). There is no mention of a postponement of the promises, "an intercalary period of history," made to Abraham. These Jewish believers, the recipients of the promises spoken by the prophets (3:24), made up "the church" " (*ekklēsia*, "assembly") (5:11). The Gospel message, "the whole message of this Life," was to be proclaimed "to the people in the temple" (5:20), that is, to Jews.

We learn later that Gentiles are to be a part of this existing Jewish assembly of believers to take part in the promises given to Israel (Acts 10:34–48). Notice Peter's conclusion: "And all the circumcised believers who had come with Peter were amazed, because the gift of the Holy Spirit had been poured out upon the Gentiles also" (10:45). "Also" implies the Holy Spirit was first poured out on the Jews. Paul makes the same point in Romans 11 when he writes that the Gentiles were grafted into an existing Jewish body of believers that Acts describes as "the church" (*ekklēsia*, "assembly") (Rom. 11:12–21).

Dispensationalists claim that their particular brand of eschatology is the only prophetic system that gives Israel her proper place in redemptive history. This is an odd thing to argue since two-thirds of the Jews will be slaughtered during the post-rapture tribulation, and the world will be nearly destroyed. Charles Ryrie writes in his book *The Best is Yet to Come* that during this post-rapture period Israel will undergo "the worst bloodbath in Jewish history."[36] The book's title doesn't seem to be very appropriate considering that during this period of time most of the Jews will die! John Walvoord follows a similar line of argument: "Israel is *destined* to have a particular time of suffering which will eclipse any thing that it has known

---

36. Charles C. Ryrie, *The Best is Yet to Come* (Chicago, IL: Moody Press, 1981), 86.

in the past.... The people of Israel ... are placing themselves within the vortex of this future whirlwind which will destroy the majority of those living in the land of Palestine."[37] Arnold Fruchtenbaum states that during the Great Tribulation "Israel will suffer tremendous persecution (Matthew 24:15–28; Revelation 12:1–17). As a result of this persecution of the Jewish people, two-thirds are going to be killed."[38]

During the time when Israel seems to be at peace with the world, she is really under the domination of the antichrist who will turn on her at the mid-point in the seven-year period. Israel waits more than 2000 years for the promises finally to be fulfilled, and before it happens, two-thirds of them are wiped out. Those who are charged with holding a "Replacement Theology viewpoint" believe in no inevitable future Jewish bloodbath. In fact, we believe that the Jews will inevitably embrace Jesus as the Messiah this side of the Second Coming. The fulfillment of Zechariah 13:8 is a past event. It may have had its fulfillment in the events leading up to and including the destruction of Jerusalem in A.D. 70. Contrary to dispensationalism's interpretation of the Olivet Discourse, Jesus' disciples warned the Jewish nation for nearly forty years about the impending judgment (Matt. 3:7; 21:42–46; 22:1–14; 24:15–22). Those who believed Jesus' words of warning were delivered "from the wrath to come" (1 Thess. 1:10). Those who continued to reject Jesus as the promised Messiah, even though they had been warned for a generation (Matt. 24:34), "wrath has come upon them to the utmost" (1 Thess. 2:16; cf. 1 Thess. 5:1–11; 2 Pet. 3:10–13).

The pre-tribulational rapture is a necessary doctrine in dispensational theology in order to maintain the Israel-Church distinction, a distinction that has been in effect for nearly two millennia, a thousand years longer that the premillennialist's supposed earthly millennium. This false distinction makes Replacement Theology an issue. The pre-trib rapture doctrine creates all kinds of theological problems. Once the pre-trib "rapture" goes, so goes everything dispensational. As I and others have pointed out, the biblical arguments for a pre-trib "rapture" are not only spurious, they are non-existent. Tim LaHaye's answer to the charge that there is no single verse that teaches the doctrine is that there's no single verse that can be found that teaches any of the other four rapture positions. (Yes, four!) This is hardly a good argument. Could it be that since there is no verse supporting any of the five rapture positions that there is no rapture and thus no Israel-Church distinction?

---

37. John F. Walvoord, *Israel in Prophecy* (Grand Rapids, MI: Zondervan, 1962), 107, 113. Emphasis added.

38. Arnold G. Fruchtenbaum, "The Little Apocalypse of Zechariah," *The End Times Controversy: The Second Coming Under Attack*, eds. Tim LaHaye and Thomas Ice (Eugene, OR: Harvest House, 2003), 262.

When I point out that there is no single verse to support the pre-trib rapture, dispensationalists will maintain that the doctrine is developed from a series of verses that when put together infer the pre-trib rapture. For example, the dispensationalist will say that the seven-year tribulation period is clearly taught in Scripture. When I ask where, I'm taken to Daniel 9:24–27. In order to get a seven-year tribulation period, the dispensationalist must first prove that there is a gap of nearly 2000 years between the 69th and 70th weeks. He must also demonstrate from these verses that the antichrist will make a covenant with the Jews during a post-rapture tribulation. Then there must be proof of another rebuilt temple that skips over the rebuilt temple that stood in Jesus' day.[39] Read Daniel 9:24–27 without the necessary dispensational preconceptions and see if you find these required dispensational distinctives in these verses.[40] Dispensationalists will argue that the "he" of 9:27 is the antichrist. Does the text say "he" is the antichrist? It does not. One would expect the antichrist of Revelation to make a covenant with the Jews during the so-called seven-year tribulation period since Revelation is an expansion of Daniel's 70th week. There is no mention of the antichrist making a covenant with anyone, either in Daniel 9:27 or in Revelation. In fact, there is not a single example of this unholy covenant in the entire Bible. It's *Jesus* who makes a covenant with the many: "this is *My* blood of the covenant, which is to be shed on behalf of the *many* for the forgiveness of sins" (Matt. 26:28). The Bible couldn't be clearer. You can read from the first verse to the last verse of Revelation and not find any mention of "antichrist" or "seven-years," let alone a seven-year tribulation period.

## Conclusion

In Jeremiah 31:35–36, God promised the following to Israel: "Thus says the LORD, Who gives the sun for light by day and the fixed order of the moon and the stars for light by night, Who stirs up the sea so that its waves roar; The LORD of hosts is His name: 'If this fixed order departs From before Me,'" declares the

---

39. The first rebuilt temple was constructed when the Jews returned to Jerusalem after the Babylonian captivity. This temple fell into disrepair during the intertestamental period and was restored and enlarged by Herod the Great, a project that started around 20 B.C. and was completed just a few years before it was destroyed in A.D. 70 by the Romans, just as Jesus had predicted (Matt. 24:1–34). The New Testament doesn't say anything about another rebuilt temple. Like the pre-trib rapture, dispensationalists admit, "There are no Bible verses that say, 'There is going to be a third temple.'" (Thomas Ice and Randall Price, *Ready to Rebuild: The Imminent Plan to Rebuild the Last Days Temple* [Eugene, OR: Harvest House, 1992], 197–198).

40. See Peter J. Gentry, "Daniel's Seventy Weeks and the New Exodus," *Southern Baptist Theological Journal* 14.1 (2010), 26–44)

LORD, 'Then the offspring of Israel also will cease from being a nation before Me forever.'" Jeremiah 31:7 continues: "Thus says the LORD, 'If the heavens above can be measured and the foundations of the earth searched out below, then I will also cast off all the offspring of Israel for all that they have done,' declares the LORD."

Jeremiah's prophecy was given more than 2000 years ago. Prior to 1948 and after A.D. 70, Israel had not been a nation. So we have a few interpretive choices of the Jeremiah passage: (1) God lied (impossible); (2) the promise was conditional (possible); the promise was postponed (always the dispensationalist answer); (4) or the fulfillment was fulfilled in the new nation that grew out of the New Covenant (most likely). Consider what Jesus tells the religious leaders of His day:

> "Therefore I say to you, the kingdom of God will be taken away from you and given to a **nation** producing the fruit of it. And he who falls on this stone will be broken to pieces; but on whomever it falls, it will scatter him like dust. When the chief priests and the Pharisees heard His parables, they understood that He was speaking about them" (Matt. 21:43–45).

Peter, quoting portions of the Old Testament related to Israel, raises the nation issue as they pertain to "the sons of Israel" (Ex. 19:6): "But you are 'a chosen race,' a royal 'priesthood, **a holy nation**, a people for God's own possession,' so that you may proclaim the excellencies of Him who has called you out of darkness into His marvelous light; for you once were 'not a people,' but now you are 'the people of God'; you 'had not received mercy,' but now you have received mercy" (1 Peter 2:9–10). Does this not fulfill what is promised to Jeremiah? There is no need of a parenthesis, a postponement of covenant promises, for a future fulfillment. Peter is clear that a new nation of believers in Jesus Christ has been founded.

# 6

# The Myth that Animal Sacrifices and Circumcision are Everlasting Rites

It was for freedom that Christ set us free; therefore keep standing firm and do not be subject again to a yoke of slavery. Behold I, Paul, say to you that if you receive circumcision, Christ will be on no benefit to you. And I testify again to every man who receives circumcision, that he is under obligation to keep the whole Law.... For in Christ Jesus neither circumcision nor uncircumcision means anything, but faith working through love (Gal. 5:1–6).

One part of the Abrahamic covenant that most dispensationalists seem to pass over is the everlasting nature of the covenant of circumcision. Like the guarantee of national existence and the land promises which are said to be everlasting covenants, the covenant of circumcision is also said to be "everlasting" (Gen. 17:13). J. Dwight Pentecost tries to separate circumcision from the other covenant promises by claiming that "the ultimate fulfillment of the Abrahamic Covenant and possession of the land by the seed is not hinged, however, on faithfulness in the matter of circumcision. In fact the promises of the land were given before the rite was introduced."[1] This is irrelevant since circumcision, like the covenant in general, is said to be everlasting: "But an uncircumcised male who is not circumcised in the flesh of his foreskin, that person shall be cut off from his people; he has broken My covenant" (Gen. 17:14).

There is nothing in the Abrahamic covenant that suggests a spiritual fulfillment for circumcision, and yet that's exactly how the Bible transfers this physical observance into a spiritual redemptive reality (Lev. 26:41; Deut. 10:16; 30:6; Jer. 6:10). Stephen, the first martyr, confirms the way circumcision is to be understood in a New Covenant redemptive context: "You men who are stiff-necked

---

1. J. Dwight Pentecost, *Thy Kingdom Come: Tracing God's Kingdom Program and Covenant Promises Throughout History* (Wheaton, IL: Victor Books, 1990), 61.

and uncircumcised in heart and ears are always resisting the Holy Spirit; you are doing just as our fathers did" (Acts 7:51).

The same wording that's used to describe the eternality of the covenant in general is used for physical circumcision in particular: "And I will establish My covenant between Me and you and your descendants after you throughout their generations *for an everlasting covenant,* to be God to you and to your descendants after you" (Gen. 17:7; cf. v. 19). Lewis Sperry Chafer states that "the Abrahamic Covenant, unlike the Mosaic Covenant which followed, was declared to be an everlasting covenant and will continue to be observed in time and eternity (vv. 7, 13, 19; 1 Chron. 16:16–17; Ps. 105:10)."[2] Notice Chafer's words: "in time and eternity."

The note on Genesis 17:9–14 in the dispensational-oriented *Believer's Study Bible*, edited by the late W. A. Criswell, avoids the problem of physical circumcision's permanence but does allude to circumcision of the heart by referencing Old and New Testament passages (Deut. 10:16; Jer. 4:4; Rom. 2:26; Col. 2:11–12).[3] Ryrie comments in the study Bible that carries his name that "For a Hebrew to refuse circumcision was to excise himself from the covenant community, Gen. 17:14."[4] Is this *forever*? Do the New Testament writers insist on physical circumcision for children of Jewish believers? Ryrie does not say.

Because the covenant of circumcision is said to be everlasting, this means that Jews born during the millennium must be circumcised because any "uncircumcised male who is not circumcised in the flesh of his foreskin, that person shall be cut off from his people; he has broken My covenant" (Gen. 17:14). The literal interpretation of Bible prophecy and the everlasting nature of the Abrahamic covenant as proclaimed by dispensationalists demand the perpetual validity and practice of *physical* circumcision. Given that the land covenant is everlasting and still requires a future fulfillment, the everlasting nature of the covenant of circumcision must also require a future fulfillment if we follow dispensational interpretive assumptions.

The comment on Genesis 17:8 in the dispensationalism oriented *Nelson Study Bible* addresses the people and land aspects of the everlasting covenant but says nothing about circumcision:

---

2. Lewis Sperry Chafer, *Systematic Theology*, John F. Walvoord, ed., 2 vols. abridged ed. (Wheaton, IL: Victor Books, 1988), 2:213.

3. W. A. Criswell, ed., *The Believer's Study Bible* (Nashville, TN: Thomas Nelson, 1991), 31.

4. Charles Caldwell Ryrie, *The Ryrie Study Bible* (Chicago: Moody Press, 1978), 31.

> The promise clearly included the Israelite people and the land (Canaan). The two are linked in the language of the covenant in ch. 15. Even though God removed Israel more than once from the land, He promised them ultimate possession of Canaan. It is an everlasting possession. The same word used of God's covenant (v. 7) is used of the land.[5]

The Old Testament note on Genesis 17:14, overseen by Old Testament editor Ronald B. Allen, professor at Dallas Theological Seminary, suggests that circumcision changes from a required physical procedure to an internal spiritual transformation when we reach the New Covenant: "Circumcision—an outward sign—stood for a thorough commitment to God—an inward reality. Hence the apostle Paul demands that the heart be circumcised to God (Rom. 2:25–29)." Dispensationalists have avoided this type of physical to spiritual transference when it comes to Israel and the land promises. Is it possible that circumcision is the key to understanding how the Abrahamic covenant can be unconditional, everlasting, and literal but not eternally physical?

## "I Haven't Really Thought About the Issue"

In preparing this chapter, I wanted to be sure about the dispensational understanding of the everlasting covenant of circumcision, so I checked all the standard dispensational books I have in my library. It was difficult to find anyone who addressed the subject. So as not to misrepresent dispensationalism, I contacted dispensational scholars and asked the following question: "Since the physical land promise is an everlasting covenant, why isn't the same true for the covenant of physical circumcision since both are said to be 'everlasting'" (Gen 17:8, 13)? Benware argues that since some of the Abrahamic covenant promises already have been fulfilled in a literal way then "all the promises will have a literal fulfillment."[6] If this is true, then physical circumcision is an everlasting rite. In response to my question, I received the following answer from a former Dallas Theological Seminary professor, the only one to respond so far:

> I haven't really thought about the issue of circumcision before in the light you have constructed your question but my initial re-

---

5. Earl D. Radmacher, gen. ed., *The Nelson Study Bible* (Nashville: Thomas Nelson Publishers, 1997), 36.

6. Benware, *Understanding End Time Prophecy*, 34.

sponse is that it **is** part of the everlasting covenant. The thing is after the millennial period and the fact that there will be no new children born, there would be no more need to have the practice for new boys born. Those Jews already circumcised will not need to be circumcised but will not lose their circumcision in their resurrected bodies.

I was surprised that he had never thought of the circumcision question since it is part of the everlasting covenant that dispensationalists use to make their case that there is a covenantal distinction between Israel and the church. In a second email, I asked if circumcision would be reinstituted during the millennium since it's during this time that the land promises are finally fulfilled given dispensational presuppositions:

Again, this is preliminary thinking on this topic for me, but I guess I would say yes to your question. I am not sure what issues of consistency, and what implications come from this view.

The implications are dramatic, and if followed consistently would overturn the New Testament teaching which states, "For he is not a Jew who is one outwardly; neither is circumcision that which is outward in the flesh. But he is a Jew who is one inwardly; and circumcision is that which is of the heart, by the Spirit, not by the letter; and his praise is not from men, but from God" (Rom. 2:28–29). For the dispensationalist, a covenantal Jew is someone who must be marked outwardly in the flesh given the demands of the Abrahamic covenant.

## Circumcision and Blood Sacrifices

Not only does dispensationalism require circumcision for Jews during the millennium but for Gentiles who want to enter the fourth temple (Ezek. 40–46). In Tim LaHaye's *Prophecy Study Bible* we read what dispensationalists claim will take place during the millennium: "No foreigner who is uncircumcised in heart and flesh may enter [the temple], neither will any descendants of the Levites conduct services, other than the godly descendants of Zadok."[7] Circumcision of the heart was an Old Covenant requirement (Deut. 10:16; 30:6; Jer. 4:4). While circumci-

---

7. Tim LaHaye, gen. ed., *LaHaye Prophecy Study Bible* (Chattanooga, TN: AMG Publishers, 2000), 886, comments on Ezekiel 44:5-15.

sion of the heart is still required under the New Covenant (Rom. 2:28–29), physical circumcision is not. Those in Christ are the "true circumcision" (Phil 3:2–3).

In addition to the reinstitution of circumcision, dispensationalism requires that animal sacrifices *for atonement* must also be reinstituted. John C. Whitcomb, in his article on "The Millennial Temple" in LaHaye's *Prophecy Study Bible*, writes that "five different offerings in Ezekiel (43:13–46:15), four of them with bloodletting, will serve God's purposes. These offerings are not voluntary but obligatory; God will 'accept' people on the basis of these animal sacrifices (43:27), which make reconciliation [atonement] for the house of Israel (45:17, cf. 45:15)."[8] Whitcomb attempts to mollify the problems associated with this unbiblical view by claiming that "the offerings will not take away sin (see Heb. 10:4), but they will be effective in sanctifying Israelites ceremonially because of His infinitely holy presence in their midst."[9]

This is an impossible interpretation for at least three reasons. First, these sacrifices are said to be "for atonement" (reconciliation) (Ezek. 45:15, 17) not, as Whitcomb claims, "as effective vehicles of divine instruction for Israel and the nations during the Millennial Kingdom."[10] Second, Jesus is the once for all sacrifice whose blood cleanses us from sin (Heb. 7:26–27; 8:13; 9:11–15; 10:5–22; 1 Peter 3:18). Third, sanctification comes by "the washing of water with the word" (Eph. 5:26) not by the washing of blood from animal sacrifices.

## Old and New Scofield

In the original *Scofield Reference Bible* (1909), a note on the nature of these blood sacrifices described in Ezekiel seeks to obscure the problem related to blood sacrifices during the thousand years of Revelation 20 by claiming that "these offerings will be memorial, looking back to the cross, as the offerings under the old covenant were anticipatory, looking forward to the cross." I wonder why the Judaizers didn't think of this argument.

A note in the *New Scofield Reference Bible* (1967) acknowledges that "a problem is posed" by the atoning nature of these sacrifices "since the N.T. clearly teaches that animal sacrifices do not in themselves cleanse away sin (Heb. 10:4) and that the one sacrifice of the Lord Jesus Christ that was made at Calvary completely provides for such expiation (cp. Heb. 9:12, 26, 28; 10:10, 14)." How do the

---

8. John C. Whitcomb, "The Millennial Temple, *Prophecy Study Bible*, 883.

9. Whitcomb, "The Millennial Temple," 883.

10. Whitcomb, "The Millennial Temple," 883.

editors solve the problem given their literal hermeneutic?: First by suggesting that the blood sacrifices "will be memorial in character,"[11] and second, "the references to sacrifices is [*sic*] not to be taken literally." Ryrie takes a similar position: "If the great festivals of Passover and Tabernacles are to be observed during the Millennium, there is no reason why sacrifices would not also be offered. Then, of course, they will be memorials of the finished sacrifice of Christ."[12] Where Jesus says "It is finished" (John 19:30), dispensationalists claim that bloodletting and blood sacrifices will continue for a future thousand years with the slain, resurrected, and glorified Jesus sitting on David's throne from Jerusalem. With His nail prints and sliced side in plain view, the people will still be sacrificing animals!

Ezekiel does not say that these sacrifices "will be memorials." The Bible clearly states that they are for "for atonement" (Ezek. 45:17, 20). This means that Ezekiel's visionary temple was either part of the Old Covenant renewal of the sacrificial system that arose during the post-exile restoration period or the fulfillment that came by way of the once-for-all redemptive work of Jesus (Luke 24:25–27, 44–45). Jesus is the fulfillment of the temple writ large.

If the sacrifices are "memorial in character," as Scofield and Ryrie claim, or are "not to be taken literally," which Whitcomb contends, then such conclusions violate dispensationalism's insistence that since "fulfilled promises have been ful-

---

11. Charles Feinberg follows the memorial approach when it comes to explaining why there will be animal sacrifices during the millennium. "The Church has had for some 1900 years a memorial of that sacrifice of Christ in the Lord's Supper; Israel as such has had none. [Animal sacrifices] will be that memorial for them primarily." Jesus stated that "this cup [filled with wine] is the new covenant in My blood" (Luke 22:20; cf. 1 Cor. 11:25). Remembrance of Jesus' shed blood is done through wine not the blood of animals. Since Jesus will be physically present, won't the nail marks in His hands and feet and the spear mark in His side be enough to remind us of His redemptive ordeal? By the way, the Lord's Supper was inaugurated with Jews. Feinberg reasons this way to justify blood sacrifices during the millennium: "If no sacrifices are needed where Christ is present, why were they permitted of God all through the earthly ministry of Christ?" The simple and obvious reason is that Jesus had not yet shed His blood. Feinberg hopes to defend his view by asking this question: "And, thirdly, greater wonder still, why, after He had assuredly perfected our salvation forever on the cross, did God allow those sacrifices to go on until 70 A.D. when the temple was destroyed?" The fact that God called for the destruction of the temple in A.D 70 is clear testimony that Feinberg's arguments are inadequate. (Charles L. Feinberg, *Premillennialism or Amillennialism?: The Premillennial and Amillennial Systems of Biblical Interpretation Analyzed and Compared*, 2nd ed. [Wheaton, IL: Van Kampen Press, 1954], 336-337).

12. Ryrie, *Ryrie Study Bible*, 1299. Note that Ezekiel doesn't say anything about a "millennium." The only place in the Bible where a "thousand years" is used to describe the reign of Christ is in Revelation 20. You will notice, however, that Revelation 20 does not say that Jesus will reign from the earth, that a temple will be built, or that animals will be sacrificed.

filled in a literal way," then "that leads to the conclusion that all the promises will have a literal fulfillment."[13]

## Dispensational Judaizing

LaHaye and Thomas Ice, given their dispensational beliefs, confirm that the millennial temple "will serve as the center for the priestly rituals and offerings" claiming that they "will provide guidance in the worship of the Messiah."[14] They admit that their literal view might seem to be "contradicting passages such as Hebrews 7:26–27 and 9:26, which teach that Jesus Christ was the perfect and final sacrifice for sin."[15] In order to keep the dispensational paradigm intact, they attempt to maneuver around their unbiblical approach by maintaining "that the sacrifices are for ceremonial purification." LaHaye and Ice quote Jerry Hullinger, a professor at Pensacola Theological Seminary, for support: "Because of God's promise to dwell on earth during the millennium (as stated in the New Covenant),[16] it is necessary that He protect His presence through sacrifice."[17] Where does the New Testament say this or intimate that such a thing is even remotely possible given what we know about the finished redemptive work of Christ? When Jesus appeared to His disciples after His resurrection, it was not necessary that He protect His presence through animal blood. Should Thomas have dipped his finger in animal blood before he put it into Jesus' side? (John 20:27). Should Jesus' disciples have slaughtered a lamb before they ate breakfast with Him? (21:12).

Contrary to what dispensationalism demands, the New Testament rejects the need for further sacrifices: "And although you were formerly alienated and hostile in mind, engaged in evil deeds, yet He has now reconciled you in His fleshly body through death, in order to present you before Him holy and blameless and beyond reproach" (Col. 1:21–22; cf. Heb. 9:11–14). LaHaye and Ice are engaged in dispensational judaizing in a vain effort to save a system that has no biblical support, if the New Testament is to be believed.

---

13. Benware, *Understanding End Times Prophecy*, 34.

14. Tim LaHaye and Thomas Ice, *Charting the End Times: A Visual Guide to Understanding Bible Prophecy* (Eugene, OR: Harvest House, 2001), 94.

15. LaHaye and Ice, *Charting the End Times*, 95.

16. There is no such promise. Revelation 20 says nothing about Jesus reigning on the earth during the thousand years.

17. Jerry M. Hullinger, "The Problem of Animal Sacrifices in Ezekiel 40-48," *Bibliotheca Sacra* 152 (July-September 1995), 289. Quoted in LaHaye and Ice, *Charting the End Times*, 95.

Charles D. Alexander summarizes the inherent theological problems associated with dispensationalism related to the everlasting nature of the Abrahamic covenant and the New Covenant's redemptive fulfillment:

> It is useless for our [dispensational] friends to tell us that this is not their error, for their interpretations require that in their so-called millennial age Gentiles must be circumcised according to the laws of Ezekiel's "temple." Hence our Savior Christ, supposedly reigning in person in Jerusalem, must preside over the subversion of His own gospel, the undoing of His work of redemption on the Cross and the dismantling of that kingdom of grace and truth which was the sole purpose of His coming into the world. In other words, the "Second Coming" according to the dispensational scheme will undo the whole purpose of the First Coming, and the Law will supplant the gospel.
>
> \* \* \*
>
> And who is now the heretic—"We who plead for a spiritual and gospel interpretation of prophecy, or our friends who reestablish circumcision, the temple, the sacrifice, the Levitical priesthood, and abolish the church and the gospel, and put Moses in the place of Christ"? When we say that the epistle to the Galatians was written to destroy this Judaistic error, we do not overstate the truth.[18]

Dispensationalism is a theological house of cards. The main reason that it remains the eschatology of choice among fundamentalists is its sensationalism factor. With its parenthesis view of history and a return to the Old Covenant rites of circumcision and animal sacrifices, it is beyond me how anyone can claim that dispensationalism is orthodox Christianity.

---

18. Charles D. Alexander, "Moses or Christ?: Paul's Response to Dispensational Error." www.graceonlinelibrary.org/full.asp?ID=440

# 7

# The Myth that the Temple Needs to be Rebuilt

A battle is raging over the Temple Mount in Jerusalem. Many Jews want to see the temple that was destroyed by the Romans in A.D. 70 rebuilt to match its former glory. But there is a big obstacle in the way. The Muslim Dome of the Rock now dominates the site, and Muslims claim the Jews have no right to the site. There are millions of Christians who believe a rebuilt temple is a mandatory prerequisite for the rise of antichrist, the great tribulation, and the final battle of Armageddon.

In order for the futurist scenario outlined by modern-day prophecy writers to take place, there must be a rapture of the church. The pretribulational rapture is the next prophetic event in the dispensational system where Israel takes centerstage in prophetic history. It supposedly sets off a series of prophetic events leading up to the millennial reign of Christ, including the rebuilding of *another* temple in Jerusalem after the destruction of the "tribulation temple." But it's in the future post-rapture "tribulation temple" that the antichrist is to take his seat (2 Thess. 2:4), place a statue of himself for people to worship (Matt. 24:15; Rev. 13:14–15), and proclaim himself to be god (2 Thess. 2:4).

But what the futurists need to support this end-time scenario is a verse that states that there will be *another* rebuilt temple, a temple different from the one that was built after the exile and renovated (rebuilt) by Herod the Great beginning in 20 B.C. and finally completed in A.D. 64. Notice how clearly the Old Testament mentions that there was a decree to rebuild the post-exilic temple (2 Chron. 36:22–23; Ezra 1:1–4; 5:6–17). The foundation stone was laid (Ezra 3:10–12) and the temple was completed (6:13–18). There was even a letter sent to the authorities of the time to determine if there had ever been a "decree to rebuild this temple" (5:1–17; 6:1–12).

Rebuilt-temple advocates Tommy Ice and Randall Price are forced to admit that "There are no Bible verses that say, 'There is going to be a third temple.'"[1] Having made this revealing concession, they go on to claim "that there will be a Jewish Temple in Jerusalem at least by the midpoint of the seven-year tribulation period."[2] Randall Price's updated 700-page book on *The Temple and Bible Prophecy* still can't produce a verse from the New Testament that actually states that another temple is prophetically required to be rebuilt.[3] Considering that there are two *books* (Ezra and Nehemiah) from the Old Testament devoted to the details of rebuilding the temple when the Jews returned from the Babylonian captivity, one would think there would be at least one *verse* in the New Testament that says something about the rebuilding of a distant post-rapture temple.

Price and Ice are not alone in making their unsupported claim for another rebuilt temple. Merrill F. Unger, writing in 1955, made a similar assertion: "The temple will be rebuilt, for the 'abomination of desolation' (Matt. 24:15) 'shall stand in the Holy Place,' in the 'Temple of God' (Jewish Temple) rebuilt (II Thess. 2:4), with an 'altar' and 'worshipers' (Rev. 11:1), and an 'outer court' in the 'Holy City' (Jerusalem, *cf.* Rev. 11:2)."[4] The problem with Unger's end-time scenario is that the temple built by Herod was still standing when these prophecies were given. Unger assumes that the mere mention of a temple in a prophetic passage must be a reference to a rebuilt temple that will be constructed during the tribulation period that follows a pretribulational rapture in what has become a nearly 2000-year delay.[5] If the temple is such a crucial piece of the end-time puzzle, why doesn't the New Testament say something about it? The silence is deafening.

---

1. Thomas Ice and Randall Price, *Ready to Rebuild: The Imminent Plan to Rebuild the Last Days Temple* (Eugene, OR: Harvest House, 1992), 197–198.

2. Ice and Price, *Ready to Rebuild*, 198.

3. Randall Price, *The Temple and Bible Prophecy: A Definitive Look at Its Past, Present, and Future* (Eugene, OR: Harvest House, 2006). Price has three chapters dealing with predictions in the New Testament on the temple, but he does not reference one verse that says anything about rebuilding the temple (255–324).

4. Merrill F. Unger, *Great Neglected Bible Prophecies* (Chicago: Scripture Press Books, 1955), 23.

5. Unger disputes Carl Friedrich Keil's contention that "the New Testament says nothing whatever concerning the rebuilding of the Jerusalem temple and the restoration of the Levitical worship." (Carl Friedrich Keil, *Biblical Commentary on the Prophecies of Ezekiel*, 2 vols. [Grand Rapids, MI: Eerdmans, 1950], 2:122). Quoted in Unger, *Great Neglected Bible Prophecies*, 23. Unger accuses Keil of following a spiritualizing methodology (23). Notice that the New Testament uses spiritual designations for the temple and its sacrifices under the new covenant: "spiritual house" and "spiritual sacrifices" (1 Pet. 2:15).

Does the Bible predict that a third temple will be built, one following Solomon's temple and the post-exile temple that was still standing in Jesus' day and was destroyed in A.D. 70 by the Romans? Don Stewart and Chuck Missler insist that the "The crucial issue boils down to how we interpret prophecy." On this, all would agree. "There are two basic ways to interpret Bible prophecy," Stewart and Missler write. "Either you understand it literally or you do not. If a person rejects the literal interpretation then they [sic] are left to their [sic] own imagination as to what the Scripture means.... We believe it makes sense to understand the Scriptures as literally requiring the eventual construction and desecration of a Third Temple."[6] The authors are careful to say that another rebuilt temple is *required*. A third temple is required only if the Bible requires it and specifically states the requirement. While dispensationalists require another temple for their prophetic system to work, as we will see, the New Testament says nothing about a rebuilt temple; not a single word.

Jesus' completed redemptive work makes the need for a rebuilt temple unnecessary. His ministry begins with the declaration that He is our tabernacle (John 1:14), "the lamb of God who takes away the sin of the world" (1:29), "the temple" (John 2:19–21), and the "chief cornerstone" (Matt. 21:42; Acts 4:11; Eph. 2:20). By extension, believers are "as living stones ... being built up as a spiritual house for a holy priesthood, to offer up spiritual sacrifices acceptable to God through Jesus Christ" (1 Peter 2:5). Those "in Christ" are the true temple of God (1 Cor. 3:16; 2 Cor. 6:16; Eph. 2:21; Rev. 21:22). Jesus and the people of God are the focus of the only temple that has any redemptive significance under the new covenant. To be "in Christ" is to be in the temple and all it stood for, "the renewed centre and focus for the people of God"[7] (Rom. 12:5; 1 Cor. 1:2, 30; Gal. 3:14, 28; 5:6). The New Testament references to the temple of stone refer only to its destruction (Matt. 24:1–2) never its physical reconstruction. It is highly significant that "Jesus never gives any hint that there will be a physical replacement for this Temple. There is no suggestion, either in the Apocalyptic Discourse [Revelation] or elsewhere, that this destruction will be but a preliminary stage in some glorious 'restoration' of the Temple."[8]

---

6. Don Stewart and Chuck Missler, *The Coming Temple: Center Stage for the Final Countdown* (Orange, CA: Dart Press, 1991), 193.

7. Timothy J. Geddert, *Watchwords: Mark 13 in Markan Eschatology* (Sheffield, England: JSOT, 1989). Quoted in Peter W. L. Walker, *Jesus and the Holy City: New Testament Perspectives on Jerusalem* (Grand Rapids, MI: Eerdmans, 1996), 9.

8. Walker, *Jesus and the Holy City*, 8.

The original temple was a shadow of things to come. It was designed to be a temporary edifice looking forward to the completed work of Jesus Christ (Isa. 66:1–3; cf. 1:11–13; Mal. 1:10–11). For dispensationalists to insist that another temple is needed to complete some type of covenantal obligation with the Jews goes against the entire New Testament and makes the "first covenant ... faultless," with "no occasion sought for a second" (Heb. 8:7). Let the Bible settle the issue:

> Now the main point in what has been said is this: we have such a high priest, who has taken His seat at the right hand of the throne of the Majesty in the heavens, a minister in the sanctuary, and *in the true tabernacle*, which the Lord pitched, not man. For every high priest is appointed to offer both gifts and sacrifices; hence it is necessary that this high priest also have something to offer. Now if He were on earth, He would not be a priest at all, since there are those who offer the gifts according to the Law; who serve a copy and shadow of the heavenly things, just as Moses was warned by God when he was about to erect the tabernacle; for, "See," He says, "that you make all things according to the pattern which was shown you on the mountain." But now He has obtained a more excellent ministry, by as much as He is also the mediator of a better covenant, which has been enacted on better promises (Heb. 8:1–6).

The writer of Hebrews declares that Jesus entered "through the greater and more perfect tabernacle, not made with hands, that is to say, not of this creation" (9:11). Since Jesus completed His redemptive work, any new temple "made with hands" is little different from a pagan temple that has no inherent life or redemptive value (cf. Acts 17:24; 19:26; 2 Cor. 5:1). "The description of the Jerusalem Temple as 'made with hands' ... is a strong means of playing down its significance. This had been a way of belittling the pagan idols (*e.g.* Ps. 115:4; *cf.* Isa. 46:6); to describe the Temple in such a fashion was potentially incendiary."[9] This is because "the author of Hebrews believed the Jerusalem Temple was but a 'shadow' of the reality now found in Christ (8:5)."[10] The "new covenant" had made the "old covenant" obsolete (8:13), and that included the temple and everything associated with it.

---

9. Walker, *Jesus and the Holy City*, 10.
10. Walker, *Jesus and the Holy City*, 208.

Stewart and Missler have made it very simple for us to determine whether the Bible addresses the issue of a rebuilt temple. If the Bible is interpreted literally, the need for a third temple should be explicitly stated. What biblical evidence do they offer to support their claim that "the Bible, in both testaments, speaks of a Temple that has yet to appear"?[11] From the Old Testament they use Daniel 9:27, 11:31, and 12:11 for support with only Daniel 9:27 being significant for their case.

Since Daniel was written *after* Solomon's temple had been destroyed by Nebuchadnezzar in 586 B.C. (2 Kings 25:8–9; Dan. 1:1–2) and *before* the *second* temple had been built by the returning exiles (Ezra 6:13–15), it stands to reason that the "sanctuary" whose "end will come with a flood" (Dan. 9:26) must refer to the second temple that had not been built at the time the prophecy was given. It was this post-exile rebuilt temple that was desecrated by Antiochus Epiphanes around 170 B.C. but not destroyed. After a period of misuse and disuse, Herod the Great restored and enlarged this second temple that was completed just a few years before it was destroyed in A.D. 70 by the Romans, just as Jesus had predicted (Matt. 24:1–34). It was this same temple that Zacharias served in (Luke 1:9), Jesus was taken to as an infant (2:27), had been under construction for forty-six years when Jesus prophesied that He would be its permanent replacement (John 2:20), Jesus cleansed of the money changers (Matt. 21:12), He predicted would be left desolate (Matt. 23:38; 24:2), whose veil was "torn in two from top to bottom" (Matt. 27:51), and that was finally destroyed by Titus in A.D. 70.

Is there any indication in the three passages from Daniel that we are to skip over what we know was a rebuilt temple, the very temple that was standing in Jesus' day, and look for another unmentioned third temple? Would Jews living in the first century have made the historical leap over the temple that was standing before them and suppose Jesus was describing yet another temple when He never used the words new or rebuilt? As Ice and Price admit, the Bible does not say anything about *another* temple. The passages from Daniel cited by Stewart and Missler and Ice and Price can easily find their fulfillment in the rebuilt temple of Ezra and Nehemiah's day that was standing during the reign of Antiochus (Dan. 11:31; 12:11) and the second temple's destruction in A.D. 70 (9:27). In fact, Ice and Price find the fulfillment of Daniel 11:31 in the sacrilegious acts of Antiochus:

> The abomination of desolation was something that took place the first time through Antiochus Epiphanes in the second century B.C. when he stopped the sacrifices and desecrated the second

---

11. Stewart and Missler, *The Coming Temple*, 194.

Temple by sacrificing an unclean pig on the altar and setting up in its place a statue of Jupiter. *This literally fulfilled Daniel 11:31.* Therefore, these future events will be similar in kind to the prototypes—they will be real, historical events in a last days' Temple.[12]

Daniel only mentions one sanctuary (8:11, 13, 26; 9:17, 26; 11:31; cf. 12:11). What indication is the reader given that two temples are in view? The temple that Jesus said would be torn down and dismantled stone by stone was the "last days" Temple, the only one mentioned by Daniel. We know that the last days were a first-century reality, not the prelude to the period of time just before a pre-tribulational rapture: "God, after He spoke long ago to the fathers in the prophets in many portions and in many ways, *in these last days* has spoken to us in His Son, whom He appointed heir of all things, through whom also He made the world" (Heb. 1:1–2; cf. Acts 2:17; James 5:3). "These last days" were the last days of the old covenant era (see 1 John 2:18; 1 Cor. 10:11). Peter confirms this: "For He was foreknown before the foundation of the world, but has appeared in *these last times* for the sake of *you*" (1 Pet. 1:20; see 4:7).

Now we are left with Daniel 9:27 as the only verse from the Old Testament that Ice and Price contend supports the need for a third temple. But there is a problem with their reasoning. They argue that "the city and sanctuary" in Daniel 9:26 refers to Herod's temple that was destroyed when Jerusalem fell and the temple was destroyed in A.D. 70 (Luke 21:6): "Jesus, seeing Himself as *the Messiah*, therefore saw the Romans as *the people ... who will destroy the city and the sanctuary*. Knowing that He would soon be *cut off* (crucified), He likewise knew that the Temple's destruction would soon occur."[13] In the span of two verses, these authors find two temples, one in Daniel 9:26 and another one in Daniel 9:27, separated by nearly 2000 years (so far). As a careful reader will note, the "sanctuary" (temple) that appears in Daniel 9:26 does not appear in 9:27. This means that Daniel 9:27 is describing events related to the already mentioned sanctuary of 9:26 which Ice and Price say refers to the temple that was standing in Jesus' day. For Ice and Price to find another rebuilt temple, Daniel 9:27 would have to say something like this: "After an unspecified period of time, he will make a firm covenant with the many for one week, but in the middle of the week he will put a stop to sacrifice and grain offering in the third sanctuary; and on the wing of abominations will come one who makes

---

12. Ice and Price, *Ready to Rebuild*, 200–201. Emphasis added.
13. Ice and Price, *Ready to Rebuild*, 68.

desolate, even until a complete destruction of the third sanctuary, one that is decreed, is poured out on the one who makes desolate." Of course, not one word of this is found in Daniel 9:27.[14]

Since, as we have seen, the Old Testament says nothing about a third temple, maybe the New Testament says something about it. Stewart and Missler and Ice and Price[15] claim to have incontrovertible biblical evidence for a rebuilt temple in three passages: Matthew 24:15; 2 Thessalonians 2:3–4; and Revelation 11:1–2. Regarding the temple mentioned in Matthew 24:15, Stewart and Missler write: "Jesus spoke of this prophecy being still future to His time (Matthew 24:15)."[16] This is true, since the prophecy was given around A.D. 30 when the temple rebuilt by Herod was still standing. It was of this temple that Jesus said, "Therefore when *you* see the abomination of desolation which was spoken of through Daniel the prophet" (Matt. 24:15). When *who* sees it? When "*you* see it," that is, when those in Jesus' audience see it. Ice and Price never explain the audience reference "you."

If Jesus had a distant future audience in view, He would have said "when *they* see the abomination of desolation." Here's their interpretation of Matthew 24:15: "'The holy place' is a reference to the most sacred room within Israel's Temple. What temple? The third Temple, since it is a future event."[17] Saying it's a "future event" does not mean that Jesus was referring to another rebuilt temple since the temple was still standing when Jesus made His prediction about the fate of the temple. We know that the temple was destroyed in A.D. 70, forty years in the future of Jesus' present audience. There is no mention of another rebuilt temple or even an implied reference to a rebuilt temple. Jesus does not say, "When *they* see the abomination of desolation which was spoken of through Daniel the prophet standing in the *rebuilt* holy place." The holy place, the sanctuary, was right before their eyes (Matt. 24:1–2). Jesus told His disciples, "'Do *you* not see *all these things*? Truly I say to *you*, not one stone *here* shall be left upon another, which will not be torn down'" (24:2). The idea of a rebuilt temple must be read into the text.

Ice and Price argue that "the apostle Paul gives us perhaps the clearest passage relating to the third Temple in *2 Thessalonians 2:3, 4*."[18] Since Paul wrote his letter before the temple was destroyed in A.D. 70, what is it in these

---

14. For an exposition of Daniel 9:24–27, see Gary DeMar, *Last Days Madness: Obsession of the Modern Church*, 4th ed. (Powder Springs, GA: American Vision, 1999), chap. 25.

15. Price, *The Temple in Bible Prophecy*, 23.

16. Stewart and Missler, *The Coming Temple*, 194.

17. Stewart and Missler, *The Coming Temple*, 199.

18. Ice and Price, *Ready to Rebuild*, 199.

verses that would indicate to the reader that the temple in which the "man of lawlessness" takes his seat is "the third temple" rather than the temple which existed already? Paul does not describe "the temple" (lit. *sanctuary*) as a rebuilt edifice. What would have led his audience to conclude that he was referring to, using Ice and Price's words, "the future third Temple," when the temple was still standing in Jerusalem when Paul wrote his letter? The "man of lawlessness" was being restrained "now," Paul writes, in *their* day (2:6, 7), and the Christians at Thessalonica knew the identity of the restrainer (2:6).[19] This doesn't even *imply* another rebuilt temple, much less *require* one.

Third-temple advocates try to muster support for their position by referencing Revelation 11:1–2. They begin by assuming that Revelation was written nearly three decades after the temple was destroyed.[20] From this unproven assumption, they conclude that John must be measuring a *rebuilt* temple. The passage says nothing about a rebuilt temple. The words "shortly" and "near" (Rev. 1:1, 3; 22:10) are used to describe the time when the events outlined in Revelation were to take place. The fact that John is told to "rise and measure the temple of God, and the altar, and those who are worshiping in it" (11:1), is *prima facie* evidence that the temple was still standing when John received the revelation. "Worshiping" is in the present tense; it's what the people were doing as John measured the temple. How could John have measured a temple that did not exist in his day? Ice and Price insist the temple that John is told to measure is the literal temple, not a "spiritual temple." "For example, in Matthew 24 Jesus is speaking about a literal Temple, since in the context of the passage he is standing and looking directly at the second Temple."[21] Following Ice and Price's argument, how could the temple John was told to measure be a literal temple if it hadn't been built yet? On the contrary, John was told to measure the literal Temple that still had worshipers in it, the same temple that Jesus stood in and Titus destroyed in A.D. 70. There is no indication that Revelation 11 is describing a future rebuilt temple.

Here's how Ice tries to explain away what Revelation 11:1–2 clearly states about the temple:

---

19. For a verse-by-verse exposition of 2 Thessalonians 2, see DeMar, *Last Days Madness*, chaps.22 and 23.

20. For a defense of a pre-A.D. 70 date of composition for Revelation, see Kenneth L. Gentry, Jr., *Before Jerusalem Fell: Dating the Book of Revelation*, 2nd ed. (Powder Springs, GA: American Vision, 1999); *The Beast of Revelation* (Powder Springs, GA: American Vision); Gary DeMar and Francis X. Gumerlock, *The Early Church and the End of the World* (Powder Springs, GA: American Vision, 2).

21. Ice and Price, *Ready to Rebuild*, 200.

It must be remembered that in the Book of Revelation John is receiving a vision about future things. He is transported in some way to that future time in order to view events as they will unfold. The word "saw" is used 49 times in 46 verses in Revelation because John is witnessing future events through a vision. It does not matter at all whether the Temple is thought to be standing in Jerusalem at the time that John sees the vision since that would not have any bearing upon a vision. John is told by an angel to "measure the temple" (Rev. 11:1). Measure what Temple? He is to measure the Temple in the vision. Even if there were a temple still standing in Jerusalem, John was on the Island of Patmos and would not have been allowed to go and measure that Temple. Ezekiel, during a similar vision of a Temple (Ezek. 40–43) was told to measure that Temple. When Ezekiel saw and was told to measure a Temple there was not one standing in Jerusalem (Preterists agree). Thus, there is no compulsion whatsoever to conclude that just because a temple is referenced in Revelation 11 that it implies that there had to be a physical Temple standing in Jerusalem at the same time.[22]

Let's deal with the obvious mistake in Ice's analysis. Ezekiel was not told to measure the temple. Ezekiel saw "a man whose appearance was like the appearance of bronze ... who measured the thickness of the wall" (Ezek. 40:3, 5). Ezekiel sees this man doing the measuring. Ezekiel is a bystander. Being a visionary temple, Ezekiel did not have access to it because it existed only in a vision, and there is no indication that it was ever designed to be built.[23]

---

22. Thomas Ice, "The Date of the Book of Revelation": www.raptureready.com/featured/DateBookRevelation.html Some commentators believe the use of temple language in Revelation 11:1–2 "is a symbol of the true church that worships the triune God" (Simon J. Kistemaker, Revelation: New Testament Commentary [Grand Rapids, MI: Baker Books, 2001], 324). The geographical context is the city where Jesus was crucified (11:8). This is a significant clue that the physical temple is in view. Mark Wilson writes: "Historically, the only group eligible to worship at the temple in Jerusalem were Jewish believers, and these are numbered earlier as part of the 144,000 (Rev. 7:4–8)." (Mark W. Wilson, "Revelation," Zondervan Illustrated Bible Backgrounds Commentary: Hebrews to Revelation, ed. Clinton E. Arnold, 4 vols. [Grand Rapids, MI: Zondervan, 2002], 4:311).

23. Ezekiel is told that the altar will be built: "These are the statutes for the altar on the day it is built, to offer burnt offerings on it and to sprinkle blood on it" (Ezek. 43:18). We know that a new temple and altar were built, animals sacrificed, and Levitical priests attended to their priestly duties after the exile (Neh. 11:11).

Mark Hitchcock makes the same mistake when he writes, "Ezekiel, like John, is told to measure the Temple he sees in his vision. The words 'measure' and 'measured' occur 44 times in Ezekiel 40–48. Ezekiel is measuring a temple that must be future to his day because no temple is standing on earth in Jerusalem for him to measure."[24] Like Ice, he fails to note who is doing the measuring. So then, since John is doing the measuring in Revelation 11, unlike Ezekiel who was with a man who measured the temple "in the visions of God" (Ezek. 40:2), we can only conclude that the temple was still standing in Jerusalem when John was given the Revelation by Jesus. The temple John is told to measure is a functioning temple with worshipers and an altar (Rev. 11:1). John saw the temple in a vision, but it was a vision of the temple that was still standing in Jerusalem in his day. The historical circumstances fit a pre-A.D. 70 Jerusalem that still would have been described as "the great city" (11:8), the place where "their Lord was crucified" (11:8), and was occupied by a foreign power (Rome) at the time (11:2). Henry Cowles (1803–1881), in his commentary on Revelation, offers the following argument:

> Here is one of the landmarks of our prophetic interpretation. We *know* that the temple, altar and holy city were standing at the time of this vision; we *know* they were on the very eve of their desolation; we *know* therefore that this desolation—so "shortly" after these visions were seen and recorded—can not possibly be any other than that effected by the Roman armies in A. D. 70.[25]

E. Earle Ellis writes that "the *present* existence of the Jerusalem temple (11:1) and its *future* desolation (11:2) are fairly strong indicators of a pre-AD 70 date for Revelation."[26] In order for a post-A.D. 70 composition and futurist interpretation of Revelation to work, a rebuilt temple must be assumed, but it cannot be proved by anyone who claims to interpret the Bible in a literal fashion.

If John can be taken to the future to measure a temple in a vision that did not exist, as Ice argues, then John could have been taken to Jerusalem in a vision to measure the temple that was still standing. The burden of proof is on Ice, Price, and Hitchcock to demonstrate from Scripture that a distant future rebuilt

---

24. Mark Hitchcock, "The Stake in the Heart—The A.D. 95 Date of Revelation," *The End Times Controversy: The Second Coming Under Attack*, eds. Tim LaHaye and Thomas Ice (Eugene, OR: Harvest House, 2003), 140.

25. Henry Cowles, *The Revelation of John* (New York: D. Appleton & Co., 1887): http://www.truthinheart.com/EarlyOberlinCD/CD/Cowles/Rev/Rev_XI.html

26. E. Earle Ellis, *The Making of the New Testament Documents* (Boston: Brill Academic Publishers, Inc., 2002), 214.

temple is in view. As was noted above, Ice and Price admit there is no mention of a rebuilt temple in the New Testament. On this point, they are correct. After the physical temple in Jerusalem (which would be destroyed a few years later in A.D. 70) had been measured, its locale changes from earth to heaven (Rev. 11:19; 14:15, 17; 15:5, 6; etc.).

## Will Ezekiel's Temple Be Built?

This brings us to the visionary temple described in Ezekiel. Keep in mind that the so-called tribulation temple, as dispensationalists describe it, is not Ezekiel's temple. Dispensationalists actually require that two temples must be built, one during the tribulation period and one during their version of the thousand years of Revelation 20. So even if Ezekiel's temple is a literal stone temple that will be built, it's not the temple of the tribulation period.

While John is told to measure the temple in Revelation 11:1, as has been noted, Ezekiel sees a vision of "a man … with a measuring rod in his hand" (40:3). Ezekiel cannot measure the temple because it's a vision. John can measure the temple because it's still standing in Jerusalem. It should be noted that nowhere in the description of the temple described in Ezekiel is it ever said that it will be built. Ezekiel's temple is an edifice that cannot be defiled (43:7–9). This temple seems to have been wholly efficacious for any who studied its description and measurement in relation to his sins (43:10–11).

Like the plans that were given to Moses to build the tabernacle (Ex. 25:9, 40; Num. 8:4), Ezekiel is given plans to rebuild the altar. This makes perfect sense since rebuilding the altar takes place during a time when there is a Levitical priesthood (Ezek. 43:19) "of the sons of Zadok" (40:46; 43:19; 44:15; 48:11) and the need for animal sacrifices. The altar is to be built but there are on instructions to build the visionary temple: "And He said to me, 'Son of man, thus says the Lord GOD, "These are the statutes for the altar *on the day it is built*, to offer burnt offerings on it and to sprinkle blood on it"'" (Ezek. 43:18). The words "build" and "built" are not found anywhere in Ezekiel 40–43:1–12 in relation to the visionary temple. We should expect to find the Hebrew word for "pattern" (*tavnyth*) used if building this visionary temple was in view as it is, for example, in Exodus 25:9 and 1 Chronicles 28:11–19. The building only refers to the altar, an old covenant shadow of new covenant realities fulfilled in the person and work of Jesus Christ (John 1:29, 36).

Dispensationalists believe that Ezekiel's temple is to be built in the future "during the earthly millennial kingdom."[27] If this is true, then why is there no mention of a temple in Revelation 20? In fact, Revelation 20 says nothing about Jesus reigning on the earth, David's throne being set up and Jesus sitting on it, animal sacrifices, the reinstitution of circumcision, or anything related to Ezekiel's temple. Former dispensationalist Philip Mauro makes an excellent series of points about how Revelation 20 is used to fix so many dispensational prophecy problems:

> The millennium [period of Revelation 20] becomes the convenient and promiscuous dumping place of all portions of Scripture which offer any difficulty.... The "postponement" system doubtless owes its popularity it enjoys to the circumstances that its method is both safe and easy. It is *safe* because, when a fulfillment of prophecy is relegated to the Millennium, it cannot be conclusively refuted until the time comes. All date-setting schemes owe their measure of popularity to the same fact. It is *easy* because it relieves the Bible student of the trouble of searching for the meaning and application of difficult passages.[28]

When the word "temple" does appear again in Revelation, we are told that "the Lord God, the Almighty, and the lamb, are [the New Jerusalem's] temple" (Rev. 21:22). What do we learn about the nature of the holy city? Notice that "the holy city, new Jerusalem" is "made ready as a bride adorned for her husband" (21:2). Not *for* a bride, but *as* a bride. The city is the bride. The New Jerusalem is made up of people. The redeemed in Christ are "a holy temple in the Lord" (Eph. 2:21). Notice the present status of this temple made of redeemed people: "in whom **you also are being built together** into a dwelling of God in the Spirit" (Eph. 2:22). The writer to the Hebrews tells his first-century audience, "But **you have come** to Mount Zion and to the city of the living God, **the heavenly Jerusalem**, and to myriads of angels, to the general assembly and church of the firstborn **who are enrolled in heaven**, and to God, the Judge of all, and to the spirits of the righteous made perfect, and to Jesus, the mediator of a new covenant, and to the sprinkled blood, which speaks better than the blood of

---

27. Tim LaHaye and Ed Hindson, gen. eds., *The Popular Bible Prophecy Commentary: Understanding the Meaning of Every Prophetic Passage* (Eugene, OR: Harvest House, 2007), 196.

28. Philip Mauro, *The Hope of Israel: What Is It?* (Boston: Hamilton Brothers, 1929), 114–115.

Abel" (Heb. 12:22–24). We are said to have been already "raised up with Him" and seated "with Him in heavenly places" (Eph. 2:6).

Jesus prepared us for Revelation's symbolism regarding the temple. The Samaritan woman thought in Old Covenant terms: "Our fathers worshiped in this mountain; and you people [*i.e.*, the Jews] say that in Jerusalem is the place where men ought to worship" (John 4:20). "Believe Me," Jesus told her, "an hour is coming when neither in this mountain **nor in Jerusalem** will you worship the Father. You worship what you do not know; we worship what we know, for salvation is from the Jews. But an hour is coming, **and now is**, when the true worshipers will worship the Father in spirit and truth; for such people the Father seeks to be His worshipers. God is spirit, and those who worship Him must worship in spirit and truth" (John 4:21–23).

Earthly Jerusalem is no longer the center of worship. Paul makes a similar point: "But the Jerusalem **above** is free; she is our mother" (Gal. 4:26). Jesus dwells with us now (Matt. 18:20). That's why John can be told to write, "Behold, the tabernacle of God is among men, and He shall dwell among them, and they shall be His people, and God Himself shall be among them" (Rev. 21:3; see John 14:23; 2 Cor. 6:16). Jesus is the eternal tabernacle who dwells among His people throughout the whole earth. Consider what Ezekiel writes in a passage that is seen as applying to Israel's yet future return to the land: "And I will make a covenant of peace with them; it will be an everlasting covenant with them. And I will place them and multiply them, and will set My sanctuary in their midst forever" (37:26). Futurists claim that Ezekiel is describing what will take place in the 1000-year period mentioned in Revelation 20. The apostle Paul sees it differently by applying Ezekiel 37:26 to events in his own day: "what agreement has the temple of God with idols? For we are the temple of the living God; just as God said, 'I will dwell in them and walk among them; and I will be their God, and they shall be My people'" (2 Cor. 6:16). What is happening in the New Testament is the fulfillment of the promise of "an everlasting covenant" and the fulfillment of all temple promises: "we are the temple of the living God." How do we know this? God dwells in His temple, the very thing that Paul says was happening in His day and continues to happen where God's people reside.

The apostle John sees "the holy city, Jerusalem, coming down out of heaven from God" (Rev. 21:10). "The picture is not, of course, intended to evoke images of space stations, or of cities literally floating in the air; rather, it indicates the divine origin of 'the City which has *foundations*, whose Architect and Builder is

God' (Heb. 11:10)."[29] The idea of a physical temple to be built a third or fourth time in Jerusalem is contrary to everything the New Testament teaches.

## Circumcision and Sacrifices

To complicate things further for the temple rebuilders, consider that Ezekiel mentions that circumcision and animal sacrifices must be reinstated during the time they say Ezekiel's temple will be built. In Tim LaHaye's *Prophecy Study Bible*, we read what dispensationalists claim will take place during the period of time outlined in Revelation 20: "No foreigner who is uncircumcised in heart and flesh may enter [the sanctuary], neither will any descendants of the Levites conduct services, other than the godly descendants of Zadok."[30] In addition to circumcision of Jews and non-Jews, dispensationalism requires that animal sacrifices *for atonement* must also be reinstituted. John C. Whitcomb, in his article on "The Millennial Temple" in the *Prophecy Study Bible*, writes that "five different offerings in Ezekiel (43:13–46:15), four of them with bloodletting, will serve God's purposes. These offerings are not voluntary but obligatory; God will 'accept' people on the basis of these animal sacrifices (43:27), which make reconciliation [atonement] for the house of Israel (45:17, cf. 45:15)."[31] Whitcomb attempts to mollify the problems associated with this unbiblical view by claiming that "the offerings will not take away sin (see Heb. 10:4), but they will be effective in sanctifying Israelites ceremonially because of His infinitely holy presence in their midst."[32]

This is an impossible interpretation for at least three reasons. First, these sacrifices are said to be "for atonement" (reconciliation) (Ezek. 45:15, 17) not, as Whitcomb claims, "as effective vehicles of divine instruction for Israel and the nations during the Millennial Kingdom."[33] The Hebrew verb *kipper* ("atonement") is used in the Ezekiel passages which is the same word and verb form used in the Pentateuch to describe sacrifices related to atonement (Lev. 6:30; 8:15; 16:6, 11, 24, 30, 32–34; Num. 5:8; 15:28; 29:5). Jesus tells His redeemed people to remember His sacrificial work in celebration of the Lord's Supper not in animal sacrifices in some

---

29. David Chilton, *The Days of Vengeance: An Exposition of the Book of Revelation* (Horn Lake, MS: Dominion Press, 2006), 552.

30. Tim LaHaye, gen. ed., *LaHaye Prophecy Study Bible* (Chattanooga, TN: AMG Publishers, 2000), 886, comments on Ezekiel 44:5–15.

31. John C. Whitcomb, "The Millennial Temple, *Prophecy Study Bible*, 883.

32. Whitcomb, "The Millennial Temple," 883.

33. Whitcomb, "The Millennial Temple," 883.

far off earthly "millennium." Second, Jesus is the once for all sacrifice whose blood cleanses us from sin (Heb. 7:26–27; 8:13; 9:11–15; 10:5–22; 1 Peter 3:18). Third, sanctification comes by "the washing of water with the word" (Eph. 5:26) not by the washing of blood that comes from animal sacrifices. Old Covenant sacrifices served only as a temporary covering of sin.

## The Meaning of Ezekiel's Temple

The book of Ezekiel begins and ends with visions. The opening visions are of God: "Now it came about in the thirtieth year, on the fifth *day* of the fourth month, while I was by the river Chebar among the exiles, the heavens were opened and I saw visions of God" (1:1). The visions of God are as intricate and specific as the visions related to the temple in Ezekiel 40–48. Any attempt to construct a physical representation of the visions of God would have missed the intended picture of glory found in the visions. Ezekiel tells us that the visions of the temple were "like the vision which I saw by the river Chebar" (43:3c). In Ezekiel 40–48, Ezekiel is shown a vision of the future in the form of a Temple and City. Like the visions in the first chapter, the elements of these visions were not to be built. The vision pictures the glories of the New Covenant that is realized in the person and work of Jesus Christ who is the ultimate manifestation of the temple, sanctuary, city, land, and people. To be "in Christ" is to be in the temple, sanctuary, city, and land. Just like the image of God is magnificent, so is the reality of the New Covenant in Christ. Only Jesus could fulfill the reality of the sanctuary, temple, land, and city:

> And He said to me, "Son of man, *this is* the place of My throne and the place of the soles of My feet, where I will dwell among the sons of Israel forever. And the house of Israel will not again defile My holy name, neither they nor their kings, by their harlotry and by the corpses of their kings when they die, by setting their threshold by My threshold, and their door post beside My door post, with *only* the wall between Me and them. And they have defiled My holy name by their abominations which they have committed. So I have consumed them in My anger" (Ezek. 43:7–8).

Israel was to see Jesus as this temple and the fulfillment of the shadows of the Old Covenant: "When He said, 'A new covenant,' He has made the first obsolete. But whatever is becoming obsolete and growing old is ready [lit. *near*] to disappear" (Heb. 8:13). It was ready to disappear in the first century because of the person and work of Jesus. The outward manifestation of the Old Covenant did soon disappear when the temple was torn down stone by stone in A.D. 70. Paul M. Hoskins, writing in *Jesus as the Fulfillment of the Temple in the Gospel of John*, argues that the combined evidence from passages like John 1:14, 1:51, 2:13–22, and 4:20–24 "suggests that the coming of Jesus inaugurates a new phase in the relationship between God and his people. In these verses, Jesus fulfills and surpasses prophecies and patterns associated with the Temple. In doing so, Jesus appears to be the fulfillment of the Temple who has come to take its place."[34] In Ezekiel 47 we read about the water that was "flowing from under the threshold of the house" (47:1). "Jesus alludes to the water flowing from Ezekiel's end-time temple in John 7:38 and interprets it of himself and of the Spirit in relation to believers, a passage that further develops the 'living water' theme of John 4."[35]

Quoting Isaiah 49:8, Paul writes, "And working together with Him, we also urge you not to receive the grace of God in vain—for He says, 'At the acceptable time I listened to you, and on the day of salvation I helped you'; behold, now is 'the acceptable time,' behold, now is 'the day of salvation'" (2 Cor. 6:1–2).[36] The New Testament brings to a climax what was promised under the directives of the Old Covenant. The New Testament, as promised, is the Old Covenant fulfilled.

---

34. Paul M. Hoskins, *Jesus as the Fulfillment of the Temple in the Gospel of John* (Eugene, OR: Wipf and Stock Publishers, [2006] 2007), 108.

35. G. K. Beale, *The Temple and the Church's Mission: A Biblical Theology of the Dwelling Place of God* (Downers Grove, IL: InterVarsity Press, 2004), 345.

36. Included in that promise is "to restore the land, to make them inherit the desolate heritages" (Isa. 49:8).

# 8

# The Myth that the Gospel Has Yet to be Preached in the "Whole World"

> Was not the gospel brought unto and published amongst the ten tribes as well as amongst the Jews when the apostle wrote this Epistle? The determination of this matter seems to conduce something towards the explaining of this chapter [Rom. 11], seeing throughout the whole chapter there is no mention of the Jews singly, but of Israel.
>
> The gospel was to be preached to the whole world before the destruction of Jerusalem [which took place in A.D. 70], Matt. xxiv. 14: and was it not to the ten tribes as well as the nations? It makes for the affirmative, that St. James directs his Epistle…, *to those ten tribes*, as well as the other two."[1]

In an article published in the November 2002 issue of *Midnight Call* magazine, Thomas Ice argues for the dispensational (futurist) position that Matthew 24:14 was not fulfilled prior to the destruction of Jerusalem in A.D. 70. While Tommy's argument is ineffective at a number of levels, he should be commended for finally doing what preterists have been asking dispensationalists to do for quite some time—deal with preterist arguments by actually interacting with preterist published works and by comparing Scripture with Scripture. I would be willing to wager that Ice's analysis of Matthew 24:14 is the first time any dispensationalist has attempted to reconcile this passage with global-language passages which indicate that the gospel had been preached to the "whole world" before Jerusalem was destroyed in A.D. 70 (Col. 1:6, 23; Rom. 1:8; 16:25–26). The language of the Bible is our interpretive key. It does not matter how we use

---

1. John Lightfoot, *A Commentary on the New Testament from the Talmud and Hebraica: Matthew—1 Corinthians*, 4 vols. (Peabody, MA: Hendrickson Publishers, [1859] 1989), 4:160.

the word "world" today; it matters only how the Bible used the words *kosmos* and *oikoumenē*, both often translated as "world."

## The Preterist Claim

Jesus concludes the first section of Matthew 24, which deals with specific signs that will take place in the lifetime of his disciples (famines, earthquakes, tribulation, war), by stating that "this gospel of the kingdom shall be preached in the **whole world** for a witness to **all the nations**, and then the end shall come" (24:14). Futurists, especially dispensationalists, maintain that the specifics of 24:14 are yet to be fulfilled because "whole world" means the entire globe as we know it today, and "all the nations" means all the nations that are in existence today. Since the gospel did not reach the entire globe prior to that first-century generation passing away, says the futurist, the passage awaits an end-time fulfillment.

Preterists, who believe the fulfillment of specific Bible prophecies took place in the *past*, offer the following reasons why they believe the events of Matthew 24:14 were fulfilled prior to the destruction of Jerusalem in A.D. 70:

1. The events of Matthew 24 are said to take place before "this generation" passes away (v. 34). Jesus always uses "this generation" in reference to His contemporaries (Matt. 11:16; 12:41, 42; 23:36; Mark 8:12; 13:30; Luke 7:31; 11:29, 30, 31, 32, 50, 51; 17:25; 21:32). The same is true for its use in Hebrews 3:10. "This generation" is never used to describe a future generation.

2. The English word "world" in Matthew 24:14 is based on the Greek word *oikoumenē* which is best translated as "inhabited earth" or "political boundary." A number of modern translations (*e.g.*, NASV and NIV) translate *oikoumenē* in Luke 2:1 as "inhabited earth," but they don't use the same translation in Matthew 24:14. The English Standard Version (ESV) follows the King James Version and translates *oikoumenē* as "world" in both cases. It's hardly possible that Rome taxed the whole wide world or that anyone had knowledge of a famine that encompassed the entire globe (Acts 11:28).

3. The use of "all the nations" is not always a reference to every nation on earth. In many cases it refers only to those known nations at that particular time in history (Matt. 24:9; Acts 2:5).

4. "The end" that Jesus refers to in Matthew 24:14 is the same end described in 24:3 and 6—the "end of the age": the end of the old covenant and the inauguration of the new (1 Cor. 10:11; Heb. 1:1–2). That first-century generation was living at the time of "the consummation of the ages" that "has been manifested" (Heb. 9:26). Peter and James confirm this when they wrote that "the end of all things is *at hand*" (1 Peter 4:7) and that "the coming of the Lord is *at hand*" (James 5:8). The use of "end" is not a reference to the end of everything but of the end of a specific period of time in redemptive history.

While Ice's article is selective in comparing verses, I have attempted to cover every element of the argument. This includes a study of older and modern commentaries on Matthew 24:14, an evaluation of the original setting and audience understanding of geography, the meaning of "all nations," how every occurrence of the Greek word *oikoumenē* is used in the New Testament, and the way global language is sometimes used as hyperbole.

## What do the Lexicons, Dictionaries, Scofield, and Darby Say?

Greek lexicons and dictionaries are nearly unanimous on the meaning of *oikoumenē*. Liddell and Scott's *Greek-English Lexicon* offers the following definition: "οἰκουμένη, (sc. γῆ ['earth' or 'land']), ἡ, inhabited region, … then the Greek world, opp. barbarian lands, … the inhabited world (including non-Greek lands, as Ethiopia, India, Scythia), as opp. possibly uninhabited regions, … our world (= Asia, Libya, Europe)."[2] *The New International Dictionary of New Testament Theology* begins by offering a definition based on the classical definition of *oikoumenē*: "It means the inhabited (earth) … in contrast to those lands inhabited by 'barbarians.' … in the Roman period … for the *imperium Romanum*—the lands under Roman rule. In other words, what had originally been a geographical and cultural concept had become a political concept in the Roman period." In the Septuagint, the Greek translation of the Hebrew Old Testament, *oikoumenē* "means the inhabited world. This is clear in Exod. 16:35 where Israel comes again into an inhabited land, *i.e.* a settled land in contrast to the wilderness where the nomads roam." The New Testament usage has little variation in meaning from

---

2. Henry George Liddell, Robert Scott, Henry Stuart Jones, and Roderick McKenzie, *Greek-English Lexicon,* 9th ed. (Oxford University Press, 1996), 1205.

its use in classical Greek and the Septuagint meaning "the inhabited world." It includes a "political and imperial usage."[3]

*The Encyclopedia of Christianity* concurs that "The term '*oikoumenē*' … means 'the inhabited earth.'"[4] Similarly, the *Greek-English Lexicon of the New Testament* begins with "*the inhabited earth, the world.*" The "world" is defined "in the sense of its inhabitants." Luke 2:1 is the primary example of this usage, which is an obvious reference to the political boundaries of the Roman Empire, "which, in the exaggerated language commonly used in ref. to the emperors, was equal to the whole world."[5] The world that was known and controlled politically at that time was the *oikoumenē*. As we will see, even the word "world" (*kosmos*) is often used in a local sense, not much different from the way we use the word today.

The entry in Wikipedia includes the following: "**Ecumene** (also spelled **œcumene** or **oikoumene**) [is] a term originally used in the Greco-Roman world to refer to the inhabited earth (or at least the known part of it). The term derives from the Greek οἰκουμένη, … short for οἰκουμένη γῆ 'inhabited world.'" Even C. I. Scofield, in his notes on Matthew 24:14, points out to his readers that "*oikoumene* = inhabited earth." He makes a similar admission in his comments on Luke 2:1: "This passage is noteworthy as defining the usual N.T. use of *oikoumene* as the sphere of Roman rule at its greatest extent, that is, of the great Gentile world-monarchies Daniel 2:7." John N. Darby made a similar notation in his translation of Matthew 24:14: "And these glad tidings of the kingdom shall be preached in the whole habitable earth, for a witness to all the nations, and then shall come the end." He did the same thing for Luke 2:1: "But it came to pass in those days that a decree went out from Caesar Augustus, that a census should be made of all the habitable world."

## What Do the Commentators Say?

A number of the early church fathers understood the meaning of Jesus' promise that the gospel would indeed be preached to the *oikoumenē* before the end of that generation. For example, in the fourth century, the church historian

---

3. Otto Flender, "Οἰκουμένη," *The New International Dictionary of New Testament Theology*, ed. Colin Brown, 3 vols. (Grand Rapids, MI: Zondervan, 1975), 1:518–519.

4. Erwin Fahlbusch and Geoffrey William Bromiley, *The Encyclopedia of Christianity* (Grand Rapids, Mich.: Eerdmans, 1999–2003), 3:821.

5. Walter Bauer, William F. Arndt, F. Wilbur Gingrich, *A Greek-English Lexicon of the New Testament and Other Early Christian Literature*, 2nd ed. (Chicago and London: The University of Chicago Press, [1958] 1979), 561.

Eusebius (*c.* 263–339) of Caesarea wrote, "Thus, under the influence of heavenly power, and with the divine co-operation, the doctrine of the Saviour, like the rays of the sun, quickly illumined the whole world; and straightway, in accordance with the divine Scriptures, the voice of the inspired evangelists and apostles went forth through all the earth, and their words to the end of the world."[6] In similar fashion, John Chrysostom (*c.* 347–407) made the following comments on Matthew 24:14 and related passages:

> "Therefore He added moreover, 'And this gospel shall be preached in the whole world for a witness to all nations, and then shall the end come,' of the downfall of Jerusalem. For in proof that He meant this, and that before the taking of Jerusalem the gospel was preached, hear what Paul saith, 'Their sound went into all the earth' [Rom. 10:18]; and again, 'The gospel which was preached to every creature which is under Heaven' [Col. 1:23]. Which also is a very great sign of Christ's power, that in twenty or at most thirty years the word had reached the ends of the world. 'After this therefore,' saith He, 'shall come the end of Jerusalem.'"[7]

Most modern commentaries fail to inform readers that in Matthew 24:14 the Greek word *oikoumenē*, often translated as "world," is not a reference to the entire globe as we know it today but the then known world. After making a study of more than a dozen representative commentaries, I found that there is rarely any comparative study of Matthew 24:14 and its use of *oikoumenē* with Acts 2:5 ("every nation under heaven"), Romans 1:8 ("throughout the whole world"), Romans 10:18 ("to the ends of the world"), Colossians 1:6 ("in all the world"), and Colossians 1:23 ("in all creation under heaven").

Few modern commentaries deal with Matthew 24:14 in a sound exegetical way. Fewer still even acknowledge that for centuries the prevalent view was to apply Matthew 24 to events leading up to and including the destruction of Jerusalem in A.D. 70.[8] Contrary to how modern commentaries handle Matthew

---

6. Eusebius, *The Church History of Eusebius* (Book II, Chap. 3, 107). In a note on this passage from Eusebius, there is this: "Compare Col. 1.6. That Christianity had already spread over the whole world at this time is, of course, an exaggeration; but the statement is not a mere rhetorical flourish; it was believed as a historical fact."

7. John Chrysostom, *Homilies on Matthew and Mark*, "Homily LXXV."

8. For example, Arno C. Gaebelein's rambling and rabidly dispensational commentary, first published in 1910, dismisses without argument any contrary view; Ed Glasscock's commentary in the Moody Gospel Commentary series (1997) assumes a futurist view of Matthew 24:14 with

24:14 and its significance in determining the timing of prophetic events, older commentaries offer detailed discussions of the passage and show how it found proximate fulfillment in the first century prior to Jerusalem's destruction in A.D. 70. What follows is merely a sample of how standard older commentaries, many still in print and used widely, interpreted Matthew 24:14.

### John S. C. Abbott and Jacob Abbott's
*Illustrated New Testament* (1878)

> *In all the world.* Before the destruction of Jerusalem, the gospel had been preached through all the regions of the then known world.

### B. W. Johnson's
*The People's New Testament Commentary* (1891)

> **This gospel of the kingdom, etc.** The gospel was preached throughout the Roman empire, 'the world' of the New Testament, before A. D. 70. **Then the end shall come.** Of the Jewish state.

### Thomas Scott's
*Commentary on the Bible* (1833)

> Not withstanding all these commotions and scandals, the gospel would soon be preached through the various nations of the Roman

---

no consideration of how the New Testament uses *oikoumenē* in other contexts; Leon Morris's *The Gospel According to Matthew* (Eerdmans, 1992) does not discuss *oikoumenē*; Craig S. Keener's massive *Commentary on the Gospel of Matthew* (Eerdmans, 1999) and his abridged commentary for InterVarsity Press (1997) assume a futurist view with no discussion of *oikoumenē* except in a footnote; in more than two pages of commentary on Matthew 24, William Hendriksen makes no mention that *oikoumenē* is used, the only time in Matthew's gospel, instead of *kosmos* (Baker 1973); dispensationalist Stanley D. Toussaint avoids any discussion of *oikoumenē* in his *Behold the King: A Study of Matthew* (Multnomah, 1980) and in his unpublished paper "A Critique of the Preterist View of the Olivet Discourse" (no date); John F. Walvoord's *Matthew: Thy Kingdom Come* (Moody, 1974), says nothing about *oikoumenē* and its possible relation to an A.D. 70 fulfillment, and there is no discussion of verse 14 in his *The Prophecy Knowledge Handbook* which claims to include "all the prophecies of Scriptures" (Victor, 1990); while Lutheran scholar R. C. H. Lenski does mention that *oikoumenē* is used, there is no discussion of its possible significance (Augsburg, 1943); the dispensational *Liberty Bible Commentary* (1982) defaults to an end-time, pre-tribulational reading of the text; the same is true for Louis Barbieri's exposition of Matthew in the *Bible Knowledge Commentary* (Victor, 1983); J. Barton Payne's only comment on Matthew 24:14 in his 754-page *Encyclopedia of Biblical Prophecy* is that it refers to "universal gospel preaching" (Harper & Row, 1973).

empire, and in the different parts of the then known world; for a witness to them, that the Messiah was come, to be 'a Light to lighten the Gentiles,' and 'to be for salvation to the ends of the earth:' and when this should be accomplished, the end of the Jewish church and state would come.

## Philip Doddridge's
## *Family Exposition of the New Testament* (1740)

*This gospel—shall be preached in all the world....* It appears from the most credible records, that the gospel was preached in Idumea, Syria, and Mesopotamia, by Jude; in Egypt, Marmorica, Mauritania, and other parts of Africa, by Mark, Simon, and Jude; in Ethiopia, by Candace's Eunuch, and Matthias; in Pontus, Galatia, and the neighbouring parts of Asia, by Peter; in the territories of the Seven Asiatic Churches by John; in Parthia, by Matthew; in Scythia, by Philip and Andrew; in the northern and western parts of Asia, by Bartholomew; in Persia, by Simon and Jude; in Media, Carmania, and several eastern parts, by Thomas; through the vast tract of Jerusalem round about unto Illyricum, by Paul; as also in Italy, and probably in Spain, Gaul, and Britain; in most of which places Christian churches were planted in less than thirty years after the death of Christ, which was before the destruction of Jerusalem.

## John Gill's
## *Exposition of the Entire Bible* (1809)

*And this Gospel of the kingdom:* Which Christ himself preached, and which he called and sent his apostles to preach, in all the cities of Judah; by which means men were brought into the kingdom of the Messiah, or Gospel dispensation; and which treated both of the kingdom of grace and glory, and pointed out the saints' meekness for the kingdom of heaven, and their right unto it, and gives the best account of the glories of it: *shall be preached in all the world*: not only in Judea, where it was now confined, and that by the express orders of Christ himself; but in all the nations of the world, for which the apostles had their commission enlarged, after our Lord's resurrection; when they were bid to go into all the world, and preach the Gospel to every creature; and when the Jews put away the Gospel from them, they accordingly turned to the Gentiles; and before the destruction of Jerusalem, it was preached to all the nations under the heavens; and churches were planted in most places, through the ministry of it: *for a witness unto all nations*: meaning either for a witness against all such in them, as should reject it; or as a testimony of Christ and salvation, unto all such as should believe in him: *and then shall the end come*: not the end of the world, as the Ethiopic version reads it, and others understand it; but the end of the Jewish state, the end of the city and temple: so that the universal preaching of the Gospel all over the world, was the last criterion and sign, of the destruction of Jerusalem; and the account of that itself next follows, with the dismal circumstances which attended it.

## Adam Clarke's *Commentary* (1810)

*And this Gospel of the kingdom shall be preached in all the world...* But, notwithstanding these persecutions, there should be a universal publication of the *glad tidings of the kingdom, for a testimony to all nations*. God would have the iniquity of the Jews published every where, before the heavy stroke of his judgments should fall upon them; that all mankind, as it were, might be brought as witnesses against their cruelty and obstinacy in crucifying and rejecting the Lord Jesus. *In all the world*, ['in all the *oikoumenē*']... Perhaps no more is meant here than the *Roman empire*; for it is beyond controversy that [the Greek 'all the *oikoumenē*,'] Luke ii. 1, means no more than the whole empire: as a decree for taxation or enrollment from Augustus Caesar could have no influence but in the Roman dominions; but see on Luke ii. 1. *Tacitus* informs us, Annal. l. xv., that, as early as the reign of Nero, the Christians were grown so numerous at Rome as to excite the jealousy of the government; and in other parts they were in proportion. However, we are under no necessity to restrain the phrase to the Roman empire, as, previously to the destruction of Jerusalem, the Gospel was not only preached in the lesser Asia, and Greece, and Italy, the greatest theatres of action then in the world; but was likewise propagated as far *north* as SCYTHIA; as far *south* as ETHIOPIA; as far *east* as PARTHIA and INDIA; and as far *west* as SPAIN and BRITAIN. On this point, Bishop Newton goes on to say, That there is some probability that the Gospel was preached in the British nations by St. Simon the apostle; that there is much greater probability that it was preached here by St. Paul; and that there is an absolute certainty that it was planted here in the times of the apostles, before the destruction of Jerusalem. See his proofs. Dissert. vol. ii. p. 235, 236. edit. 1758.[9] St. Paul himself speaks, Colossians i. 6, 23, of the Gospel's being come into ALL THE WORLD, *and preached* TO EVERY CREATURE *under heaven*. And in his Epistle to the Romans, Rom. x. 18, he very elegantly applies to the lights of the Church, what the psalmist said of the lights of heaven *Their sound went into* ALL THE EARTH, *and their words unto the* END *of the* WORLD. What but the wisdom of God could foretell this? and what but the power of God could accomplish it? ...*Then shall the end come*. When this general publication of the Gospel shall have taken place, then a period shall be put to the whole Jewish economy, by the utter destruction of their city and temple.

## John Lightfoot's
## *Hebrew and Talmudical Exercitations* (1658–1674)

[*And this gospel of the kingdom shall be preached in all the world.*] Jerusalem was not to be destroyed before the gospel was spread over all the world: God so ordering and designing it that the world, being first a catechumen in the doctrine of Christ, might have at length an eminent and undeniable testimony of Christ presented to it; when all men, as many as ever heard the history of Christ, should understand that dreadful wrath and severe vengeance which was poured out upon that city and nation by which he was crucified.

## Matthew Henry'
## *Commentary on the Whole Bible* (1706–1721)

It is intimated that the gospel should be, if not heard, yet at least heard of, throughout the then known world, before the destruc-

---

9. Thomas Newton, *Dissertations on the Prophecies* (London: J. F. Dove [1758], 1838), 341.

tion of Jerusalem; that the Old-Testament church should not be quite dissolved till the New Testament was pretty well settled, had got considerable footing, and began to make some figure. Better is the face of a corrupt degenerate church than none at all. Within forty years after Christ's death, the *sound of the gospel was gone forth to the ends of the earth,* Romans 10:18. St. Paul *fully preached the gospel from Jerusalem, and round about unto Illyricum;* and the other apostles were not idle. The persecuting of the saints at Jerusalem helped to disperse them, so that they *went every where, preaching the word,* Acts 8:1–4. And when the tidings of the Redeemer are sent over all parts of the world, then shall come the end of the Jewish state. Thus, that which they thought to prevent, by putting Christ to death, they thereby procured; all men *believed on him, and the Romans came, and took away their place and nation,* John 11:48. Paul speaks of the gospel being *come to all the world, and preached to every creature,* Colossians 1:6, 23.

## John Wesley's *Explanatory Notes of the New Testament* (1754)

*This Gospel shall be preached in all the world*—Not universally: this is not done yet: but in general through the several parts of the world, and not only in Judea. And this was done by St. Paul and the other apostles, before Jerusalem was destroyed. *And then shall the end come*—Of the city and temple. Josephus's *History of the Jewish War* is the best commentary on this chapter. It is a wonderful instance of God's providence, that he, an eyewitness, and one who lived and died a Jew, should, especially in so extraordinary a manner, be preserved, to transmit to us a collection of important facts, which so exactly illustrate this glorious prophecy, in almost every circumstance. Mark 13:10.

## Milton Terry's *Biblical Apocalyptics* (1898)

It seems like the persistent blindness of a dogmatic bias to insist that 'preaching of the gospel in all the world for a testimony to the nations' must needs included all the missionary operations of the Church during the Christian centuries.... This 'world' did not signify to Galilean fishermen or to learned Jewish rabbis what it does to a modern reader, familiar every day with telegraphic communications from remote continents and islands. Nor does Paul's comprehensive phrase, 'all creation under heaven,' require us to interpret it with any more rigid literalism than we do in the statement at the close of John's gospel, that 'the world itself would not contain the books that should be written.' Such expressions are usually understood to contain an element of hyperbole and are common in all the languages of men.[10]

The above examples do not come from obscure commentators, nor do they speak for a single evangelical tradition. Gill was a Baptist, Clarke and Wesley were in the Methodist tradition, Lightfoot and Henry were Presbyterian, Scott an Anglican, and Doddridge an evangelical mixture. By the end of the nineteenth century, the preterist view of Matthew 24 was a common feature of most commentaries that followed a lengthy interpretive tradition that is too comprehensive to rehearse here. The reason for the near agreement was because they followed a grammatical-historical methodology, the same methodology outlined by the standard hermeneutical manual of the twentieth century, Milton Terry's *Biblical Hermeneutics*.

Terry's text is important since non-dispensationalists and dispensationalists consider it to be the standard work on the subject of hermeneutics. Dispensationalist Robert L. Thomas, an ardent critic of preterism, contrasts "new hermeneutical principles with traditional grammatical-historical hermeneutics"[11] with Terry as the standard by which all other hermeneutical systems should be measured. Thomas quotes the following from Terry's classic work:

> In the systematic presentation, therefore, of any scriptural doctrine, we are always to make a discriminating use of sound hermeneutical principles. We must not study them in the light of modern systems of divinity, but should aim rather to place ourselves in the position of the sacred writers, and study to obtain the

---

10. Milton S. Terry, *Biblical Apocalyptics: A Study of the Most Notable Revelations of God and of Christ* (Grand Rapids, MI: Baker Book House, [1898] 1988), 233.

11. Robert L. Thomas, "The Hermeneutics of Progressive Dispensationalism," *The Master's Perspective on Contemporary Issues*, Robert L. Thomas, gen. ed (Grand Rapids, MI: Kregel, 1998), 190.

impression their words naturally have made upon the minds of the first readers.[12]

To be sure, dispensationalism is one of the many "modern systems of divinity" in vogue today. And as we will see in our study of Matthew 24:14, dispensationalist commentators do not place themselves in the position of the sacred writers. Instead, they do what Terry decries; they allow themselves "to be influenced by hidden meanings, and spiritualizing processes, and plausible conjectures."[13]

If Thomas and other dispensationalists are such fans of Terry's hermeneutical model, and they should be, why do they ignore Terry's extended non-dispensational comments on eschatology? In terms of Ice's study of Matthew 24:14 and his claim that preterists have distorted its meaning, how do he and Thomas deal with Terry's nearly four-page exposition of this verse, the conclusion of which is quoted above? Matthew 24:14 is not the only place where we find this kind of hyperbole in the Bible. We learn from Luke that "men from **every** nation" heard Peter preach the gospel (Acts 2:5, 9–11, 14). The progression of the Gospel's spread began in Jerusalem and made its way "throughout **all** Judaea" (Acts 10:37). Paul says he had "**fully preached** the gospel" from "Jerusalem and round about as far as Illyricum" (Rom. 15:19). He even says that his preaching has brought "salvation to **all men**" (Titus 2:11).

## The Original Setting

An indispensable rule in Bible interpretation is understanding a text in terms of its original setting and audience, always asking the question, "How would those who first picked up copies of the gospels and epistles have understood what they were reading?" Louis Berkhof, following Milton Terry's injunction that we should "place ourselves in the position of the sacred writers," stresses that the interpreter

> must place himself on the standpoint of the author, and seek to enter into his very soul, until he, as it were, lives his life and thinks his thoughts. This means that he will have to guard carefully against the common mistake of transferring the author to the present day and making him speak the language of the twentieth century. If he does not avoid this, the danger exists, as McPheeters

---

12. Milton S. Terry, *Biblical Hermeneutics*, 2nd. ed. (Grand Rapids, MI: Zondervan, n.d.), 595. Quoted in Thomas, "The Hermeneutics of Progressive Dispensationalism," 190.

13. Terry, *Biblical Hermeneutics*, 152.

expresses it, that "the voice he hears (will) be merely the echo of his own ideas."[14]

Reading modern-day concepts, whether scientific, geographical, or academic,[15] back into the Bible can cause insurmountable interpretive problems. For example, how many times have you heard a minister claim that the gospel is like "dynamite"? The comparison is made because the Greek word *dunamis*, translated "power" (Rom. 1:16), is the same word Alfred Nobel chose in 1866 to name his explosive concoction. Since "power" and "dynamite" share the same Greek word (*dunamis*), the New Testament use of "power" must share the characteristics of dynamite. D. A. Carson describes this as "an appeal to a kind of reverse etymology,"[16] reading modern definitions of words back into ancient writings. The effects of dynamite were unknown by the New Testament writers. Paul was not thinking of exploding sticks of dynamite when he used *dunamis* to describe the power of the gospel any more than he was thinking about the power expended when the Space Shuttle takes off from Cape Canaveral. Our understanding of the biblical use of *dunamis* has to be understood in terms of how it was understood in Paul's day. "[Gordon] Fee and [Douglas] Stuart rightly emphasize that 'the true meaning of the biblical text for us is what God originally intended it to mean when it was first spoken.'[17] We must first determine what a text meant 'in their town' before we can determine what it means and how we should apply that meaning to our own time and culture."[18]

In a similar way, we should not read twenty-first century geographical knowledge into the Bible. For example, were the cartographers of Jesus' day wrong when they called the Sea of Galilee a sea rather than a lake (Matt. 4:18)? Our definition of "sea" should not be the interpretive standard for the New Testament. Many commentators misinterpret what Jesus meant when He stated that He would be "three days and three nights in the heart of the earth" (12:40) because they

---

14. Louis Berkhof, *Principles of Biblical Interpretation* (Grand Rapids, MI: Baker Book House, [1950] 1974), 115.

15. By academic I mean "scientific precision." While estimates and over-generalizations might not be suited for today's academic research papers, they are perfectly appropriate for conveying God's redemptive covenant.

16. See D.A. Carson, *Exegetical Fallacies*, 2nd ed. (Grand Rapids, MI: Baker Book House, 1996), 34.

17. Gordon D. Fee and Douglas Stuart, *How to Read the Bible for All Its Worth: A Guide to Understanding the Bible*, 2nd ed. (Grand Rapids, MI: Zondervan, 1993), 26.

18. J. Scott Duvall and J. Daniel Hays, *Grasping God's Word: A Hands-On Approach to Reading, Interpreting, and Applying the Bible* (Grand Rapids, MI: Zondervan, 2001), 97.

do not understand the statement in terms of Jerusalem-centered geography or in terms of Herbaic idiom.[19] Equally so, we should not read into the Bible our conception of what we now know about our world.

## All the Nations and all the Earth

Jesus tells His disciples that the gospel must be preached in the "whole world for a witness *to all the nations*" (Matt. 24:14). Ice does not deal with how "all the nations" is often used in a restrictive sense. He asserts, because of his futurist presuppositions, that "all nations," by definition, must refer to a global fulfillment. The interpreter would be making a serious mistake if every time he read "all nations" he concluded that the biblical writer had every nation around the globe in mind. The following examples will show that "all nations" and "all kingdoms" often have a limited geographical application:

- Cyrus, the king of Persia, said, "The Lord, the God of heaven, has given me *all the kingdoms of the earth*" (Ezra 1:2; 2 Chron. 36:23).

- David writes, "*All nations surrounded me*" (Ps. 118:10).

- God "brought the fear of [David] *on all the nations*" (1 Chron. 14:17).

- It is written of Hezekiah king of Judah "that he was exalted *in the sight of all nations* …" (2 Chron. 32:23).

- The Chaldeans are said to "march throughout the earth" (Hab. 1:6).

- "The people from *all the earth* came to Egypt to buy grain from Joseph" (Gen. 41:57).

- "*All the earth* was seeking the presence of Solomon" (1 Kings 10:24).

- "And *all the nations* shall serve him [Nebuchadnezzar], and his son, and his grandson, until the time of his own land comes" (Jer. 27:7).

- Nebuchadnezzar addresses his decree as "the king to all the peoples, nations, and men of every language that live in all the earth" (Dan. 4:1).[20]

---

19. "Heart of the earth" has reference to Jerusalem which was considered to be the center of the world. "Three days and three nights" most likely refers to Thursday night in the Garden of Gethsemane to His burial through Sunday morning. See Ralph Woodrow, *Three Days and Three Nights—Reconsidered in the Light of Scripture* (Riverside, CA: Ralph Woodrow Evangelistic Association, Inc., 1993).

20. "*All the earth*]—*i.e.*, the known, inhabited world, from Elam and Media in the east to Egypt and the Mediterranean seacoasts in the west. Cf. Jer. 25:26; 27:5–6). The Assyrian and

- At Pentecost "there were Jews living in Jerusalem, devout men, from *every nation under heaven*" (Acts 2:5).
- Jesus told His *disciples* that they would be "hated by *all nations*" (Matt. 24:9).[21]

Using "all" and "every" in a narrow sense when referring to nations and kingdoms is neither unusual nor non-literal. We must be equally careful when we see "all the earth." The Hebrew *eretz* and the Greek *gē* can be translated "earth" or "land" depending on the context (Gen. 47:13; 1 Sam. 17:46; Luke 23:44).

Consider how "all" is used in Luke 17:26–29. Jesus first compares the days of Noah with the days of the Son of Man. In Noah's day

> they were eating, they were drinking, they were marrying, they were being given in marriage, until the day that Noah entered the ark, and the flood came and *destroyed them all* (Luke 17:27).

For those who believe in a global flood, "destroyed them all" refers to everybody on the face of the earth. Only the eight in the ark were saved. Local flood advocates would understand "all" to be limited to the geographical extent of the flood. But if "all" means everyone without exception, then when the days of the Son of Man are always compared to "the days of Lot," there is a problem:

> they were eating, they were drinking, they were buying, they were selling, they were planting, they were building; but on the day that Lot went out from Sodom it rained fire and brimstone from heaven and *destroyed them all* (17:29).

It's obvious from this passage that "all" only refers to those in Sodom and cannot in any way be understood globally. If the New Testament writers saw and described their world as only encompassing what they knew of the Roman Empire and those nations bordering the empire, then we as modern-day interpreters should not impose our expanded understanding of our world on their writings.

---

Babylonian kings regarded themselves as kings of all the earth, and in their inscriptions were accustomed thus to speak of themselves. This practice was also in vogue among Persian rulers." (Edward J. Young, *The Prophecy of Daniel: A Commentary* [Grand Rapids, MI: Eerdmans, 1949], 97).

21. It's obvious that "all nations" refers to all the nations in which they had access. Rome was an empire of conquered nations similar to the way the land of Canaan was home to "seven nations" (Acts 13:19; Deut. 7:1).

## The Immediate Context of *Oikoumenē*

Ice begins his study of Matthew 24:14 by stating correctly, "While it is true that 'world,' or *oikoumenē*, is used in the New Testament to refer to 'the Roman Empire of the first century,' its basic meaning is that of 'inhabited earth.'" But that's just the point. Those living in the first-century saw only their world as the inhabited earth. Also, Ice does not deal with the way that global language ("all" and "every") is used to specify a more restricted contemporary geographical area (see above). The following points by Ice do not resolve the problem that confronts dispensationalists on the extent of gospel proclamation described by Jesus in Matthew 24:14:

> Clearly *oikoumenē* can be used globally, even though it may have a more restricted use. The deciding factor is the context. Thus, if Matthew 24:14 was fulfilled in A.D. 70, then it would have a localized meaning as noted by [Gary] DeMar. However, if it will be fulfilled in the future, then it has the meaning of the entire inhabited world at some future date, which would clearly include much more than the old Roman Empire.

Ice states the obvious: Jesus is either describing events in the *near* future, or He is describing events in the *distant* future. So then, by Ice's own admission *oikoumenē* can and usually does refer to a localized meaning. For Ice, the question remains as to how Jesus is using the word in Matthew 24:14. Since Jesus tells His disciples later in the chapter that "this generation will not pass away until *all these things take place*" (24:34), and every time "this generation" is used by Jesus it means the generation to whom He is speaking, then *oikoumenē* most probably refers to the first-century Roman Empire since it falls within the time frame of "this generation."[22]

It's significant that Matthew uses *oikoumenē* only in 24:14, while he uses *kosmos*, a word that can have a more global meaning, eight times.[23] In fact, we read later in Matthew's gospel: "Truly I say to you, wherever this gospel is preached in the whole world [*kosmos*], what this woman has done shall also be spoken of in memory of her" (26:13). The Greek construction in 24:14 is identical except that in 26:13

---

22. For a study of "this generation," see Gary DeMar, *Last Days Madness: Obsession of the Modern Church*, 4th ed. (Powder Springs, GA: American Vision, 1999), 55–60.

23. In Matthew 13:32, the Greek word translated "world" in the NASB is *aion*, best translated as "age." In Matthew 13:35, *kosmos* is understood. It is not found in the Greek text.

*kosmos* is used for "world" instead of *oikoumenē*. Matthew chooses *oikoumenē* over *kosmos* in 24:14 because he wants to emphasize its local geographical fulfillment within the time frame of "this generation" in contrast to a universal fulfillment not bound by geography or time as is the obvious case in 26:13.

Notice also that Jesus tells His disciples that the things outlined in Matthew 24 will happen to them. Jesus makes this point by His continual use of the second person plural "you":

- "And **you** will be hearing of wars and rumors of wars" (24:6).
- "Then they will deliver **you** up to tribulation" (24:9).
- [And they] will kill **you**" (24:9).
- "And **you** will be hated by all nations on account of My name" (24:9).
- "Therefore when **you** see the abomination of desolation ... standing in the holy place" (24:15).

Sandwiched between 24:6, 9 and 24:15 is "And this gospel of the kingdom shall be preached in the whole world [*oikoumenē*] for a witness to all the nations, and then the end shall come" (24:14). If, as Ice correctly notes, "the deciding factor is the context," then as the above passages demonstrate, the context is decidedly pre-A.D. 70, the generation to whom Jesus was speaking.

By placing ourselves in historical context of the first-century writers, we can conclude that it was perfectly natural to use "all nations" and "inhabited earth" as references to the geography of their day. Since the time when the events of Matthew 24 are to take place are contemporary with Jesus' audience, we can come to no other conclusion than that the gospel was preached to the nations round about the Roman Empire prior to that generation passing away. To read Matthew 24:14 any other way is to strip the text from its context. R. T. France offers a helpful summary on the proper contextual meaning of the text:

> Those who interpret the "end" here [Matt. 24:14] as the *parousia* and the final judgment have sometimes taken this saying as a spur to evangelism in our day: in the early twentieth century there was an influential missionary slogan, "Evangelize to a finish to bring back the King!" The phrase "all the nations" has also been pressed into a program to bring the gospel to every known nation and tribe in the modern world (including those unknown to the Eurasian world of Jesus' day) so as to hasten the *parousia*. But that

is to take this text quite out of context. In particular, this passage does not speak of worldwide evangelization as the cause of the "end," but as a necessary preliminary. And we have argued at v. 6 [in Matthew 24] that the "end" (*telos*) in view here is not the "end (*synteleia*) of the age" but the destruction of the temple, which happened long ago.[24]

## *Oikoumenē* as "Inhabited World"

The case can be made that *oikoumenē* is used exclusively for the geographical area generally limited to the Roman Empire of the first-century and the territories immediately adjacent which were known and accessible to first-century travelers. When first-century Christians read the word *oikoumenē*, they thought of what they knew of their world. Francis Sampson offers a concise definition:

> The classic usage of [*oikoumenē*] gives the sense of "the inhabited earth," especially as settled by Greeks. By people of the Roman empire, it was currently used to express the empire (as in Luke 2:1,...), by a sort of arrogant exaggeration, as though the empire embraced the whole world.[25]

In time, the definition came to include the world in which people lived, the inhabited world. Its meaning did not encompass what we know of the world today. Henry Cowles, in his commentary on Matthew, explains how the *oikoumenē* definition developed in the context of the first century:

> "All the world" is literally all the inhabited—*i.e*, to the extent of what is peopled. But in usage, "all the world" to the Romans was the Roman Empire: to the Greeks it meant the countries at the utmost where their tongue was spoken: to the Jew it was primarily Palestine; but ultimately became coextensive with the range of their dispersions. That is to say, the usage of the word made its scope rather national than universal.

---

24. R.T. France, *The Gospel of Matthew* (Grand Rapids, MI: Eerdmans, 2007), 908–909.

25. Francis S. Sampson, *A Critical Commentary on the Epistle to the Hebrews* (New York: Robert Carter and Brothers, 1856), 85–86.

The New Testament usage may be seen in Luke 2:1— "All the world enrolled for taxation"—which could not extend beyond the limits of the Roman Empire. Also Acts 11:28—"Great dearth [famine] *throughout all the world*"—foretold by Agabus. This was probably less in extent than the whole Roman Empire.—This restricted usage appears also in profane classic writers.

\* \* \*

Thus we do no violence either to the sense of these words or to the historic facts, if we hold that this prophecy had its fair fulfillment before the fall of the doomed city.[26]

This is generally the way *oikoumenē* is used throughout the New Testament. The word rarely if ever has a universal application as we will see in the following examples.

## *Oikoumenē* in *Luke's Gospel* and *Acts*

Luke uses *oikoumenē* eight times, more than any other New Testament author, three times in his gospel and five times in Acts. All commentators agree that its use in Luke 2:1 refers to the boundaries of the Roman Empire in the first century. The use of *oikoumenē* in Luke 21:26 fits well with how preterists interpret the Olivet Discourse since it takes place before verse 32: "Truly I say to you, this generation will not pass away until all things take place."[27] The imminent conflagration predicted by Jesus is not world-wide but is confined to the surroundings of Judea (Matt. 24:16; Luke 21:21). This includes "the expectation of the things which are coming upon the world [*oikoumenē*]" (Luke 21:26).

*Oikoumenē* is used in Luke 4:5 where Jesus is shown "all the kingdoms of the world," while Matthew uses *kosmos* in the parallel passage in his gospel (Matt. 4:8). Why the difference? As we will see, *kosmos* is often used in a non-universal way similar to *oikoumenē*, as some dispensational commentators readily admit (*e.g.*, Rom. 1:8 and Col. 1:6). Luke may have chosen *oikoumenē* "to bring out the political sense in a way that Matthew's use of *kosmos* (Mt. 4:8) does not."[28] This

---

26. Henry Cowles, *Matthew and Mark: With Notes Critical, Explanatory, and Practical* (New York: D. Appleton & Co., 1881), 210, 211.

27. See Gary DeMar, *Last Days Madness: Obsession of the Modern Church*, 4th ed. (Powder Springs, GA: American Vision, 1999).

28. Leland Ryken, James C. Wilhoit, and Tremper Longman, gen. eds., "World," *Dictionary*

is the opinion of Otto Flender, whose article on *oikoumenē* appears in the *New International Dictionary of New Testament Theology*:

> The *oikoumenē* is the inhabited world in the sense that all its population has to suffer under Satanic powers for religious, but mainly political, reasons. Equally in the story of Christ's temptation, the replacement in Lk. 4:5 of 'kosmos' by *oikoumenē* suggests a strong political connotation, even though "the kingdoms of the world" prevents a direct identification with the Roman empire.[29]

In Acts, Luke describes a "great famine" that would be "all over the world [*oikoumenē*]" (Acts 11:28). The geographical area of the famine is no larger than that required of Luke 2:1 where we learn "that a decree went out from Caesar Augustus, that a census be taken of all the inhabited earth [*oikoumenē*]." Famines are generally confined to limited geographical areas and are often brought on by governmental policies. While there might be a famine in one part of the world, other parts have an abundance (*e.g.*, Gen. 41–43). Simon Kistemaker points out that the famine has a limited geographical scope in Luke's account:

> The famine that Agabus predicted occurred during the reign of Emperor Claudius, who ruled from A.D. 41 to 54. Luke calls it a severe famine, for in varying degrees it affected the entire Roman empire. Egypt sold grain for the benefit of the people in famine-stricken Jerusalem. Cyprus supplied figs, and the Christians in Antioch sent aid to the believers in Judea (v. 29). Different parts of the Roman empire suffered famines. Therefore, we interpret Luke's description, "a severe famine all over the Roman world," not in a literal but in a broad sense.[30]

Later in Acts we learn that Jews at Thessalonica were so upset at the effects of the preaching of the gospel that they dragged Jason and some of his friends before the city officials and made the following charge: "These men who have upset the world [*oikoumenē*] have come here also" (Acts 17:6). This use of *oikoumenē* is even

---

*of Biblical Imagery* (Downers Grove, IL: InterVarsity Press, 1998), 968.

29. Otto Flender, "*Oikoumenē*," in the *New International Dictionary of New Testament Theology*, ed. Colin Brown, 3 vols. (Grand Rapids, MI: Zondervan, 1979), 1:519.

30. Simon J. Kistemaker, *New Testament Commentary: Exposition of the Acts of the Apostles* (Grand Rapids, MI: Baker Book House, 1990), 425. For a summation of the famines during Claudius's reign, see F. F. Bruce, *The Book of Acts* (NICNT), rev. ed. (Grand Rapids, MI: Eerdmans, 1988), 230, note 39.

more limited in scope, for it's obvious that Paul and Silas had not even upset the entire Roman world by this time. Everett F. Harrison calls its use in this context "a hyperbole."[31]

In addition to political threats, the preaching of the gospel upset the worshipers of the Greek goddess Artemis who is said to have been worshiped by "all of Asia and the world [*oikoumenē*]" (Acts 19:27). This is hardly possible if *oikoumenē*'s meaning is global. But its use in this context makes perfect sense if the Roman Empire and its immediate environs are in view.

Near the end of Acts we read that Paul is described as "a real pest … who stirs up dissension among all the Jews throughout the world [*oikoumenē*]" (Acts 24:5). Jews were not in every part of the world in the first century.

This brings us to Luke's use of *oikoumenē* in Acts 17:31: "He has fixed a day in which He will judge the world [*oikoumenē*] in righteousness through a Man whom He has appointed, having furnished proof to all men by raising Him from the dead." Ice sees this use of *oikoumenē* as a reference to a distant future end-time global event. "Surely this speaks of the whole globe," Ice writes, "even though it may have a more restricted sense." Like Luke's use of *oikoumenē* in his gospel and elsewhere in Acts, I believe it has the same meaning: a reference to the world at that time. It was their world that God would judge. As F. F. Bruce notes, "Greek thought had no room for such an eschatological judgment as the biblical revelation announces."[32] By using *oikoumenē* instead of *kosmos*, Paul was warning the Athenians that even they would come under God's judgment. There would be no exceptions. The Greeks would have accepted Paul's denouncement of the *kosmos* (everyone but them) as appropriate. The same is true of the Romans: "The inhabited world, or the *oikoumenē*, is not all the earth, but the world that is organized and controlled by the Roman Empire. Everything else is the world of the barbarians."[33] J. A. Alexander's comments put the meaning of *oikoumenē* in its proper historical perspective:

> *Throughout all the world*, literally, *on* (or *over*) *the whole inhabited* (*earth*) [Acts 11:28]. This phrase, though strictly universal in its import, is often used in a restricted sense. The Greeks in their par-

---

31. Everett F. Harrison, *Acts: The Expanding Church* (Chicago, IL: Moody Press, 1975), 262.
32. Bruce, *The Book of Acts*, 340–341.
33. Pablo Richard, *Apocalypse: A People's Commentary on the Book of Revelation* (Maryknoll, NY: Orbis Books, 1995), 61.

ticular pride of race, applied it to their own country; the Romans, in like manner, to the empire.[34]

Paul removes all pretense of Athenian superiority by telling them that even their world will be judged.

## *Oikoumenē* in *Romans*

Like Matthew, Paul uses *oikoumenē* once in Romans 10:18 in dealing with how far the gospel message has been preached. Some might claim that "they have never heard." Paul disputes this assertion: "Their voice has gone out into all the earth, and their words to the ends of the world [*oikoumenē*]" (10:18). How could this be? Douglas Moo's explanation is helpful:

> How could Paul assert, in A.D. 57, that the gospel has been proclaimed "to the whole earth"? Two implicit qualifications of Paul's language are frequently noted. First, as the word *oikoumenē* in the second line of the quotation might suggest, Paul may be thinking in terms of the Roman Empire of his day rather than of the entire globe. Second, Paul's focus might be corporate rather than individualistic: he asserts not that the gospel has been preached to every person but to every nation, and especially to both Jews and Gentiles. Both these considerations may well be relevant. But perhaps it would be simpler to think that Paul engages in hyperbole, using the language of the Psalm to assert that very many people by the time Paul writes Romans have had the opportunity to hear.[35]

Once again there is no need to follow Ice's forced exegesis in the use of *oikoumenē* in the New Testament. It is obvious that the gospel had not gone global in Paul's day. David L. Turner claims that Matthew 24:14 might have a universal application in spite of Paul's use of *oikoumenē* in Romans 10:18 because this verse and others in the same genre (*e.g.*, Col. 1:6, 23) "should be read in view of Romans 15:19; 16:23ff. which indicate that Paul still wished to take the gospel

---

34. J. A. Alexander, *Acts of the Apostle* (Carlisle, PA: Banner of Truth Trust, [1857] 1980), 438.

35. Douglas Moo, *The Epistle to the Romans* (NICNT) (Grand Rapids, MI: Eerdmans, 1996), 667.

to previously unreached regions (Spain)."³⁶ This is hardly likely. Paul writes about his original intentions. The book of Romans was written nearly thirty years after Pentecost. At the birth of the New Testament church there were Jews "from every nation under heaven" (Acts 2:5). Surely someone had taken the gospel to Spain and beyond by A.D. 57 (8:4). And if not, there were still thirteen years before Jerusalem would be destroyed and "this generation" passed away (Matt. 24:14).

## *Oikoumenē* in *Hebrews*

The writer of Hebrews uses *oikoumenē* twice. In Hebrews 1:6 we read of a prophetic word regarding the incarnation: "And when He again brings the firstborn into the world [*oikoumenē*], He says, 'And let all the angels of God worship Him.'" Jesus most importantly enters the world to a particular people and only secondarily to the world in general (Heb. 10:5): "To the Jew first, and also to the Greek" (Rom. 1:16; 2:10). Jesus entered a certain place, the world of Israel (John 1:11), when time and conditions were perfect: "But when the fullness of the time came, God sent forth His Son, born of a woman, born under the law, in order that He might redeem those who were under the Law, that we might receive adoption as sons" (Gal. 4:4).³⁷ In time, however, we know that the gospel was to go to the nations.

Following the lead of seventeenth-century commentators John Owen (1616–1683) and William Gouge (1578–1653), the use of *oikoumenē* in Hebrews 2:5 is most probably a reference to the habitation of "the whole number of God's elect,"³⁸ "the days of the Messiah"³⁹ or, according to Francis Sampson, "the gospel

---

36. David L. Turner, "The Structure and Sequence of Matthew 24:1–41: Interaction with Evangelical Treatments," *Grace Theological Journal*, 10:1 (Winona Lake, IN: Grace Theological Seminary, Spring 1989), 7.

37. "The Son, as the firstborn, enters the inhabited world of men. The word *world* is Hellenic and was used in ordinary speech to refer to the populated world." (Simon J. Kistemaker, *New Testament Commentary: Exposition of Hebrews* [Grand Rapids, MI: Baker Book House, 1984], 38).

38. William Gouge, *Commentary on Hebrews* (Grand Rapids, MI: Kregel Publications, [1655] 1980), 113.

39. John Owen, *An Exposition of the Epistle to the Hebrews*, 7 vols. (Grand Rapids, MI: Baker Book House, [1855] 1980), 3:324. "But the world here intended is no other but the promised state of the church under the gospel. This, with the worship of God therein, with special relation unto the Messiah, the author and mediator of it, administrating its heavenly things before the throne of grace, thereby rendering it spiritual and heavenly, and diverse from the state of the worship of the old testament, which was worldly and carnal, was 'the world to come' that the Jews looked for, and which in this place is intended by the apostle" (324).

dispensation."⁴⁰ Philip Edgcumbe Hughes concurs: "The coming age, here called *the world to come*, is the age of the Messiah in which the messianic promises and prophecies of old find their fulfillment."⁴¹ John Brown notes that "There is a great possibility ... that there is an allusion to the land of Canaan as enjoyed by the Israelites, which is called [*oikoumenē*], Luke ii. 1; Acts xi. 28; and the peaceful enjoyment of which was a type of the New Testament state."⁴² It's obvious, therefore, that *oikoumenē* in this context is not being used for the worldwide physical world as we know it today.

## *Oikoumenē* in *Revelation*

How *oikoumenē* is interpreted in Revelation is often determined by whether a person holds to an early pre-A.D. 70 or a late mid-A.D. 90 date for the book's composition. This debate cannot be settled here. I've taken the position that Revelation was written some time in the mid 60s A.D., during the reign of Nero.⁴³ The use of *oikoumenē* by John helps to support this conclusion.

In Revelation 3:10, John states that an "hour of testing ... is about to come upon the whole world [*oikoumenē*]." John is writing to the first-century church of Philadelphia. Notice the time reference: "which is about to come." Robert Mounce states that the Greek word translated "about to" (*mellō*) "points to what is about to happen rather than what is destined to be."⁴⁴ "Earth" can also be translated as "land," that is, the land of Israel, or more broadly, the land in which people live. The author of the Revelation commentary in *An Illustration of the New Testament*, published in 1760, concludes that "by *all the World* here, as in other Places of the *New Testament*, is meant the *Roman* Empire, as *Ch.* ii.6."⁴⁵

Satan is said to be one "who deceives the whole world" (12:9). Once again, Revelation describes those things which must "shortly take place" (1:1) "for the

---

40. Sampson, *A Critical Commentary on the Epistle to the Hebrews*, 86.

41. Philip Edgcumbe Hughes, *A Commentary on the Epistle to the Hebrews* (Grand Rapids, MI: Eerdmans, 1977), 82.

42. John Brown, *Hebrews* (Carlisle, PA: Banner of Truth Trust, [1862] 1972), 89.

43. For a comprehensive study of the dating question, see Kenneth L. Gentry, Jr., *Before Jerusalem Fell: Dating the Book of Revelation*, 3rd ed. (Powder Springs, GA: American Vision, 1998) and *The Beast of Revelation* (Powder Springs, GA: American Vision, 2002).

44. Robert H. Mounce, *The Book of Revelation* (NICNT), rev. ed. (Grand Rapids, MI: Eerdmans, 1998), 103, note 23.

45. *An Illustration of the New Testament, by Notes and Explications, etc.* (London: R. Baldwin, 1760), 923.

time is near" (1:3). The world (*oikoumenē*) that is being deceived is the one to which the seven churches are written (2–3). Certainly the devil deceives more than this area, but the point of Revelation is to describe what's about to happen to within a shortened time frame.

We know from history that Jerusalem was surrounded and destroyed by the heathen armies of Rome in A.D. 70, therefore, the use of *oikoumenē* is appropriate in this context. The world of Old Covenant Judaism was about to come to an end when John received the Revelation. Philip Carrington's comments on Revelation 16:14 are helpful in this regard:

> The name Armageddon is significant because it is at Megiddo that the Jewish King Josiah was defeated and killed by an Egyptian army under the Pharaoh; and Titus had just returned from Egypt. Armageddon means Mountain of Megiddo; but Megiddo is a valley. It is the Mountain of Sion which has become Mountain of Megiddo or Mountain of defeat. The name, anyhow, shows that the field of battle is in Palestine....[46]

The way *oikoumenē* is used in Revelation goes with the larger debate over the dating of the book. Based on the time texts (1:1, 3; 22:10), the local geography of the seven churches (2–3), and the fact that the temple is still standing (11:1–2) when John wrote, demonstrates that only the *oikoumenē* is in view.

## "The Whole World"

In Romans 1:8 Paul writes that the faith of the Romans "is being proclaimed throughout the whole world," that is, the *kosmos*. While Ice does not deal with this verse, its use is important to help students of the Bible understand how global language is often used to describe non-global events. *Kosmos* is often used in the Bible to describe "their world" events. How does dispensational commentator John A. Witmer interpret "the whole world" of Romans 1:8?:

> For the Romans he [Paul] rejoiced that news of their **faith** had spread **all over the world**, a hyperbole meaning throughout the Roman Empire.[47]

---

46. Philip Carrington, *The Meaning of the Revelation* (London: SPCK, 1931), 265.

47. James A. Witmer, "Romans," in *The Bible Knowledge Commentary: New Testament (An Exposition of the Scriptures by Dallas Seminary Faculty)*, John F. Walvoord and Roy B. Zuck, eds. (Wheaton, IL: Victor Books, 1983), 440. Also see Douglas Moo, *The Epistle to the Romans*

Dispensationalist Woodrow Michael Kroll takes a similar approach when he states that Paul speaks of the Romans' faith in "world-wide terms," a common expression for "'everyone.'"[48] Its language is universal but its application is only to the world of Paul's day.

Ice claims that in Colossians 1:6 "Paul is saying that the Gospel has come, or been introduced to the Colossian believers, just as it has come, or been introduced in all the world." Exactly! Once we determine how the gospel came to the Colossians, we will know how it came, to use Paul's words, "in all the world." Ice continues: "So this is not a statement about whether the Gospel has been preached to a certain area per se; it is a statement about the arrival of the Gospel as a global message." Wrong. The gospel had come to the Colossians "*just as* in all the world." Paul says much more than Ice's minimalist approach tries to argue:

> [The gospel] which has come to you, just as in all the world [*kosmos*] also it is constantly bearing fruit and increasing, even as it has been doing in you also since the day you heard of it and understood the grace of God in truth (Col. 1:6).

Not only had the gospel come or been introduced to the Colossians where it was bearing fruit, but it was doing the same thing "in all the world." It's not just the arrival of the gospel that Paul describes, it's the effect that it was having "in all the world [*kosmos*]," that is, the world of Paul's day in the first century. In his article, Ice quotes R. C. H. Lenski in support of his position, but he does so selectively: "The Colossians are to remember that its range is world-wide, the very opposite of the little Judaistic sectlet that has somehow appeared in their midst."[49] But Lenski goes on to comment that "the gospel is bearing fruit and growing 'in all the world' even as the Colossians themselves have witnessed this since the day on which they got to hear it.... What they witnessed in Colosse is happening 'in all the world.' ... The whole world, nothing less, is the field for this activity of the gospel."[50]

---

(NICNT) (Grand Rapids, MI: Eerdmans, 1996), 57.

48. Woodrow Michael Kroll, "The Epistle to the Romans," *The Liberty Bible Commentary: New Testament* (Lynchburg, VA: Old-Time Gospel Hour, 1982), 340.

49. R. C. H. Lenski, *The Interpretation of St. Paul's Epistles to the Colossians, to the Thessalonians, to Timothy, to Titus and to Philemon* (Minneapolis, MN: Augsburg Publishing House, [1937] 1964), 26.

50. Lenski, *The Interpretation of St. Paul's Epistles to the Colossians, to the Thessalonians, to Timothy, to Titus and to Philemon*, 26–27. Lenski notes that "the commentators call the phrase a popular hyperbole" (26–27).

Dispensational commentator Edward R. Roustio writes that "in all the world" means that the "gospel was spreading all over the Roman Empire."[51] This is what preterists claim for the extent of the preaching of the gospel in Matthew 24:14. It's interesting that Ice quotes J. B. Lightfoot on Colossians 1:23 below, but he does not quote him on 1:6 where Lightfoot states that "in all the world" is "hyperbole," comparing it to Romans 1:8 ("throughout the whole world"), 1 Thessalonians 1:8 ("in every place"), and 2 Corinthians 2:14 ("in every place").[52] Ice takes a similar approach with Colossians 1:23 which states:

> If indeed you continue in the faith firmly established and steadfast, and not moved away from the hope of the gospel that you have heard, *which was proclaimed in all creation under heaven*, and of which I Paul was made a minister.

Although this passage does not use *kosmos*, Ice links it with Colossians 1:6. He quotes several commentators who actually agree with what preterists believe. James R. Gray, for example, denies that the passage is literal, but then admits that the gospel is "bearing fruit in the world—not that the gospel has been preached in all the world.... Paul is talking about the sphere of preaching, not that every creature was preached unto."[53] Gray understands that the language is universal, and he also knows that he cannot interpret it literally. Of course, I can't understand how Gray can maintain that the gospel is bearing fruit in the world if it had not been preached in all the world.

No preterist has ever claimed that these passages teach that the gospel has been preached to every creature in the whole wide world but only that the gospel had made its way throughout the then known world "as a witness to the nations" (Matt. 24:14).

Lightfoot comments that Colossians 1:23 is the "fulfilment of the Lord's last command, ['Go into all the world and preach the gospel to all creation'] Mark xvi. 15.... For the hyperbole ['in all creation'] compare I Thess. i.8 ['in every place']. To demand statistical exactness in such a context would be to require what is never required in similar cases."[54] Let's allow dispensational commentator Norman L. Geisler to address the meaning of the passage:

---

51. Edward R. Roustio, "The Epistle to the Colossians," *Liberty Bible Commentary*, 589.

52. J. B. Lightfoot, *St. Paul's Epistles to the Colossians and Philemon* (Peabody, MA: Hendrickson, [1875] 1993), 134.

53. James R. Gray, *Prophecy On The Mount* (Chandler, AZ: Berean Advocate Ministries, 1991), 62.

54. Lightfoot, *St. Paul's Epistles to the Colossians and Philemon*, 163.

**to every creature under heaven.** This is obviously a figure of speech indicating the universality of **the gospel** and its proclamation, not that every person on the globe heard Paul preach. In Acts 2:5 this phrase describes countries without including, for example, anyone from North or South America (cf. Also Gen. 41:57; 1 Kings 10:24; Rom. 1:8).[55]

All the commentators Ice quotes understand that the passage is not meant to be interpreted literally. Unlike Ice, they admit that these global phrases mean nothing more than the world in which Paul and the early church lived. Ice is so intent in defending dispensationalism against its many interpretive problems that he selectively quotes commentators. His use of Lightfoot is the most egregious example. Paul was using hyperbole simply to make the case that "the gospel did spread with remarkable swiftness in the comparatively few years after Pentecost, and no one can state precisely just where its geographical limits were."[56] This is why dispensational commentator Homer A. Kent, Jr. can also claim that "the statement is a legitimate use of literary hyperbole, and should be regarded as a generalization not requiring statistical exactness."[57]

These passages state what Ice denies. They couldn't be any more clear and they harmonize perfectly with what Jesus told His disciples in Matthew 24:14.

## Every Nation and Tribe and Tongue and People

Ice believes that Matthew 24:14 and Revelation 14:6–7 are parallel passages. This is a surprising admission since in terms of language, they are quite dissimilar. In Matthew 24:14 Jesus says that "the gospel of the kingdom shall be preached in the inhabited earth [*oikoumenē*] for a witness to all the nations" and in Revelation 14:6 we read, "And I saw another angel flying in midheaven, having an eternal gospel to preach to those who live on the earth, and to every nation and tribe and tongue and people." "Nations" seems to be the only common word. Ice claims that "global evangelization will take place just before the middle of the seven-year Tribulation." There is no "seven-year Tribulation" in Revelation. The words "seven years" appear only once in the New Testament, and it has

---

55. Norman L. Geisler, "Colossians," *Bible Knowledge Commentary*, 675.

56. Homer A. Kent, Jr., *Treasures of Wisdom: Studies in Colossians and Philemon* (Grand Rapids, MI: Baker Book House, 1978), 57.

57. Kent, *Treasures of Wisdom*, 57.

nothing to do with a tribulation period.⁵⁸ Ice is forced to squeeze the Bible into the dispensational mold. This means that he often fails to compare Scripture with Scripture. He lets his system guide his judgment.

Of course, there is no need to rehearse the arguments that have already been developed that demonstrate that *oikoumenē* and even *kosmos* are not universal in their geographical scope. But even with the seemingly universal scope of John's language, this does not mean that he is recording anything more than what other global passages are saying (Rom. 1:8; Col. 16, 23; etc.). Notice how almost identical language is used in Daniel: "Nebuchadnezzar the king to all the peoples, nations, and men of every language that live in all the earth" (Dan. 4:1). Is this meant to be taken in a global way? Not at all.

But let's assume that John is describing the world-wide global preaching of the gospel. The parallel is more with Matthew 24:31 than with 24:14. It's after the fall of Jerusalem that God's elect are gathered "from the four winds, from one end of heaven to the other" (24:31).⁵⁹ Similarly, in Revelation 14:6 we learn that the "eternal gospel" is to be preached (Rev. 14:6) when "Babylon the great" is fallen (14:8). Babylon the great is first-century Jerusalem, and it fell in A.D. 70. In terms of parallels, notice also that in Revelation 14:6 and Matthew 24:31 angels are involved in the gospel being sent forth.⁶⁰ It seems to me that this passage best describes a post-A.D. 70 world after the immediate fall of Jerusalem.

With Jerusalem no longer the redemptive focus, the gospel is to go worldwide: "But you shall receive power when the Holy Spirit has come upon you; and you shall be My witnesses both in Jerusalem, and in all Judea and Samaria, and even to the remotest part of the earth" (Acts 1:8). Prior to the destruction of Jerusalem the gospel was to go into the "inhabited world" of the first century as a "witness to all the nations" (Matt. 24:14). Later in the Olivet Discourse, Jesus describes a more universal spreading of the gospel "from one end of the sky to the other" (24:31). Prior to Jesus' ascension, Jesus tells His disciples to "make disciples of all the nations" (28:19). Notice that there is no time reference as there is in Matthew 24:14 ("this generation").

But there is another interpretive possibility. Like Revelation 12 which seems to look back to earlier New Testament history, John may be doing the same thing in Revelation 12:6. Arthur M. Ogden suggests:

---

58. DeMar, *Left Behind*, 39–42.

59. For a discussion of Matthew 24:31, see Gary DeMar, *Last Days Madness: Obsession of the Modern Church*, 4th ed. (Powder Springs, GA: American Vision, 1999), 173–177.

60. R. T. France, *The Gospel of Mark* (NIGTC) (Grand Rapids, MI: Eerdmans, 2002), 536–537.

> The Lamb is standing on Mount Sion with the 144,000 ready for the beginning of the New Testament order. John watches as an angel flies through the midst of heaven with the everlasting gospel to preach to all nations. The scene is Pentecost, 30 A.D. (cf. Heb. 12:22–24). This is when the gospel began to be preached under the authority of the great commission (cf. Matt. 28:18–20; Mr. 16:15–16; Lk. 24:46–49) and the power of the Holy Spirit (Acts 1:8, 2:1–4, 33; 1 Pet. 1:12). From here the gospel was preached to every nation, kindred, tongue, and people (cf. Matt. 24:14; Mk. 13:10; Rom. 1:16; 10:18; Col. 1:23).[61]

While we can't be definite, Acts 2:5 may be the key to understanding the significance of Revelation 14:6 since there were "Jews living in Jerusalem, devout men, from every nation under heaven." They heard the gospel "in his own language" (Acts 2:6). Within a period of forty years, the gospel had made its way beyond the borders of Israel to every place a caravan or ship could take a person.

## To All the Nations

One last argument that needs to be dealt with is Ice's understanding of Romans 16:26. In *Last Days Madness* and *Left Behind: Separating Fact from Fiction* I claim that this passage fulfills the demands of Matthew 24:14 since "Paul declared that the gospel had 'been made known to all nations,' a direct fulfillment of Matthew 24:14 (Rom. 16:26)."[62] Ice disagrees by stating the following:

> As virtually every commentary will tell you, the purpose of Paul's mystery about the Gospel is so that it reaches throughout the world.[63] H.P. Liddon says that "to all the nations" speaks "of the range of destination. Among all the heathen peoples."[64] "Having revealed this truth to Paul, God ordered it preached to all the Gentile nations."[65] This passage informs us that the Gospel message

---

61. Arthur M. Ogden, *The Avenging of the Apostles and Prophets: Commentary on Revelation*, 2nd ed. (Somerset, KY: Ogden Publications, 1991), 292–293.

62. DeMar, *Left Behind: Separating Fact from Fiction*, 85. Also see *Last Days Madness*, 89.

63. Leon Morris, *The Epistle to the Romans* (Grand Rapids, MI: Eerdmans, 1988), 547.

64. H. P. Liddon, *Explanatory Analysis of St. Paul's Epistle to the Romans* (Minneapolis, MN: James and Klock, [1899] 1977), 307.

65. Randolph O. Yeager, *The Renaissance New Testament*, 18 vols. (Gretna, LA: Pelican, 1983), 12:282.

has been introduced into the entire world and was intended for every human being throughout all creation. This statement could have been made on the day of Pentecost when the Church was born since it speaks to the fact that the Gospel mystery tells us that it is not just for Jews, but will include Gentiles as well.

How many times have we seen Paul use global language to express what he states again in his doxology at the conclusion of Romans? He thanks God for the Christians in Rome (1:5) because their "faith is being proclaimed throughout *the whole world*" (Rom. 1:8). He tells them that "their voice has gone out *into all the earth*, and their words *to the ends of the world*" (10:18). We have seen how Colossians 1:6 and 1:23 use similar language. Given Ice's penchant for being a literalist, it's rather surprising to read how he dances around these global-language texts.

Ice's claim that "the purpose of Paul's mystery about the Gospel is so that it reaches throughout the world" states the obvious and says nothing about this debate. The question remains: Did the gospel reach throughout the then-known world prior to that pre-A.D. 70 generation passing away? Paul and other New Testament writers say it did! To admit this, Ice would have to abandon dispensationalism.

Once again, Ice quotes the commentators selectively. For example, he references Morris as saying the "mystery about the Gospel is so that it reaches throughout the world." I agree. But as we've seen over and over, the New Testament's understanding of "world," whether *oikoumenē* or *kosmos*, says this is a done deal in terms of what people understood these words to mean in their day. Contrary to Ice, Morris also writes that "the gospel has been made known, and been made known to the Gentiles (cf. 1:5)."[66]

But let's suppose for the moment that Ice is correct, that Paul only had the hope of the gospel's extent in mind, so that it "reaches throughout the world." In effect, Paul is only stating what will be, not what has been accomplished. Of course, such an interpretation would contradict what Paul says elsewhere in Romans (Rom. 1:8; 10:18), passages which Ice does not discuss. Furthermore, since Paul was writing around A.D. 57, and Colossians was not written until A.D. 63, there is perfect harmony. By the time Paul writes to the Colossians, the gospel had been preached "in all creation under heaven" (Col. 1:23). In reality, Jesus said that the gospel would be preached "in the whole world for a witness to all the nations" (Matt. 24:14) before "this generation" passed away, that is, prior to the

---

66. Morris, *Epistle to the Romans*, 547.

destruction of Jerusalem in A.D. 70. In one of his later letters, written around A.D. 64, Paul writes to Timothy that Jesus was "proclaimed among the nations, believed on in the world" (1 Tim. 3:16). Can the Bible be any more clear?

## Conclusion

While Ice makes an attempt to shore up the walls of collapsing dispensationalism with his article on Matthew 24:14, he has inflicted yet more damage. He fails to make a comprehensive study of how *oikoumenē* is used in the New Testament, he selectively cites passages and commentators that do not support his view, he often refutes what he attempts to defend in his own position, and he makes no attempt to interpret the pertinent passages in light of their historical context. If Ice's article is standard dispensational fare, then dispensationalism is in deep trouble. These are merely signs of its imminent collapse.

# 9

# The Myth that Earthquakes Are Signs of the End Times

For decades now, modern-day prophecy writers have been claiming that the increase and severity of earthquakes are sure indicators that the rapture is near. Carl G. Johnson wrote in 1972 that "the greatest earthquakes that have ever shaken this world have all come since the close of World War I. Several of them shook the whole earth."[1] Peter LaLonde claims that the number of earthquakes per decade "has roughly doubled since the 1950's." David Allen Lewis offers a similar statistic: "There have been more earthquakes in the last 50 years than in the previous 1,500 years." Michael D. Evans, whose book *The American Prophecies* is touted as an end-time *tour de force* by a number of dispensational advocates, wrote in an earlier prophecy work that "The magnitude and frequency of earthquakes sets [the decade of the 1990s] apart from any other time in spiritual history." Jack Van Impe argued in a similar way: "History shows that the number of killer quakes remained fairly constant until the 1950s—averaging between two to four per decade. In the 1950s, there were nine. In the 1960s, there were 13. In the 1970s, there were 51. In the 1980s, there were 86. From 1990 through 1996, there have been more than 150."[2] As we will see, statistically there has not been an increase in the number of earthquakes in the past 100 years or an increase in their severity.

## Great Earthquakes

Like clock work, when news reports started coming in about the deep-sea earthquake that created a massive tsunami that has killed more than 150,000

---

1. Carl G. Johnson, *Prophecy Made Plain for Times Like These* (Chicago: Moody Press, 1972), 86.

2. These citations were taken from Richard Abanes, *End-Time Visions: The Road to Armageddon?* (New York: Four Walls Eight Windows, 1998), 258–267.

people, I predicted that prophecy writers would connect this tragic event to an end-of-the-world scenario. Hal Lindsey was one of the first to make the inevitable connection.[3] Lindsey concentrates on Luke's account of Jesus' prophecy in the Olivet Discourse:

> When Jesus was asked what the signs of His return would be, He painted a picture of a world torn by ethnic strife and war, famine in the midst of plenty, rocked by great earthquakes and ravaged by pestilences.

Lindsey uses Luke 21:11 for his apocalyptic reference point: "And there will be great earthquakes, and in various places plagues and famines; and there will be terrors and great signs from heaven." He claims that Jesus is referring to what will take place at a distant time, in a period just before the "rapture" and the great tribulation.

Lindsey has pulled the earthquake card before. He started in 1970 with the publication of *The Late Great Planet Earth*.[4] In 1997, he wrote, "Earthquakes continue to increase in frequency and intensity, just as the Bible predicts for the last days before the return of Christ."[5] In 1994, he published similar statistics in the first edition of *Planet Earth 2000 A.D.* The source for Lindsey's statistics is the authoritative United States Geological Survey in Boulder, Colorado. "But he does not give details of the report (report name, author, date, location, etc.)."[6] Those who consider earthquakes to be a sign of *our* end of the age and the nearness of the rapture are missing some crucial biblical and historical data. First, the end of the age was a first-century event (1 Cor. 10:11; Heb. 1:1–2; 9:26; 10:24–25). Second, the sign of earthquakes only has meaning within the time context of the generation to whom Jesus was addressing (more about this below). Third, the statistics used by Lindsey, LaLonde, Van Impe, *et al.* cannot be substantiated by a study of the data.

---

3. Hal Lindsey, "Stingy Sam" (Dec. 30, 2004) www.worldnetdaily.com/news/article.asp?ARTICLE_ID=42171

4. Hal Lindsey, *The Late Great Planet Earth* (Grand Rapids, MI: Zondervan, 1970), 52.

5. Hal Lindsey, *Apocalypse Code* (Palos Verdes, CA: Western Front Ltd., 1997), 296.

6. Steven A. Austin and Mark L. Strauss, "Are Earthquakes Signs of the End Times?: A Geological and Biblical Response to an Urban Legend," *Christian Research Journal*, 21:4, 32. Through careful analysis, the authors refute the claim that there has been an increase of earthquakes in the periods stated by the above prophecy writers. In fact, the authors conclude, "Graphical plots of global earthquake frequency indicate overall a decreasing frequency of earthquakes" (38). A more detailed analysis can be found online at www.icr.org/research/sa/sa-r06.htm

A majority of prophecy writers begin with Jesus' longest prophetic statement most often referred to as the Olivet Discourse (Matt. 24; Mark 13; Luke 21). In fact, Jesus is describing what took place before that first-century generation passes away: "Even so you, too, when you see these things happening, recognize that the kingdom of God is near" (21:31). Notice the audience reference: "Even so *you* … when *you* see these things happening" (cf. Matt. 24:33). Jesus was informing His present audience about what *they* would see and experience. If Jesus had a future generation in view, He would have said, "When *they* see these things happening."

## Whose Generation?

In addition, notice how Jesus says, "*this* generation will not pass away until all these things take place" (Luke 21:32). Each and every time "this generation" is used in the gospels, it refers to the generation to whom Jesus is speaking (Matt. 11:16; 12:41–42; 23:36; Mark 8:12; Luke 7:31; 11:30–32, 50–51; 17:25; cf. Gen. 7:1; Ps. 12:7; Heb. 3:10). "This generation" is never used as a reference to a future generation. Again, if Jesus had a future generation in mind, He would have said, "*that* generation will not pass away."

Jesus is referring to world conditions in His day. The near demonstrative "this" is always used to describe what is near in terms of time and place. "The demonstrative[s] … are of two kinds: near and distant. The near demonstratives, as the name denotes, points to someone or something 'near,' in close proximity. They appear as the singular word 'this' and its plural 'these.' The distant demonstratives, as their name suggests, appear as 'that' (singular), or 'those' (plural)."[7] The near demonstrative always refers to something present-day as Greek lexicons and grammars demonstrate in their definitions.

- "This" refers "to something comparatively near at hand, just as *ekeinos* [that] refers to something comparatively farther away."[8]
- "Sometimes it is desired to call attention with special emphasis to a designated object, whether in the physical vicinity or the speaker or the literary context of the writer. For this purpose the demonstrative construction is used.… For that which is relatively near in actuality or thought the *immediate* demonstrative [*houtos*] is used.… For that which is

---

7. Cullen I K Story and J. Lyle Story, *Greek To Me: Learning New Testament Greek Through Memory Visualization* [New York: Harper, 1979], 74).

8. William F. Arndt and F. Wilbur Gingrich, *A Greek-English Lexicon of the New Testament and Other Early Christian Literature*, 4th ed. (Chicago, IL: The University of Chicago Press, 1952), 600.

relatively distant in actuality or thought the *remote* demonstrative [*ekeinos*] is used."[9]

As we will see, there is ample historical evidence that these earthquakes did take place before that first-century generation passed away. In fact, as history records, killer quakes, tsunamis, and hurricanes have a long history.

## We've Seen this Before

A great deal of attention has been focused on the number of hurricanes that struck the United States in 2005 and the tsunami that hit Asia in 2004. Many believe that these are signs of the end based on Luke's account of the Olivet Discourse where he writes about the "perplexity at the roaring of the sea and the waves" (Luke 21:25). The Mediterranean Sea floor is littered with ships that broke apart and sank because of storms. We read of one such incident in Acts 27. The storm is described as a "Euraquilo," that is, "a northeaster" (27:14). Luke writes that they did not see the sun or stars "for many days" (27:20). The ship finally ran aground where it was "broken up by the force of the waves" (27:41). The Roman historian Tacitus describes a series of similar events in A.D. 65:

> The gods also marked by storms and diseases a year made shameful by so many crimes. Campania was devastated by a hurricane ... the fury of which extended to the vicinity of the City, in which a violent pestilence was carrying away every class of human beings ... houses were filled with dead bodies, the streets with funerals.[10]

The natural disasters described by Matthew, Mark, and Luke, common to every age, pointed specifically to the coming of Jesus in judgment upon Jerusalem before that first-century generation passed away.

The August 27th, 1883 eruption of Krakatoa resulted in the deaths of 40,000 people, almost all of whom died from 100-foot tsunamis generated by the shock waves. Through eyewitness accounts, we learned that the explosion was heard thousands of miles away, and the eruption's shock wave traveled around the world. The effects of the disaster were far-reaching and long-lasting:

---

9. H. E. Dana and Julius R. Mantey, *A Manual Grammar of the Greek New Testament* (New York; Macmillan, 1957), 127–128, sec. 136.

10. George Edmundson, *The Church in Rome in the First Century* (London: Longmans, Green and Co., 1913), 143.

## The Myth that Earthquakes are Signs of the End Times 155

> Beyond the purely physical horrors of an event that has only very recently been properly understood, the eruption changed the world in more ways than could possibly be imagined. Dust swirled round the planet for years, causing temperatures to plummet and sunsets to turn vivid with lurid and unsettling displays of light. The effects of the immense waves were felt as far away as France. Barometers in Bogotá and Washington, D.C., went haywire. Bodies were washed up in Zanzibar. The sound of the island's destruction was heard in Australia and India and on islands thousands of miles away. Most significant of all—in view of today's new political climate—the eruption helped to trigger in Java a wave of murderous anti-Western militancy among fundamentalist Muslims: one of the first outbreaks of Islamic-inspired killings anywhere.[11]

What's unique about tsunamis in our day is how quickly we learn about them through television, satellite transmission, and the Internet. News of the devastating effects of Krakatoa was transmitted by Morse Code. If, as Lindsey himself states, the December 26, 2004 "catastrophic tsunami was caused by the fourth most powerful undersea earthquake on record," then there were three that were more powerful that we know about and possibly others that we don't know about. It seems that there are more earthquakes today because of several factors:

> A partial explanation may lie in the fact that in the last twenty years, we have definitely had an increase in the number of earthquakes we have been able to locate each year. This is because of the tremendous increase in the number of seismograph stations in the world and the many improvements in global communications. In 1931, there were about 350 stations operating in the world; today, there are more that 4,000 stations and the data now comes in rapidly from these stations by telex, computer and satellite. This increase in the number of stations and the more timely receipt of data has allowed us and other seismological centers to locate many small earthquakes which were undetected in earlier years, and we are able to locate earthquakes more rapidly. The NEIC now locates about 12,000 to 14,000 earthquakes each year or approximately 35 per day. Also, because of the improvements in communications and the increased interest in natural disas-

---

11. http://www.amazon.com/exec/obidos/tg/detail/-/0066212855/qid=1104773777/sr=1-1/ref=sr_1_1/103-5583319-4472647?v=glance&s=books

ters, the public now learns about more earthquakes. According to long-term records (since about 1900), we expect about 18 major earthquakes (7.0–7.9) and one great earthquake (8.0 or above) in any given year.[12]

As history attests, devastating earthquakes are not new. In addition, the latest disaster could have been averted through an early warning system that is presently available.[13]

Lindsey continues: "Jesus indicates that all the natural disasters will begin to increase in frequency and intensity in concert with each other shortly before His return. And it is as these 'birth pains' begin to take place that believers in Jesus are to know that their deliverance is near." There is no mention of an increase in the frequency or intensity of earthquakes in what Jesus says, only that they will occur "in various places" before "this generation," that is, the generation of Jesus' day, passed away.

The biblical record shows that earthquakes occurred before Jerusalem was destroyed in A.D. 70. Two earthquakes are mentioned in Matthew: When Jesus was crucified (27:54) and when the angel came down to roll the stone away from the tomb where Jesus was buried (28:2). This second earthquake is said to have been "severe." Luke records in Acts that "a great earthquake" that shook "the foundations of the prison house" (Acts 16:26). In Revelation 11:13 we read: "And in that hour there was a *great earthquake*, and a tenth of the city fell; and seven thousand people were killed in the earthquake, and the rest were terrified and gave glory to the God of heaven." The temple was still standing when John recorded this event (11:1–2). For us, this great earthquake is a past event and is another fulfillment of what Jesus predicted in the Olivet Discourse.

Secular historians of the time support the biblical record. "And as to earthquakes, many are mentioned by writers during a period just previous to 70 A.D. There were earthquakes in Crete, Smyrna, Miletus, Chios, Samos, Laodicea, Hierapolis, Colosse, Campania, Rome, and Judea. It is interesting to note that the city of Pompeii was much damaged by an earthquake occurring on February 5, 63 A.D."[14] Henry Alford compiled the following list:

---

12. http://earthquake.usgs.gov/faq/myths.html#8

13. Daniel Lapin, "Don't blame God for Asian casualties," www.worldnetdaily.com/news/article.asp?ARTICLE_ID=42212

14. J. Marcellus Kik, *Matthew Twenty-Four: An Exposition* (Philadelphia, PA: Presbyterian and Reformed, 1948), 93.

> The principal *earthquakes* occurring between this prophecy and the destruction of Jerusalem [in A.D. 70] were, (1) a great earthquake in Crete, A.D. 46 or 47; (2) one at Rome on the day when Nero assumed the manly toga, A.D. 51; (3) one at Apamaea in Phrygia, mentioned by Tacitus, A.D. 53; (4) one tat Laodicea in Phrygia, A.D. 60; (5) one in Campania.[15]

Notice the tight geographical area of these earthquakes within a period of just 12 years. Their severity and frequency have not been eclipsed in modern times.

Flavius Josephus, an eyewitness to the events surrounding Jerusalem's destruction, describes an earthquake in Judea of such magnitude "that the constitution of the universe was confounded for the destruction of men."[16] Of course, he was speaking metaphorically, using hyperbole, something the Bible often does to describe local catastrophes (Ps. 18; 2 Sam. 22; Zeph. 1:1–4, 14–18), because of the devastation brought to the holy city and sanctuary that were the identity of the Jewish people. Josephus goes on to write that the Judean earthquake was "no common" calamity, indicating that God Himself had brought it about for a special purpose. One commentator writes: "Perhaps no period in the world's history has ever been so marked by these convulsions as that which intervenes between the Crucifixion and the destruction of Jerusalem."[17] Since the generation between A.D. 30 and 70 is past, there is no reason to attach prophetic significance to earthquakes in our day as a fulfillment of Matthew 24:7. They are not signs of the imminency of Jesus' return in our generation, but they were a prelude to the coming of Jesus in judgment upon Jerusalem in the generation of the apostles.

## The End of the World?

"I thought it was the end of the world." Cesar Jamorawon believed the thunderous eruptions from Mount Pinatubo in the Philippines in July of 1991 were a punishment from God. "I thought that this must be a punishment from God because the world has forgotten Him. I have never experienced a graver crisis than

---

15. Henry Alford, *The New Testament for English Readers* (Chicago, IL: Moody Press, n.d.), 163.

16. Quoted in Thomas Scott, *The Holy Bible Containing the Old and New Testaments, According to the Authorized Version; with Explanatory Notes, Practical Observations, and Copious Marginal References,* 3 vols. (New York: Collins and Hannay, 1832), 3:108.

17. Edward Hayes Plumptre, "The Gospel According to St. Matthew," *Ellicott's Commentary on the Whole Bible*, ed. Charles John Ellicott, 8 vols. (London: Cassell and Company, 1897), 6:146.

this in my life."[18] From Jamorawon's perspective, the eruption of Mount Pinatubo was a unique eschatological experience, but was it a sign of coming prophetic events?

This was not the first eruption from the mouth of Mount Pinatubo. The volatile mount had erupted in 1380. There is little doubt that those who witnessed Pinatubo's fury more than six centuries ago expressed sentiments like those of Cesar Jamorawon. A similar reaction was heard in Kobe, Japan, in January 1995. Minoru Takasu "thought it was the end of the world"[19] when a devastating earthquake struck. It wasn't the end of the world then, and it's probably not a "sign" of the end of the world now.

Of course, we should see in events like earthquakes, volcanoes, famines, and floods a reminder that God does respond to a world that "has forgotten Him." John Wesley wrote of "The Cause and Cure of Earthquakes" in 1750:

> Of all the judgments which the righteous God inflicts on sinners here, the most dreadful and destructive is an earthquake. This he has lately brought on our part of the earth, and thereby alarmed our fears, and bid us "prepare to meet our God!" The shocks which have been felt in divers places, since that which made this city tremble, may convince us that the danger is not over, and ought to keep us still in awe; seeing "his anger is not turned away, but his hand is stretched out still," Isa. x, 4.[20]

Wesley's assessment of earthquakes as an immediate judgment of God is quite different from saying that such events should be tied to texts that indicate the timing of a so-called rapture or the Second Coming. In 1756, Gilbert Tennent observed that earthquakes were "extraordinary in respect of number and dreadful Effects"[21] *in his day*. He saw them as indicators that "some extraordinary Revolutions [might] be near at Hand," not as signs of the soon coming of Jesus. James West Davidson writes:

> Ministers in 1755 as well as 1727, New Light as well as Old, accepted the prevailing assumptions that earthquakes were naturally caused, that they were inescapably meant as moral judgments, and that (most important) they were compatible with other moral

---

18. Eileen Guerrero, "I thought this was the end of the world," *Marietta Daily Journal* (17 June 1991), 1A.

19. "'The end of the world,'" *Marietta Daily Journal* (18 January 1995), 1A.

20. John Wesley, "The Cause and Cure of Earthquakes" (1750), *Sermons on Several Occasions*, 2 vols. (New York: Carlton & Phillips, 1853), 1:506.

21. Gilbert Tennent (1703–1764) quoted in James West Davidson, *The Logic of Millennial Thought: Eighteenth-Century New England* (New Haven, CT: Yale University Press, 1977), 102.

judgments which God accomplished by using human instruments. They saw natural disasters as one proper part of the climax of history, not because of a preference for any specific millennial chronologies (once again a wide range of opinion appeared on that subject), but because catastrophes fell under the more general category of moral judgment, which was a necessary part of ultimate deliverance.[22]

News of earthquakes in our day seem to hold prophetic significance "because we are to such an extent 'strangers to the past,' [thus] we easily read into the events and circumstances of our own day a distinctiveness and uniqueness that may not actually be there."[23] Much of the speculative nature of today's Bible prophecy hysteria can be linked to "generational provincialism," that is, the belief that nothing has prophetic significance unless it happens to the present generation. Many who take this approach seem to be unaware that wars, earthquakes, famines, and plagues have been a part of the human condition since the fall. At various crucial periods in human history, God has used these phenomena as warnings of impending judgment or as retribution for covenantal unfaithfulness (Num. 16:30, 32, 34; 26:10; Deut. 11:6). Of course, not every earthquake or famine has such a *special* meaning. Each occurrence, however, ought to serve as a reminder that we are sinners and our world has been ravaged by the effects of rebellion (John 9:1–3). Political tyranny and religious apostasy are not necessarily signs of impending eschatological destruction.

## The Lisbon Earthquake

What about the Lisbon earthquake of 1755? Surely, if the Black Plague was not a prelude to the end, Lisbon's encounter with the power of the earth and the "wrath of God" had to be a sign that the end was near. Had not Jesus told His audience that "there will be great earthquakes" (Luke 21:11)? "The estimates of the death toll range from about 15,000 to more than 75,000. Modern historians incline to believe that the correct figure is probably about 30,000, which

---

22. Davidson, *Logic of Millennial Thought*, 97.

23. Carl Olof Jonsson and Wolfgang Herbst, *The "Sign" of the Last Days—When?* (Atlanta, GA: Commentary Press, 1987), x. This book is filled with statistical and historical information that easily refutes the notion that our era is unique when it comes to earthquakes, wars, and famines.

would be more than ten percent of the city's population, the equivalent of nearly a million in contemporary New York."[24]

Modern date setters do acknowledge past great earthquakes. But to make *our* generation unique in the annals of Bible prophecy, those engaged in predicting the time of the end assert that we should calculate the *frequency* of earthquakes. Again, the present must be seen as unusual to make the prophetic system work. Hal Lindsey wrote: "There have been many great earthquakes throughout history, but, according to surprisingly well-kept records, in the past they did not occur very frequently. The 20th century, however, has experienced an unprecedented increase in the frequency of these calamities. In fact, the number of earthquakes per decade has roughly doubled in each of the 10-year periods since 1950."[25] No statistical evidence is offered.

In fact, Lindsey is wrong. There is nothing unique about the number of earthquakes that the world is now experiencing. Certainly there are better detection devices. These alone would make their occurrences *seem* more numerous. In addition, because of a worldwide news network, communication satellites, and instant news analysis, we read about even the slightest seismic tremor in the morning paper.

The way some prophecy analysts talk, only a dozen or so major earthquakes have been recorded over the centuries. This is far from the truth. The Roman writer Seneca, in A.D. 58, stated that frequent earthquakes had been a characteristic of the ancient world:

> How often have cities in Asia, how often in Achaia, been laid low by a single shock of earthquake! How many towns in Syria, how many in Macedonia, have been swallowed up! How often has this kind of devastation laid Cyprus in ruins! How often has Paphos collapsed! Not infrequently are tidings brought to us of the utter destruction of entire cities.[26]

Notice the date of Seneca's writing—A.D. 58—just twelve years before the destruction of Jerusalem and twenty-eight years after Jesus' prophecy about earthquakes. After A.D. 70, earthquakes no longer have the same prophetic significance.

---

24. Friedrich, *End of the World*, 188.

25. Lindsey, *The 1980s*, 30.

26. *Seneca Ad Lucilium Epistulae Morales,* trans. Richard M. Gummere, vol. 2 (London: 1920), 437. Quoted in Jonsson and Herbst, *The "Sign" of the Last Days—When?*, 75.

# 10

# The Myth that Oil in Israel Is a Prophetic Sign

Hal Lindsey claims that the Bible predicts that oil will be discovered in Israel.[1] Now there is a book that attempts to make the same case: *Breaking the Treasure Code: The Hunt for Israel's Oil*.[2] The book's description reads as follows:

> A treasure map was hidden in the Bible more than three thousand years ago. The treasure, a gift from God to Israel, was buried in the sands of the Promised Land to ensure her prosperity and protection. "Breaking the Treasure Code" pieces the map together and reveals the clues that lead to a vast oil reserve; the source of Israel's wealth and the key to her survival in the last days.

That's the good news. Now the bad news. Israel will be invaded. "The interesting thing is," Lindsey writes, "that this invasion will be triggered by the enormous wealth that the nation accumulates in this time." Israel just can't win. The Arab countries have been swimming in oil for decades and living the luxurious life from the accumulated revenue, but as soon as Israel discovers the long-buried energy source, she's going to be invaded! Bummer.

Israel may in fact discover oil. This would not be too surprising since the region is glutted with the black gold. But can a *biblical* case be made for the prophetic significance of oil as it relates to Israel and a future end-time scenario made popular by writers like Lindsey? Let's follow Lindsey's line of logic through Scripture to see if he has made his case.

---

1. Hal Lindsey, "Israel, nation of miracles" (April 1, 2004): http://tinyurl.com/4l67b4

2. James R. Spillman and Steven M. Spillman, *Breaking the Treasure Code: The Hunt for Israel's Oil* (Travelers Rest, SC: True Potential Publishing, Inc., 2005).

## Israel's Birth Dearth

Lindsey quotes part of Genesis 49:25 (in italic) which describes the blessings that will come to Joseph: *"From the God of your father who helps you, and by the Almighty who blesses you with blessings of heaven above, blessings of the deep that lies beneath,* blessings of the breasts and of the womb." Lindsey says of this verse: "Note that it predicts his great blessing will come from '*the deep that lies beneath*' his land." By "deep," Lindsey means oil buried deep in the ground!

A careful reader would have looked up the verses quoted by Lindsey (Acts 17:11) and noticed that he conveniently left out "blessings of the breasts and of the womb." The dispensational oriented *Bible Knowledge Commentary* states that this phrase refers to "abundant offspring."[3] Henry M. Morris, a noted dispensationalist, agrees and writes that it's a promise of "an abundance of healthful progeny, of both man and animal."[4] Gerhard Charles Aalders, not a dispensationalist, concurs with the above authors: "'Blessings of the breast and womb' certainly refer to abundance in the bearing and feeding of children, as well as for human children as for the young of the livestock."[5]

Earlier in Genesis we read of a promise of an increase in population that would result in Israel being as numerous "as the stars of the heavens, and as the sand which is on the seashore" (22:17; cf. 32:12).[6] And when was this fulfilled?:

- "And Thy servant is in the midst of Thy people which Thou hast chosen, a great people who cannot be numbered or counted for multitude" (1 Kings 3:8).

- "Judah and Israel were as numerous as the sand that is on the seashore in abundance" (1 Kings 4:20).

If Genesis 49:25 refers to the distant future, as Lindsey speculates, then there is a problem. By the year 2020, Arnon Sofer of the University of Haifa forecasts about 6.4 million Jews will live in Israel, "based on population growth and an average 50,000 Jewish immigrants a year. He expects the Arab population to

---

3. Allen P. Ross, "Genesis," *The Bible Knowledge Commentary: Old Testament*, John F. Walvoord and Roy B. Zuck (Wheaton, IL: Victor Books/Scripture Press, 1985), 99.

4. Henry M. Morris, *The Genesis Record: A Scientific and Devotional Commentary on the Book of Beginnings* (Grand Rapids, MI: Baker Book House, 1976), 660.

5. Gerhard Charles Aalders, *Genesis: Bible Student's Commentary*, trans. William Heynen, 2 vols. (Grand Rapids, MI: Zondervan, 1981), 2:287.

6. "As numerous as the sands of the sea and the stars of heaven" are hyperbolies (Gen. 41:49).

reach around 8.5 million, in addition to 1 million non-Jews of other origins."[7] The most optimistic projections show Jews and Palestinians about even in population in 25 years.[8] Beyond the borders of Israel, there are more than a hundred million non-Jews. It seems by present-day demographics that in comparison, it's the wombs of Israel's *enemies* that have been blessed.

## "The Deep that Lies Beneath"

Lindsey believes the phrase "the deep that lies beneath" is a reference to crude oil. As far as I can tell, he's the first person to make this discovery. If the "deep" refers to oil, then what are the "blessings of heaven above"? He doesn't say. You can see that Genesis 49:25 is a classic example of Hebrew parallelism. How does one of Lindsey's fellow dispensationalists interpret the passage? "Blessings from heaven above" is a reference to "rain for crops," while "from the deep" refers to "streams and wells for water"[9] (Gen. 7:11; 8:2; Deut. 33:13). H. C. Leupold captures the meaning of the Hebrew imagery:

> The following blessings are specialized: first "blessings of the heavens above"—those would be such blessings as the heavens hold within their grasp—rain, sunshine and pleasant breezes. Then follow "blessings of the deep," *i.e. tehom*, the deep source of the subterranean waters, which is pictured as being "that coutheth (or croucheth) beneath" the earth. This involves the waters stored in the earth that are so essential to all vegetable growth as well as the sources of the much needed streams and of the fountains.[10]

Contextually, this interpretation makes sense since the lack of rain and dry wells, especially for people living in a region not far from desert conditions, would invariably lead to failed crops and depleted livestock. There is nothing in all of Genesis 49 that would lead the interpreter to conclude that crude oil is buried in the deep. Lindsey is reading modern-day geo-politics and technology into the text. He did a similar thing in his 1973 book *There's a New World Coming* when

---

7. Phil Brennan, "Israel's Population Bomb in Reverse," www.newsmax.com (October 19, 2002).

8. Ben Wattenberg, "Israel Needn't Worry About a Population Implosion" (May 18, 2002). www.tzemachdovid.org/Facts/demography.shtml

9. Ross, "Genesis," 99.

10. H.C. Leupold, *Exposition of Genesis*, 2 vols. (Grand Rapids, MI: Baker Book House, [1942], 1976), 2:1196.

he seems to accept the identification of the locusts that came up out of the pit in Revelation 9 as Vietnam-era "Cobra helicopters."[11]

## "Let Him Dip His Foot in Oil"

Lindsey continues by appealing to Deuteronomy 33:24 to support his crude oil theory: "And of Asher he said, 'More blessed than sons is Asher; may he be favored by his brothers, *and may he dip his foot in oil*.'" Once again, Lindsey takes a verse meant for an ancient context and setting, and projects the distant future onto it to fit his system of interpretation. The "oil" of this verse is a reference to "olive oil." Jack S. Deere, writing on Deuteronomy in the dispensational oriented *Bible Knowledge Commentary*, states that "to bathe one's **feet in oil** rather than simply to anoint them would be an extravagant act. Thus the tribe of Asher would experience abundant fertility and prosperity."[12] Jan Ridderbos makes a similar observation: "his land will be so rich in oil that it is possible, so to speak, to wade in it. Indeed, Galilee, Asher's territory, was rich in olive trees."[13] J. A. Thompson adds further insight to the meaning of the passage:

> The last phrase in verse 24, *He dips* (or, may he dip) *his feet in oil* is to be understood as a wish that Asher may enjoy prosperity. The Galilean highlands were famous for olives and both Josephus and one of the Jewish Midrashim refer to this fact. The latter contains the saying, 'It is easier to raise a legion of olives in Galilee than to bring up a child in Palestine.'[14]

"The land of Asher was agriculturally rich, and is still known for its olive groves."[15] Once again, determining the context and setting are crucial in determining the meaning of a text.

Did the prophecies concerning Asher come to pass? Throughout the Old Testament, Asher is identified as a tribe blessed by God (1 Chron. 7:40; 12:36) and

---

11. Hal Lindsey, *There's a New World Coming* (Santa Ana, CA: Vision House, 1973), 138–139. You can find the quotation in the Bantam paperback edition in chapter 9, page 124.

12. Jacks S. Deere, "Deuteronomy, *Bible Knowledge Commentary: Old Testament*, 322.

13. Jan Ridderbos, *Deuteronomy: The Bible Student's Commentary*, trans. Ed M. van der Maas (Grand Rapids, MI: Zondervan, 1984), 311.

14. J. A. Thompson, *Deuteronomy: An Introduction and Commentary* (Downers Grove, IL: InterVarsity Press, 1974), 316.

15. Cyril J. Barber, "Tribe of Asher," *Baker Encyclopedia of the Bible*, ed. Walter A. Elwell, 2 vols. (Grand Rapids, MI: Baker, 2:212.

a protector of the nation (Judges 6:1–8, 35; 7:23; 1 Sam. 11:7; 1 Chron. 12:23, 36). Asher is one of the few tribes even mentioned in the New Testament. While many Israelites were "dispersed abroad" (James 1:1), a descendant from the tribe of Asher was waiting for the promised Messiah in Jerusalem (Luke 2:36), a wonderful fulfillment of prophecy.

## The Bible and Petroleum

When the word "oil" appears in the Bible, it is never a reference to crude oil or petroleum but olive oil.[16] Petroleum substances (bitumen) were known and used in Bible times, but they were not identified as "oil." There were pools of an asphalt-like material often translated as "pitch" or "tar" (KJV: "slime"): "Now the valley of Siddim was full of tar pits…" (Gen. 11:14). The "pitch" or "tar" was used for waterproofing (Gen. 6:14; Ex. 2:3) and mortar (Gen. 11:3). If God wanted to identify a future discovery of crude oil in Genesis 49:25 and Deuteronomy 33:24, He could have chosen any of the Hebrew terms already in use at that time to make the point.

## Crude Oil in Job

Given the way dispensationalists continually read the Bible through the lens of modern-day events and refuse to acknowledge the time texts and the contemporary context of so many passages, the Bible can be made to say almost anything. Consider this verse: "He reveals mysteries from the darkness, and brings the deep darkness into light" (Job 12:22). The use of oil as a fuel to run automobiles, buses, trucks, and other motorized vehicles would have been a "mystery" to the people of Job's day. Drilling into the earth to get out the oil would have been inconceivable. Of course, because oil is deep in the ground, it's in perpetual "darkness"—the darkest of the dark since oil itself is dark. But the oil drillers bring the darkness into light. Once oil is struck, it gushes into the brightness of day. Job was prophesying about the discovery of oil! It says so right in the Bible!

---

16. See entry of "Oil" in Leland Ryken, James C. Wilhoit, and Tremper Longman III, *Dictionary of Biblical Imagery* (Downers Grove, IL: InterVarsity Press, 1998), 603–604.

## Conclusion

Dispensationalists like Hal Lindsey insist that they interpret the Bible literally, and everyone else is an allegorizer. Tim LaHaye tries to sell this point in the Introduction to Mark Hitchcock and Thomas Ice's *The Truth About Left Behind*:

> Jerry [Jenkins] and I have unashamedly taken the position that all prophecy should be interpreted literally whenever possible. We have been guided throughout by the golden rule of interpretation: *When the plain sense of Scripture makes common sense, seek no other sense. Take every word at its primary, literal meaning unless the facts of the immediate context clearly indicate otherwise.*[17]

If only it were so. Lindsey, who follows the same "golden rule," is certainly not applying the principle in Genesis 49:25, Deuteronomy 33:24, and Ezekiel 38–39, and neither are LaHaye, Ice, and Hitchcock in their interpretation of Ezekiel 38–39 where ancient weapons are said to be descriptions of Russian MIG fighters. Like snake-oil salesmen, these modern-day prophetic hucksters are selling false remedies to a gullible audience willing to believe anything their prophetic heroes say about their product.

---

17. Tim LaHaye, "Introduction," Hitchcock and Ice, *The Truth Behind Left Behind*, 7.

# Appendix A

# "Church" or "Congregation"? A Choice of Deadly Consequence

English translations have obscured the biblical and historical meaning of *ekklēsia* by translating it as "church" rather than "assembly" or "congregation." It's unfortunate that John Wycliffe (c. 1324–1384) and the translators of the Geneva Bible (1560) chose to translate *ekklēsia* as "church" rather than the more accurate "assembly" or "congregation." And it's a shame that the scholars who were chosen to develop what has come to us as the King James Version were *forced* to translate *ekklēsia* as "church." The English word "church" is not related to the Greek word *ekklēsia* but is derived from the Greek *kyriake* (*oikia*)[1] "Lord's (house)," from *kyrios* "ruler, lord."

> The English term *church*, along with the Scottish word *Kirk* and German *Kirche*, is derived from [Anglo-Saxon and Latin from] the Greek *kuriakon*, which is the neuter adjective of *kurios*, "Lord," and means, "belonging to the Lord." *Kuriakon* occurs only twice in the New Testament, neither time with reference to the church as commonly used today.[2]

It's my contention that the use of "church" instead of "congregation" or "assembly" has gone a long way to create the myth of an Israel-Church distinction because it was viewed as a new thing rather than an extension of what the Old Testament had made obvious, both in the Hebrew and its Greek translation, the Septuagint. In all of the many definitional uses of *ekklēsia* in the New Testa-

---

1. "The word *oikia*, house, being omitted and understood." (Melvin E. Elliott, *The Languages of the King James Bible: A Glossary Explaining its Words and Expressions* [Garden City, NY: Doubleday & Company, Inc., 1967], 35).

2. Saucy, *The Church in God's Program*, 11.

ment—Melvin Elliott lists six[3]—not one of them fits the definition given by dispensationalists as an newly created category of believers that had the result of creating an Israel-Church distinction. The Tyndale New Testament, the first English translation to use the original languages of Hebrew and Greek, did not use the word "church." William Tyndale (1494–1536) chose words "assembly" and "congregation"[4] to translate *ekklēsia*, and ecclesiastical authorities took notice of it, not because such a translation would nullify an Israel-Church distinction but because "certain aspects of Tyndale's translation were instantly perceived as a threat by more conservative English Catholics."[5] More and others in the church believed that these translation changes would give credence to arguments by Protestants that the Church could be questioned and reformation might be in order.

Here is how Tyndale's translation handled the first two appearances of *ekklēsia* in the New Testament (spelling modernized):

- "…And upon this rock I will build my congregation: and the gates of hell shall not prevail against it (Matt. 16:18).[6]

- "If he hear not them, tell it unto the congregation: if he hear not the congregation, take him as an heathen man, and as a publican" (Matt. 18:17).[7]

The Catholic Church protested Tyndale's use of "congregation" as the proper translation of *ekklēsia* since at that time "church" signified an "organized body of the clergy" and a place to worship[8] and resulted in a clear distinction between the clergy and laity. In 1529, Sir Thomas More (1478–1535) published *Dialogue Concerning Heresies,* a frontal assault on Tyndale's New Testament translation. "At bottom, More asserts that Tyndale's offence has been to give the people

---

3. Elliott, *The Languages of the King James Bible*, 35–36. Also see James Bannerman, *The Church of Christ: A Treatise on the Nature, Powers, Ordinances, Discipline and Government of the Christian Church*, 2 vols. (Carlisle, PA: The Banner of Truth Trust, [1869] 1960), 1:5–17.

4. William Tyndale, "Answer to Sir Thomas More's Dialogue" in *The Works of William Tyndale*, 2 volume work (Carlisle, PA: The Banner of Truth Trust, [1849–1850], 2:13–16.

5. Alister McGrath, *In the Beginning: The Story of the King James Bible and How it Changed a Nation, a Language, and a Culture* (New York: Doubleday, 2001), 75.

6. "…And apon this rocke I wyll bylde my congregacion. And the gates of hell shall not prevayle ageynst it."

7. "If he heare not them tell it vnto the congregacion. If he heare not the congregacion take him as an hethen man and as a publican."

8. Benson Bobrick, *Wide as the Waters: The Story of the English Bible and the Revolution It Inspired* (New York: Simon & Schuster, 2001), 114.

Paul in English, and to translate key words in their Greek meanings as 'senior' [*presbuteros*],[9] 'congregation' [*ekklēsia*], 'love' [*agape*] and 'repent' [*metanoia*], instead of the Church's 'priest', 'church', 'charity', and 'do penance.'"[10] More wanted to insure that the hierarchy of the church was protected and the division of the clergy and laity maintained. It's no wonder that More attacked Tyndale on the translation of specific words that would have called into question the hierarchical division. The common reader could have seen, in addition to how *ekklēsia* was translated, that the English word "priest"[11] referred either to Jewish or pagan priests and not elders in the Church. "As a result, many New Testament references that could have been taken as endorsing the institution of the Church were now to be understood as referring to local congregations of believers."[12] More believed that Tyndale's translation undermined "the authority of Tradition,"[13] that is, the ecclesiastical traditions of the Roman Catholic Church.

> Like Wycliffe, Luther, and others, Tyndale believed that the invisible Church of the faithful was the only true Church, and that, as C.S. Lewis observed, "the mighty theocracy with its cardinals, abbeys, pardons, inquisition, and treasury of grace" connoted by the word "Church" was "in its very essence not only distinct from, but antagonistic to, the thing that St. Paul had in mind whenever he used the Greek word *ekklesia*. More, on the other hand, believed with equal sincerity that the 'Church' of his own day was in essence the very same mystical body which St. Paul addressed."[14]

For his efforts, Tyndale was strangled and burned at the stake in 1536 for defying church authority, opposing the Church by promoting doctrines such as *sola Scriptura*, justification by faith alone, the denial of purgatory, questioning the number of sacraments, and translating particular words that could lead the laity to believe that the Church's authority was limited. Tyndale's most pernicious "attack" on the Church was his insistence that *ekklesia* should be translated "congregation" rather than "church":

---

9. In a later edition, Tyndale translated *presbuteros* as the more accurate "elder."

10. David Daniell, *The Bible in English: It's History and Influence* (New Haven, CT: Yale University Press, 2003), 149.

11. The Greek word *hiereus*, not *presbuteros*, is translated accurately as "priest."

12. McGrath, *In the Beginning*, 75.

13. Bobrick, *Wide as the Waters*, 115.

14. Bobrick, *Wide as the Waters*, 115–116.

In his major defense of his translation, *An Answer to Sir Thomas More's Dialogue*, Tyndale begins with *ekklesia* in its relation to the English word *church*. He announces that "This word *church* hath divers [many] significations" (PS 3.11).[15] He then sets out ... three senses of the English word: first, a building; second, the clergy; and third, "a congregation; a multitude or a company gathered together in one, of all degrees of people" (PS 3.12).[16] He rejects *church* as a translation of *ekklesia*, because the first two senses do not appear in the New Testament, and the last is "little known among the common people [now-a-days]" (PS 3.12).[17] They would thus be misled into thinking that "church" referred to the bishops, monks, and priests, rather than to themselves as a collectivity. He therefore prefers *congregation*, which carries the third sense clearly, and the first and second not at all.[18]

As William Stafford writes, it was understood by the laity and church officials that "it was the clergy who were the *ecclesia*, the church."[19] But as Tyndale saw it, "the church was not the clergy, nor was it the hierarchical, legal, and ceremonial edifice sustaining the clergy, but rather the congregation of all who responded to the word of God."[20] This hierarchical understanding of *ekklēsia* did not stop with protests against Tyndale's more accurate translation of the word. One of the *Rules to be Observed in the Translation of the [King James] Bible* required the following: "The old Ecclesiastical Words to be kept, *viz.* the Word *Church* not to be translated *Congregation &c.*"[21] It seems that church officials, this time "the Anglican establishment,"[22] wanted to impose on *ekklēsia* a contemporary "ecclesiastical" understanding of the word rather than its biblically contextual definition.

---

15. William Tyndale, *An Answer to Sir Thomas More's Dialogue* (Cambridge: The University Press, [1536] 1850), 11.

16. Tyndale, *An Answer to Sir Thomas More's Dialogue*, 12.

17. Tyndale, *An Answer to Sir Thomas More's Dialogue*, 12.

18. Matthew Decoursey, "The Semiotics of Narrative in *The Obedience of a Christian Man*," *Word, Church, and State: Tyndale Quincentenary Essays*, eds. John T. Day, Eric Lund, and Anne M. O'Donnell (Washington, D.C.: The Catholic University of American Press, 1998), 77.

19. William S. Stafford, "Tyndale's Voice to the Laity" in *Word, Church, and State: Tyndale Quincentenary Essays*, 105.

20. Stafford, "Tyndale's Voice to the Laity," 106.

21. Quoted in Daniell, *The Bible in English*, 439.

22. McGrath, *The Story of the King James Bible*, 172.

Because of Rule 3, the hands of the translators were tied since they were in the employ of the king.

> [Bishop Richard] Bancroft was determined to ensure that the translation process was judiciously guided, and limit the freedom of the translators. The translators were instructed to follow strict "rules of translation," drawn up by Bancroft and approved by [King] James, designed to minimize the risk of producing a Bible that might give added credibility to Puritanism, Presbyterianism, or Roman Catholicism.[23]

Whether translated "church" or "congregation," neither Tyndale nor the ecclesiastical powers of his day had any notion of the modern-day dispensational understanding of 'church.' Even so, it's unfortunate that some of these early English translations—the Geneva Bible (1560) and the King James Version (1611)—translated *ekklēsia* as "church" since the word obscured its biblical definition of "assembly." In a similar way, because dispensationalists did not make a formal study of the translation issue, they developed a foreign understanding of *ekklēsia* that had more to do with the state of the church in the 18th century then with the actual meaning of the word. Similar to the Roman Catholic Church that read into the word *ekklēsia* their traditional understanding of the word "church," dispensationalists read back into the word "church" their newly formulated dispensational view. Robert Saucy is correct when he writes, "The use of *ekklesia* in the New Testament is limited to the senses of the local and universal church [as it is in the Old Testament]. Other connotations which have arisen with the English term *church* are not found with the New Testament word."[24] This would include the way dispensationalists understand the meaning of "church."

---

23. McGrath, *The Story of the King James Bible*, 173.
24. Saucy, *The Church in God's Program*, 18.

# Appendix B

# "False Teaching About the Last Days"

from We Can Have Revival Now
by Evangelist John R. Rice

Thousands of tracts, magazine articles, sermons and radio messages tell the people, "Jesus is coming soon!" "These last days of this dispensation" and similar phrases are very common in the Christian magazines. "Time is running out!" writes one Christian, who means that in a very short time Jesus is certain to come. "The last great mission opportunity before Jesus comes" is the way one mission field is described. A widely-known seminary professor on the west coast is quoted as saying recently, "I believe we are seeing the very closing days of this dispensation." Some Christian writers regard the atomic bomb, the rise of Russia, the founding of the new Israel state, the last world war (as they regarded the first world war), as evidence that we are in the very last days before Jesus comes.

All these people, usually faithful Bible believers, earnest Christians, have been influenced and misled by a heresy that has become widespread in recent years. This mistaken teaching holds that we are now, according to what are regarded as definite signs, in the very last few weeks or months or years before Jesus must come; that this period which they call "the last days" is more difficult than ever. They believe that sinners are harder hearted, that Satan deceives people more than ever, that world conditions make it harder to reach people with the gospel, and that for all these reasons great revivals are less likely than ever, if not impossible.

A noble and greatly-used man of God says about the blessed Billy Graham revival in Los Angeles late in 1949: "For these three thousand we are profoundly grateful to God, and our confidence in the power of mass evangelism to sweep folks into the kingdom of God has been restored."

Our brother agrees that the day of mass evangelism has not passed, though it took the Los Angeles revival to prove it. But it is noteworthy that many other people like this noble brother had been led to feel that mass evangelism had been outdated, no longer able "to sweep folks into the kingdom of God." We thank God that his confidence in this matter has been restored, but we need to face the false teaching, so prevalent, which has undermined the confidence of the people that great revivals and mass evangelism are possible today.

Again and again godly men have asked me how the work in the revival field goes. "Isn't it getting harder to have revivals?" they ask. And they are astonished when I tell them that it is not. And many others who are defeated lament that they cannot get the publicity that evangelists could once get, that local conditions like the competition of movies and radio and sports and the grip of modernists on the churches is unfavorable to revivals. And in the case of literally thousands of preachers these thoughts are connected with the teaching they have absorbed that the Lord Jesus is certain to return soon, and that in the immediate period before His return we will be unable to have great revivals.

"The great apostasy is on," people say, and they mean that they think the modernism of today proves that the end of gospel opportunity is about at hand, forgetting that great waves of infidelity have come to the world and even to the church down through many centuries, as it was in England before the Wesleyan revivals, as it came in France before that, as it came even in the early church in the first centuries of the Christian era.

The defeatism of Christians, who are not bold in preaching nor bold in prayer because they believe that Christian work is less effective than ever before, that the gospel does not bring the results that it did before, and that great revivals are less likely than ever before, is tragic indeed. And it is especially sad to see this defeatism springing up because of misinterpretation of Scriptures by Christians who really believe the Bible and love Jesus Christ.

This ultradispensational teaching that Jesus is certain to come soon, that certain signs prove the age is rushing to an early end, that the apostasy, world conditions and increased activity of Satan make gospel efforts less fruitful and revivals more difficult and unlikely, is a distressing perversion of a great truth. It is true that Jesus may come at any moment, but the ultradispensationalists do not preach the emphasis that Jesus urged, "Watch therefore, for ye know neither the day nor the hour wherein the Son of man cometh" (Matt. 25:13), and the Bible doctrine often stated and inferred that Jesus might have returned any time since Pentecost and may return now at any time. Instead, they emphasize world conditions and so-called signs, and spend their time in study of the technical details of prophecy and speculation rather than on the soul-winning work which Jesus clearly told us to be about until He should return.

Jesus would have us to watch for His coming simply because He commanded us to watch. However, the custom has grown up among a lot of premillennial Christians of looking for Christ's return because we have had the first or the second world war, or of looking for Christ's return because Zionists and infidel Jews have established the modern nation Israel in Palestine. Some are moved more by newspaper accounts than by the plain command of the Lord Jesus.

And earnest Christians ought to recognize that this ultradispensational outlook is largely a retreat from alarming conditions which Christians are not willing to face and for which they think the gospel is not sufficient. Too many Christians see the wickedness of the human heart, as expressed in Hitler's murderous career and in the far worse wickedness of communism, and their faith wavers. Instead of an attitude of aggressive evangelism with the gospel which is really the dynamite of God, sufficient for any generation, they declare that such a generation as this is too hard for God, that Satan is too active, that the apostasy is too great and conditions too unfavorable for a revival.

Let us face this defeatism for what it is. Let us recognize the lack of faith, the powerlessness for the retreat of Christians from the battle which seems hard.

Indeed, some Christians rationalize the situation and subconsciously evade the facts of their powerlessness and unbelief with the doctrine that we are in the last days, and it is impossible to win souls in any great numbers. That is bad enough, but many such Christians are actually not much concerned about soul-winning and would much rather examine the Scriptures with a kind of morbid curiosity, hoping to be thought wise, when really they shed no tears for souls and never wait before God pleading for revival or His mighty Pentecostal power.

Learned men say to the people, "Let us gather around the Word," and then they examine the Word of God as if it were a museum piece. It is as if, in a museum; soldiers gather around a sword, talk with interest of its history, how it was made, who wielded it, and tell what exploits were wrought with it in the past, yet never take this same sword to battle. So do many "Bible teachers" and "Bible students" use the Word of God. The Bible is not simply to be the object of dispassionate, technical interest and investigation. It is not a museum curiosity! It is the sword of the Spirit which ought to be used to cut sinners to the heart. It contains the gospel, the dynamite of God which is the power of God unto salvation to everyone that believeth. "Is not my word like as a fire? … and like a hammer that breaketh the rock in pieces?" (Jeremiah 23:29), the Lord asks. So all the searching of the Bible and the searching of the daily newspapers to find some "signs" that prove Christ will come within a certain specified time is contrary to the spirit of the Scriptures and does dishonor to the Lord Jesus Christ who left us here simply to get the gospel to every creature.

## I. The Bible Doctrine That Christ's Return Is Imminent Cannot Be Reconciled With the Teaching That He Could Only Return After Modern Events

There are two theories about the premillennial coming of Christ which are contradictory. Both of them cannot be true.

One theory is that Jesus will not come until certain signs have appeared. Some think Jesus cannot come until the gospel is preached again to all the world. Some think Jesus could not come until what they call "the budding of the fig tree," the re-establishment of the nation Israel as it has recently been reestablished in Palestine. Others think that Jesus could not return until the so-called "great apostasy," the wave of modernism in the church which has occurred in America in the last fifty years and is now possibly past its climax. Many would say that the first and second world wars are signs of the soon coming of Christ. If that be true, then Jesus could not have come before these wars. Others believe that certain earthquakes, that famine following the wars, that the present capital-labor controversy encouraged by socialists and communists everywhere are signs of Christ's coming, and that therefore Christ could not have come before these clashes occurred and communism and socialism reached their present popularity. I want you to see that this first and popular theory I am discussing is simply that Jesus was to come only after certain definite signs should appear.

The other and contradictory theory is that Jesus might have returned any time after Pentecost. No one knew when He would return, so it would have been possible for Him to have returned before the first or second world wars, before the evolution theory became widely prominent and the present great rage of modernism developed. He might have come before the modern missionary movement. Or he may come now at any moment. This theory, or doctrine, we will call it, is the doctrine of the imminency of Christ's return. But note carefully that this doctrine of the immanency of Christ's return contradicts the doctrine that Jesus could not come until a certain set time in a program and that He must come after a number of specified signs are fulfilled. The teaching that Christ must come at a set time or in a particular generation and only after a certain program of signs is fulfilled is entirely different from the doctrine of the imminent coming of Christ. And the imminent coming of Christ is clearly taught in the Scriptures.

I beg your patience as I state it again. It is important for us to see that one cannot hold to the imminency of Christ's return, that is, that He may come at any moment, that He might have come at any time since Pentecost as far as any one then could know, and that Christians, all through the ages, were right to expect Christ to come at any moment, and to watch for His coming, and to believe at the same time that certain signs must come first. That doctrine that Christ's coming is imminent, the time of His coming unknown and unknowable, is clearly taught in the Bible. But one cannot hold to the imminency of Christ's return, and at the same time believe that there had to be a first world war before Christ could return, or that Christ could not return before the nation Israel was established in Palestine; or that Christ could not return before the present wave of modernism and worldliness. Every reader may take his choice; he can believe in Christ's imminent return, as taught in the Scriptures, or he can believe that Christ's coming had to await certain events. The two doctrines are irreconcilable. They cannot be harmonized. The intelligent Bible believer cannot hold to both positions. And the Bible certainly clearly teaches the imminent return of Christ, that is, that Christ may return at any moment.

That being true, it will naturally be impossible for anybody to tell when we are in the last days of this dispensation. That being true, there can be no signs which definitely show the approach of the return of Christ. If Christ had to wait until certain signs appear before He can return, then His return is not imminent. On the other hand, if Paul was right to expect the Lord's return in his day, as he did, speaking of "we who are alive and remain unto the coming of the Lord" (I Thess. 4:15), then all are wrong who think that Christ's coming is now indicated by the first and second world war, the great falling away of these days, the founding of the nation Israel in Palestine recently, etc. Either Christ might have come at any moment, as He taught, or He could not return until certain other events occurred. Both cannot be true. If Christ cannot now return until the gospel is preached to some tribes in the Amazon valley, then the imminent coming of Christ could not be true.

But, let me say again, the imminency of Christ's coming is clearly taught in the Bible. To the disciples on Mount Olivet and to all succeeding generations of Christians, Jesus commanded, "Watch therefore: for ye know not what hour your Lord doth come" (Matt. 24:42). Again He said to them and to us, "Therefore be ye also ready: for in such an hour as ye think not the Son of man cometh" (vs. 44). Again He said to these disciples, and to all Christians who come after them, "Watch therefore, for ye know neither the day nor the hour wherein the Son of man cometh" (Matt. 25:13). Then He told them, "And what I say unto you I say unto all, Watch" (Mark 13:37). If these Scriptures are to be taken at honest face value, then all Christians, including those first disciples and including Christians of all ages, have been commanded to watch for Christ's return, since He might come at any moment.

Christ's second coming, then, does not now wait, and never did wait, on any world events.

## II. No One Knows Even Approximately When Jesus Will Come

In the Olivet discourse the Saviour discusses the second coming. The clearest point in all His teaching on the second coming is that no one knows when it will be. Consider Mark 13:32-37:

> "But of that day and that hour knoweth no man, no, not the angels which are in heaven, neither the Son, but the Father. Take ye heed, watch and pray: for ye know not when the time is. For the Son of man is as a man taking a far journey, who left his house, and gave authority to his servants, and to every man his work, and commanded the porter to watch. Watch ye therefore: for ye know not when the master of the house cometh, at even, or at midnight, or at the cock crowing, or in the morning: Lest coming suddenly he find you sleeping. And what I say unto you I say unto all, Watch."

**Now observe the clear teaching of the Saviour that no man can know the time:**

1. The angels do not know when Jesus will come.

2. The Lord Jesus Himself while on earth did not know when He would return.

3. Jesus said His second coming was so wholly unpredictable that it was illustrated by the servants waiting for their master's return. The master might come in the evening, midnight, cock-crowing or in the morning. In this world no one can foretell even approximately when Jesus will return and when this age will end. If the more than nineteen hundred years which have

already elapsed since Christ promised to return be divided up into four watches or periods to represent evening, midnight, cock-crowing and morning, we find that Jesus is saying that no one can know even within centuries of the time of His return.

4. The all-important teaching of Jesus about His return is that He may come at any moment. His coming is imminent.

Jesus may not come for one hundred years, for five hundred years, for one thousand years. People often say, "Jesus is coming soon." That cannot be proven by Scripture. It is not what Jesus said. Jesus said, "Behold, I come quickly" (Rev. 22:7). We know Jesus will come suddenly. Whether He will come soon or late, we do not know. Whether He will come at evening or at midnight or at cock-crowing or in the morning, we do not know. Jesus said plainly that we are not to know. We are simply to wait. We are to expect His coming, to be ready for His coming and to be doing His blessed will in carrying the gospel to every creature but we do not know even the approximate time of His coming, nor of the end of this age.

This same strong teaching is given in Matthew 24:36-39. Again we have the clear statement of Jesus that no one can know even the approximate time of His coming. Read it carefully:

"But of that day and hour knoweth no man, no, not the angels of heaven, but my Father only. But as the days of Noah were, so shall also the coming of the Son of man be. For as in the days that were before the flood they were eating and drinking, marrying and giving in marriage, until the day that Noah entered into the ark, And knew not until the flood came, and took them all away; so shall also the coming of the Son of man be."

Again Jesus plainly says that no man can know the day or hour of His return. He repeats that even the angels in Heaven do not know the time, and then He illustrates the total lack of information which any man can have about the time of the second coming. As it was in the days before the flood when people ate, drank, married, and gave in marriage and had no hint of the time when the flood would come until "the flood came and took them all away," just so surprising and unforeseen will be Christ's second coming. Before the flood they did not know even one day ahead of time when it would come. So from the words of the Lord Jesus Himself, we properly infer that we cannot know even one day ahead of time when Jesus will come. Again this question of Christ's return and the restoration of the kingdom to Israel was brought up by the disciples after Christ's resurrection. Read the discussion in Acts 1:5-7:

> "For John truly baptized with water; but ye shall be baptized with the Holy Ghost not many days hence. When they therefore were come together, they asked of him, saying, Lord, wilt thou at this time restore again the kingdom to Israel? And he said unto them, It is not for you to know the times or the seasons, which the Father hath put in his own power."

Jesus had told the disciples to tarry and wait there until they were endued with power from on high. They were to be baptized with the Holy Ghost and so supernaturally empowered for soul-winning.

Do you ever find Christians more concerned about the technical details of prophecy, more concerned about speculation as to the time of Christ's return than about soul-winning? Well, the twelve apostles before they were Spirit-filled had the same carnal viewpoint. Instead of rejoicing that they were to be filled with the Spirit for soul-winning, they immediately jumped to the hopeful conclusion that Christ referred to His return, the restoration of David's throne and the future independence of Israel. So they said, "Lord, wilt thou at this time restore again the kingdom to Israel." Then Jesus in strong and emphatic language told the disciples that the time and season of His glorious return and the restoration of Israel were not within their province at all, not matters for them to know. He said:

> "It is not for you to know the times or the seasons, which the Father hath put in his own power. But ye shall receive power, after that the Holy Ghost is come upon you: and ye shall be witnesses unto me both in Jerusalem, and in all Judaea, and in Samaria, and unto the uttermost part of the earth." Acts 1:7, 8.

It is well to remember that the carnal mind seizes on externals rather than spiritual internals. The carnal nature is more concerned with incidentals than fundamentals. Men would rather be baptized than born again. Men would rather talk in tongues than have the mighty soul-winning power of the Holy Spirit. Just so, modern speculating, ultradispensationalists prefer to look for signs rather than to obey the Great Commission and to win souls.

Let us clearly understand what Jesus taught. He said, "It is not for us to know the times or seasons" concerning the second coming. Not the day, nor the hour, not the year, not the era of the second coming can be foreseen. Jesus expressly said that the Father deliberately kept this secret and it is not one that Christians should seek to know.

## III. Date-Setting, Speculation, an Embarrassing Heresy

How it appeals to foolish human pride for a man to think, "In my superior wisdom I have figured out something others do not know!" And particularly, Bible teachers like to show their superior understanding of the Scriptures and the times, because, first if 'the discovery' is sensational and will help get a crowd of excited hearers and second, if it will be a good alibi for man's powerlessness and fruitlessness in soul-winning. Men try to make the headlines by predicting when the next war will begin and when the next depression will be upon us. One can arouse more excitement and attract more attention if he can give plausible evidence that he has discovered approximately when the Saviour will return. That indicates that such a Bible teacher is more spiritual and more discerning and more everything that a proud carnal heart desires to appear to be! It is not surprising therefore that we have constantly recurring efforts to set the approximate date of the Lord's return.

For example, more than a century ago a farmer in New York state, named Miller, started to read his Bible and discovered, he thought, what the scholars had overlooked. By making a day mean a year (which it never does) he took some of the prophecies of Daniel from out of their setting and figured that Jesus must return on a certain day in 1846. He convinced many of his neighbors that he was right and these Millerites made them white robes and got ready for the rapture; but they waited in vain on hilltops and haystacks for the Saviour to catch them away.

One day last summer I sat at dinner with Dr. Lowe, a professor of Biblical Interpretation at the Practical Bible Training School, Johnson City, New York. He told me that his people lived in the community of Farmer Miller and many of them had been convinced that Jesus was coming on the day announced by Miller. One uncle planted no crops. Why should he when he wouldn't be there to gather them? He showed his faith by sitting on his front porch while others toiled. But Jesus did not come and that winter thirteen of his cows starved while he and his family barely lived on the milk from one cow and from corn meal given by a neighbor.

Seventh-Day Adventists are the spiritual descendants of the Millerites, and many of them still try to figure the time of the Lord's return by misinterpretation of Daniel's prophecy.

How foolish to think that the secret of the date of Christ's return is given in the book of Daniel and that Jesus and none of His disciples knew it!

The British-Israel cult could not find the date of Christ's return in the Bible so they turned instead to the Great Pyramid and they count it an inspired revelation like the Bible. In the ascending passage leading to the tombs of the kings in the pyramid they figured that one larger portion with a higher ceiling would represent the time of Christ's return; so they took a tape measure from the supposed original edge of the pyramid through the passage to the enlargement. They counted every inch a year and so began to foretell when Jesus would come!

One greatly-heralded British-Israel teacher in Los Angeles predicted that Jesus would come September 16, 1936, as I recall. Needless to say, his prophecy was proved wrong and his influence was broken. Date-setting for the return of the Saviour has always been a heresy which turns out with embarrassment.

In my boyhood I saw in the old opera house at Gainesville, Texas, a picture prepared under the direction of "Pastor Russell" of the "Millenial Dawn" cult. He predicted, "Millions now living will never die," and his books agreed that Jesus would come in 1914. When 1914 brought not the return of the Saviour but the First World War, Pastor Russell said Jesus came invisibly. The Russellites, later called Rutherfordites, now called Jehovah's Witnesses, still teach this heresy. But they still die!

Since speculation as to the date of the return of Christ has proved so foolish in the past and always is connected with heresy, it seems that Bible-believing Christians would take seriously the word of Jesus, "It is not for you to know the times or the seasons, which the Father hath put in his own power" (Acts 1:7).

Such speculations are carnal, not spiritual, and grow out of human pride and from misinterpretation of the Bible. No one knows even approximately when Jesus will return. No one knows the day, the year, the generation when Jesus will return. He may come today. Praise His name, I would be glad to see Him; but there is no way for any honest Bible student to foretell whether Jesus will come soon or after hundreds of years.

# IV. There Are No "Signs" of Christ's Coming by Which We May Know It Is Near

In my early ministry I sometimes preached on "Signs of Christ's Second Coming." I have a chapter on that subject in my book, The Coming Kingdom of Christ. In a second edition I was compelled to modify the chapter. I was compelled to see that the next thing on God's program, as far as Bible prophecy is concerned, is Christ's coming in the air to receive His saints when the Christian dead shall be raised and living saints changed and called up to meet Him in the air. That event is imminent; that means it may occur at any time. If Christ may come at any moment, then obviously we need not wait for any signs. And any signs could not make Christ's coming other than imminent, could not prove He would come this year or day and could not prove He would not come this year or day. The Bible teaching is that Jesus may come at any moment, signs or no signs. He could have come even in apostolic days before any recent events could have occurred.

But did not Jesus speak about signs of His coming? Jesus spoke particularly of one sign but that was not a sign of the first phase of His coming and the rapture but a sign which will occur after the rapture, at the close of the tribulation period, before Christ comes visibly, triumphantly, to the earth to reign.

This sign is mentioned in the Olivet discourse of Jesus. In Matthew 24:3 we have the disciples' question, "Tell us, when shall these things be? and what shall be the sign of thy coming, and of the end of the world?"

You see, the disciples asked, "What shall be the sign of thy coming, and of the end of the world?" Or better translated, "What is the sign of thy coming, and of the end of the age?" In Luke 21:25-27 Jesus answered as follows about signs:

> "And there shall be signs in the sun, and in the moon, and in the stars; and upon the earth distress of nations, with perplexity; the sea and the waves roaring; Men's hearts failing them for fear, and for looking after those things which are coming on the earth: for the powers of heaven shall be shaken. And then shall they see the Son of man coming in a cloud with power and great glory."

It is similar to the passage in Matthew 24:29,30 where Jesus mentioned the sign in these words:

"Immediately after the tribulation of those days shall the sun be darkened, and the moon shall not give her light, and the stars shall fall from heaven, and the powers of the heavens shall be shaken: And then shall appear the sign of the Son of man in heaven: and then shall all the tribes of the earth mourn, and they shall see the Son of man coming in the clouds of heaven with power and great glory."

**Note the following facts about Jesus' answer:**

1. The sign is to be "immediately after the tribulation.; I understand from the Scriptures that the tribulation cannot begin till after the rapture, so Jesus must come into the air to receive His saints before the Great Tribulation. "The sign" is after Christ's coming for His saints, not before.

2. We see that Christ's coming referred to by the prophets was His coming to the earth to reign after the rapture. Jews would naturally look forward to the part of Christ's coming that will affect them, when Jews will be regathered from all the earth, when the "angels...shall gather together his elect from the four winds, from one end of heaven to the other" (Matt. 24:31), when Christ will destroy all the enemies of the Jews and overthrow all Gentile dominion and restore David's throne in Jerusalem and sit on David's throne. It is this kingdom that the apostles asked about in Acts 1:6: "Wilt thou at this time restore again the kingdom to Israel?" Gentile Christians are naturally more concerned about the rapture, the first phase of Christ's coming. But Old Testament prophecies in the interest of Jews center mainly in the second phase of Christ's coming, His revelation to Israel.

After the world is in the Great Tribulation time it will be very simple for those who know the Bible to learn when Jesus will return. There must be seven years in Daniel's seventieth week. The Great Tribulation time itself is clearly announced to continue 3 1/2 years, 42 months, 1,260 days. (Dan. 7:25; Rev. 11:2, 3; Rev.12:14.) The terrifying reign of the Man of Sin is definitely limited. After the first phase of Christ's second coming, the rapture, the second phase must come within a specified time. And just before Jesus returns to the earth with saints and angels to fight the Battle of Armageddon and set up His kingdom, the sign of His coming will appear in the heavens.

There is no sign of Christ's coming promised before the rapture. No preacher has a Scriptural warrant, I think, for preaching that current events are signs of Christ's soon return. Mussolini was not the Antichrist, as some Bible teachers said, and they will be as foolish if they so designate Stalin or Tito.

We are not to believe Christ is coming because of some "signs" but because He said so!

## V. Christ's Coming for His Saints Does Not Await the Preaching of the Gospel to Every Creature

A great missionary leader, a friend whom I greatly admire and love, has recently published a book in which he pictures an imaginary scene. Satan is pictured as in counsel with the princes of darkness, the leading demons who supervise his work in various countries. Some demons report proudly that the gospel is not being preached in the countries over which they bear evil sway, and all gloat that Christ cannot now return until these people hear the gospel. Missionaries shot down or discouraged before they can enter Afghanistan, and the failure of missionary groups to reach other isolated tribes, is cited. And then Satan himself and his demons are pictured as being greatly distressed and defeated because at last there is prospect of the gospel being preached to every creature. Now, though they have defeated Christ's planned return so long, it appears that the gospel will be preached to every creature and the Saviour will return.

It is here taught that Jesus cannot return to take away His saints until the gospel is again preached to all the world. But I believe that this is an entirely wrong interpretation of Scripture. The gospel has already been preached to all the world in early Christian times, if not in this generation. And if Jesus could not return until the gospel is preached to every tribe again, then His plain commands to watch, that He might come at any time, would seem out of place and misleading, if not actually dishonest. That surely we cannot concede. The imminent coming of Christ, so clearly taught in the Scripture, means that He might have come at any moment, may come at any moment now, whether the gospel is preached again to all the world or not.

Mistaught people sometimes think that Matthew 24:14 refers to a sign of Christ coming. It says, "this gospel of the kingdom shall be preached in all the world for a witness unto all nations; and then shall the end come." But the context shows that this is a message primarily for Jews who will be living in the tribulation time and not for us today. The next verse mentions the Abomination of Desolation, when the Antichrist will stand in the temple in Jerusalem claiming to be God, which event must come after the rapture and which begins the Great Tribulation time. The following verse speaks of the flight of the Jews from the Man of Sin in those days, and verse 21 plainly says, "For then shall be great tribulation, such as was not since the beginning of the world to this time, no, nor ever shall be."

So during the Great Tribulation time the gospel of salvation will be preached to the world in view of Christ's literal return. The preaching of the gospel to all the world mentioned in Matthew 24:14 will be after the first phase of Christ's coming, not before.

The simple truth is that the gospel has already been preached to all the world. I remember that Dr. R.A. Torrey called attention to two or three Scriptures which show that the gospel has already been preached to all the world. In Acts 2:5, "there were dwelling at Jerusalem Jews, devout men, out of every nation under heaven" and these men heard the gospel at Pentecost. In Romans 1:8 Paul says "that your faith is spoken of throughout the whole world," and how could people have heard of the wonderful faith of the fine Christians at Rome if they had not heard the gospel? Colossians 1:4-6 also says that the gospel had come to all the world in Paul's time. So Matthew 24:14 could not teach and does not teach that the gospel is to be yet preached in all the world before Jesus comes.

Besides, if the preaching of the gospel to some unknown tribe in Central America or the Amazon valley is an event that must occur before Jesus can come, then Christ's coming could not be imminent and the Scriptural warning that we must watch since Jesus may come any day or year would be foolish.

Let us say again there are no signs that will indicate when Jesus is to come and there is not a single prophetic event which must come before the rapture of the saints.

## VI. The Modern Establishment of a Nation Israel in Palestine Not "the Budding of the Fig Tree," Not a Sign of Christ's Soon Return

Some months ago Editor Meldau, of Christian Victory magazine, my esteemed friend, wrote me and about a dozen well-known Bible teachers, asking us to prepare a statement for a forthcoming issue of his good magazine on a subject something like this, "Is the Re-establishment of Israel as an independent nation in Palestine recently, the budding of the fig tree mentioned in Matthew 24:32, 33, and a sign of Christ's coming?" I was glad to give my answer, and glad indeed when the symposium came out in the good magazine that nearly all the Bible teachers agreed that the recent establishing of an independent nation of Jews in Palestine did not fulfill the prophecy of the budding of the fig tree as foretold in Matthew 24:32, 33, and was not especially a sign of Christ's soon return.

Since that matter has often been misunderstood, let us read the passage involved and see clearly what the Saviour said in that Olivet discourse, about the budding of the fig tree. Matthew 24:29-34 reads as follows:

> "Immediately after the tribulation of those days shall the sun be darkened, and the moon shall not give her light, and the stars shall fall from heaven, and the powers of the heavens shall be shaken: And then shall appear the sign of the Son of man in heaven: and then shall all the tribes of the earth mourn, and they shall see the Son of man coming in the clouds of heaven with power and great glory. And he shall send his angels with a great sound of a trumpet, and they shall gather together his elect from the four winds, from one end of heaven to the other. Now learn a parable of the fig tree; When his branch is yet tender, and putteth forth leaves, ye know that summer is nigh: So likewise ye, when ye shall see all these things, know that it is near, even at the doors. Verily I say unto you, This generation shall not pass, till all these things be fulfilled."

**Let us note very simply some of the things which Jesus taught in this passage:**

1. The time discussed is at the close of the Great Tribulation, and some time after the rapture of the saints. It is "immediately after the tribulation of those days…" (vs. 29). So the parable of the fig tree does not apply to these days before the rapture and before the Great Tribulation, but to the days "immediately after the tribulation." Nothing before the tribulation period could be meant here. The recent developments in Palestine are not meant, it is quite clear, since they did not happen "immediately after the tribulation of those days…"

2. The meaning of the parable is clearly explained. Certain events which will follow the Great Tribulation are like a fig tree whose branch is tender and which puts forth leaves in the spring. These events are the appearing of the sign of the Son of man in Heaven, when Christ starts to return, and the sight of the Son of man coming in the clouds of Heaven; and the sending of the angels to regather Israelites from all over the world. Then verse 33 says, "So likewise ye, when ye shall see all these things, know that it is near, even at the doors." When converted Israelites at the close of the Great Tribulation time, or other saints converted in that tribulation time, see Christ coming in the clouds of Heaven with power and great glory to set up His throne at Jerusalem and reign on the earth, and when they see the angels of God sent out miraculously around the world with the great sound of a trumpet to regather the elect, God's chosen nation Israel, from among all the lands of the earth, then these troubled people may know that Christ's coming and reign is immediately at hand. So there would be no use in speculating about the matter, because the meaning of the parable is clearly given in the words of the Saviour Himself.

And we should distinguish between the present immigration of godless Jews into Palestine, unconverted and unrepentant, and going by human means and with human purposes, from that other great gathering when every Jew left alive in the world will be gathered by the angels and brought to Palestine at Christ's return. The present movement in Palestine is human. It is not particularly a subject of Bible prophecy. It has no particular significance except that the Scripture indicates that some Jews will be in Palestine and will make a treaty with the Antichrist in the tribulation time. The present influx of Jews into Palestine is not the great regathering which will be done miraculously by the angels of God when Jesus returns in person to reign, after the rapture and after the tribulation period.

3. We must make sure to notice, too, that the coming of Christ here mentioned is the second phase of His coming. It is not His coming into the air invisibly to raise the Christian dead and receive them and us together, and carry us away for a honeymoon in Heaven. This is not the coming of Christ for His

saints. It is the coming of Christ with the raptured saints, after the tribulation is over. The rapture will come, as most reputable premillennial Bible teachers agree, before the Great Tribulation time. Then after the Great Tribulation (which will occur in Daniel's seventieth week, as I believe), Christ will return with these saints and with angels to fight the battle of Armageddon, to destroy the kingdom of the Antichrist, and to set up His throne at Jerusalem and reign on the earth for a thousand years of joy and peace. There are two separate phases of Christ's coming. That for which we wait is His coming into the air to receive His saints. Then after the tribulation time, those who will have been converted on the earth will long for Christ's return, with us, to set up His kingdom. It is this second phase of Christ's coming, when He shall come literally to the earth to take charge and to reign, that is discussed in this passage.

4. Jesus said in verse 34, "Verily I say unto you, This generation shall not pass, till all things be fulfilled." I rather think that "this generation" means the race of Jews and the race will not be destroyed despite all the Hitlers and Antichrists. Dr. Scofield's notes on this verse say about generation:

> Gr. *genea*, the primary definition of which is, 'race, kind, family, stock, breed.' (So all lexicons.) That the word is used in this sense here is sure because none of 'these things,' *i.e.* the world-wide preaching of the kingdom, the great tribulation, the return of the Lord in visible glory, and the regathering of the elect, occurred at the destruction of Jerusalem by Titus, A.D. 70. The promise is, therefore, that the generation-nation, or family of Israel—will be preserved unto 'these things'; a promise wonderfully fulfilled to this day.

But if the word generation here means people living in one particular life-span, it still could mean only that group living "immediately after the tribulation of those days…" as Jesus Himself places them in verse 29. The so-called "budding of the fig tree" cannot happen until after Christ comes for His saints, after the Great Tribulation.

I am glad personally that there is now a land where oppressed Jews will be welcomed. But these Jews, going back in unbelief, have possession of only a very small portion of the land of Israel. They do not even have undisputed possession of Jerusalem. They have not gone back under the blessing and forgiveness of God. Blindness in part is still upon Israel.

The veil is not yet taken away from their faces. The great future regathering and conversion of Israel will take place by supernatural means after the tribulation time. And the establishment of a little state called Israel in recent months is not a sign that Christ may come soon. Christ may come very soon, but it needs no sign such as that to prove it. He may not come for long years. No one knows.

Let me stress with all my soul that current events do not especially affect the simple fact, clearly taught throughout the Bible, that we can have revival now, that God is in the saving business, and that any time God's people meet God's requirements, they may have His glorious power and the manifestation of it in the saving of multitudes of souls, in great revivals. Those who go by the newspapers and are greatly excited by current events may feel that the atomic bomb, the hydrogen bomb, the upsurge of communism, the modernism in many churches, the possibility of a third world war, and the establishment of the modern nation Israel, mean we are in "the last days," and that therefore great revivals are impossible. But those who steadfastly depend upon the words of Christ will remember that "The grass withereth, and the flower thereof falleth away: But the word of the Lord endureth for ever" (I Pet. 1:24, 25). The harvest is still great and the labourers few. If God's people, called by His name, shall humble themselves, and pray, and seek His face, and turn from their wicked ways, God will hear from Heaven, will forgive their sin, and heal their land, as He promised in II Chronicles 7:14. All of God's promises are still true. God's tender heart toward sinners still yearns for them to be saved. God's Holy Spirit has all the convicting and saving power He ever had. The Word of God is still quick and powerful and sharper than a two-edged sword. The blessed promise of Jesus, "He that believeth on me, the works that I do shall he do also; and greater works than these shall he do; because I go unto my Father" (John 14:12), is still true. Do not let false teachings and heresies about these so-called "last days" keep you from believing the Word of God, that we can have revivals now!

# Index

## A

**Abbott, John S. C. and Jacob Abbott**
   on *oikoumenē* 124
**Abrahamic covenant, the**
   as everlasting, yet conditional 68
   as everlasting, yet postponed 65
   circumcision and 95–98
   for Abraham's true descendants 8, 77
   land promises fulfilled 72, 75
   refuting postponement theories 69–71
   related to the Noahic covenant 67
**Alexander, J. A.**
   on *oikoumenē* 139–140
**Allen, Ronald B.**
   on circumcision's transition 97
**animal sacrifices**
   ended by Antiochus Epiphanes 108
   Ezekiel's temple and 113–114
      reinstatement of ceremonial laws in 116–117
   fulfilled in Christ 75–77, 105
   reinstatement of
      as heresy 102
      "as memorials" 100–101
      "for atonement" 99, 116
   unnecessary in the New Covenant 83, 86
**Antichrist, the**
   dealings with Israel during Great Tribulation
      biblical silence on covenants 93
      purported covenants with Israel 29
   not the "he" of Daniel 9:27 93
   Revelation's silence on 93
**Aquinas, Thomas** 51
**Armageddon**
   explained in its historical context 143
   name-dropped by futurists 30, 37, 38, 39, 86, 185, 189

## B

**Bancroft, Bishop Richard**
   promoting ecclesiastical hegemony 171
**Berkhof, Louis**
   concerning historical context 130–131
**Beza, Theodore** 52
**Boyd, Alan Patrick**
   on the church fathers and Israel 51
**Brightman, Thomas** 53
**Brown, John**
   on *oikoumenē* 142
   on the future of the Jews 61–62
**Bucer, Martin** 52

## C

**Calvin, John**
   on the future of the Jews 52
**Carrington, Philip**
   on Armageddon 143
**Chafer, Lewis Sperry**
   on Israel's dispersions and restorations 78, 86
   on the Abrahamic versus the Mosaic covenant 96
   Seven Biblical Signs of the Times 36
**"Church Age," the**
   as a parenthesis in prophecy 22, 34, 43, 85
   beginning at Pentecost 90
   Israel-Church distinction and 35
   seven churches of Revelation 1 and 33
      Laodicean 32
   the rapture as the end of 25
   the weeks of Daniel and 11
**church fathers, the** 51
**circumcision**
   Ezekiel's prophetic reinstatement of
      as problematic for dispensationalists 116

Jesus as the fulfillment of 76
of the heart 8
the "everlasting" nature of 96
   dispensational silence on 97–98
the Millenial reinstatement of 95–96
   as contrary to Christ's finished work 98–99, 102
   lack of dispensational thought on 97–98
   Revelation 20's silence on 114

**Clarke, Adam**
on *oikoumenē* 126

**continuity of God's covenants, the**
Gentiles also 19, 82, 91
the church as extension 19–23
the meaning of "everlasting" 65–67
   according to dispensationalists
      Allan MacRae 70
      Arnold G. Fruchtenbaum 69
      John H. Walton 70
   circumcision as an "everlasting covenant" and 95–98
   Israelite land and 36, 75
   refuting postponement theories 71–72, 102
unconditionality 79, 97

**Cowles, Henry**
on Jeremiah 33:22 77
on *oikoumenē* 136–137
on the temple John measured 112

**Cyril of Alexandria**
*Explanatio in Epistolam ad Romanos* 51

# D

**Dabney, Robert L.** 62
**Dallas Theological Seminary**
the future of dispensationalism and 4
**DeJong, J. A.** 63
**dispensationalism's Holocaust problem** 86–87
**dispensational Judaizing** 101
**Doddridge, Philip**
on *oikoumenē* 125

# E

**earthquakes as prophetic signs**
as God's judgment in all ages 158
dispensationalist claims 151
   Michael D. Evans 151
   Carl G. Johnson 151
   Peter LaLonde 151
   David Allen Lewis 151
   Hal Lindsey 152, 159
   Jack Van Impe 151
not becoming more frequent 154–157
   seem frequent due to modern detection and media 160
Olivet Discourse and 152–153
   "this generation" means this generation 153–154

**Edwards, Jonathan**
on the future of the Jews 59–60
preterism, the future conversion of Jews and 63

*ekklēsia*
as common to both Testaments 14
as "congregation" rather than "church" 167–171
*qāhāl* and 15
"Replacement Theology" and 83
the continuity of the covenant and 9, 12–23

**Elliott, Melvin**
biblical uses of *ekklēsia* 168

**Ellis, E. Earle**
on dating the book of Revelation 112

**English, E. Schuyler**
espousing "intercalary periods" 28
on the Church replacing Israel 89

**Ezekiel's Temple** 113–118

# F

**Falwell, Jerry**
on Israel and the imminent Rapture 30

**Flender, Otto**
on *oikoumenē* 138

**Fruchtenbaum, Arnold G.**
on Israel's dispersions and restorations 78, 86
on the future Jewish Holocaust 2, 92
on the meaning of "everlasting" 69–70

**future conversion of the Jews, the**
Charles Hodge on 61
the church fathers on 51
Elnathan Parr on 55
Iain Murray on 53–54
J. A. DeJong on 63
John Brown on 61

John Calvin on 52
John Murray on 62
John Owen on 55
Jonathan Edwards on 59
Martin Bucer on 52–53
Martin Luther on 52
Peter Martyr on 54
the Reformers on 49
Richard Sibbes on 55
Robert Haldane on 60
Robert L. Dabney on 62
Samuel Rutherford on 55
Theodore Beza on 52
The Savoy Declaration on 58
Thomas Aquinas on 51
Thomas Brightman on 53
Thomas Goodwin on 59
Thomas Ridgeley on 56–57
Thomas V. Moore on 61
Walter Smith on 58
Westminster Directory for Public Worship on 57
Westminster Larger Catechism on Question 191 56
William Perkins on 55

**futurism**
"all the earth" and 132
as opposed to preterism 120
Matthew 24 and Jerusalem's destruction 119
necessitating a Millenial temple 112–113
necessitating a pre-trib Rapture 103

## G

**Gaebelein, Arno C.**
dismissing preterism (footnote) 123
premillennialism and Anti-Semitism 88
**Geisler, Norman L.**
on "every creature under heaven" 146
***Geneva Bible***
on the future conversion of Jews 49
on the future conversion of the Jews 54
translating *ekklēsia* as "church" 167, 171
**Gill, John**
on *oikoumenē* 125
**Goodwin, Thomas** 59
**Gouge, William**
on *oikoumenē* in Hebrews 2:5 141
**Gray, James M.**
premillennialism and Anti-Semitism 87–88

**Gray, James R.**
on the unfulfilled sign of the global gospel 145
**Great Tribulation, the**
Anti-Semitism and 87
as a distinctive of dispensational premillennialism 1
as after the Rapture 184
as a future Jewish Holocaust 56, 92
as restarting the "prophetic clock" 11, 42–43
as the restarting of the "prophetic clock" 85
Daniel 9:24-7 and 93
the "fig tree" and 187–188
the rebuilt temple and 104

## H

**Haldane, Robert** 60
**Henry, Matthew**
on *oikoumenē* 128
**Hitchcock, Mark**
against "the fig tree" representing Israel 45
altering his predictions based on current events 38
equivocating on Rapture signs 30
on Daniel's weeks 25
on Ezekiel and John measuring the temple 112
on signs of the imminent Rapture 31, 39, 40
on the church replacing Israel 89
**Hodge, Charles** 61
**Hodges, Zane C.**
on the fulfillment of Joel's prophecy at Pentecost 18–19
**Horner, Barry** 84
**Hughes, Philip Edgcumbe**
on *oikoumenē* 141–142
on the continuity of the assembly of believers 13–14, 23
**hyperbole**
"all creation under heaven" and 146
as described by "literalist" 73
Flavius Josephus using 157
found throughout the Bible 130
*kosmos* and 143
Milton Terry on 129
*oikoumenē* and 121, 139, 140

## I

**Ice, Thomas**
    against date-setting the rapture 31–32
    on "literal interpretation" 166
    on "stage-setting" for the rapture 42–43
    on the future of dispensationalism 4
    on the gospel being preached to the "whole world" 119
    on the reinstatement of ceremonial laws 101
    on the temples in Ezekiel and John 111–112
    on the third temple 104
    on unfulfilled promises to Israel 22, 89–91
    putting words in Peter's mouth 17

**intercalary periods of history** 21, 28, 89, 91

**Ironside, H. A.**
    on parenthetical periods (footnote) 68
    on the "Church Age" as a parenthesis 11

**Israel-Church distinction**
    Anti-Semitism and 83
    as a distinctive of dispensational premillenialism 1, 2, 11–12
    definition of 11
    ekklesia and 12–13, 167–168
    the Rapture and 92, 93

**Israel, The modern State of**
    as a purported fulfillment of Bible prophecy 31, 34, 35, 39, 45, 78
    refutation 94
    "fig tree" and 44–46

## J

**Jenkins, Jerry**
    claiming "literal interpretation" 166
    giving signs of the signless 33
    on the "fig tree" 45

**Jeremiah, David**
    on the present state of Israel 84
    signs of a signless Rapture
        church attendee's confusion 41–42

**Johnson, B. W.**
    on *oikoumenē* 124

**Josephus, Flavius**
    on olive trees in Galilee 164
    on the destruction of Jerusalem 128, 157

## K

**Kaiser, Jr., Walter C.** 72
    on "Replacement Theology" 81

**Kent, Jr., Homer A.**
    detecting hyperbole in Colossians 1:23 146

***King James Bible, the***
    mistranslating *ekklēsia* in Acts 7:38 16
    mistranslating *oikoumenē* in Matthew 24:14 120
    Rules to be Observed in the Translation of 170
    translation of *ekklēsia* 167, 171

***kosmos* (world)**
    absent in Colossians 1:6 145
    absent in Matthew 24:14 134
    compared to *oikoumenē* 137–139
    importance of historical context 120, 149
    Matthew 24:14 compared to 26:13 135
    interpreted as "known world" 144
    sometimes locally limited 122, 137, 143, 147

## L

**LaHaye, Tim**
    altering predictions based on current events 34
    defending the Rapture's lack of biblical support 93
    giving signs of the signless 33, 39
    on modern Israel's rebirth as "Super Sign" 26, 44
    on "stage-setting" the Rapture 42
    on the church replacing Israel 89
    on the "fig tree" as modern Israel 45
    on the "literal interpretation" of the Bible 166
    on the past imminency of the Rapture 33
    on the rebuilt temple 114
    on the reinstatement of ceremonial laws 98, 101, 116
    on the signlessness of the Rapture 32
    putting words in Peter's mouth 90

**Lewis, C. S.**
    on *ekklēsia* and the invisible church 169

**Lightfoot, J. B.**
    on hyperbole in Colossians 1:23 145–146
    selectively quoted by Thomas Ice 145–146

# Index

**Lightfoot, John**
   on *oikoumenē* 127
   on the gospel to the whole world 119
**Lindsey, Hal**
   charging preterists with Anti-Semitism 83
   inisting falsely on his "literal" interpretation 166
   locusts from the pit= Cobra helicopters 164
   on earthquakes as prophetic signs 152
   on modern Israel as "super-sign" 35
   on the frequency of earthquakes 159
   predicting oil in Israel 161
**literal interpretation**
   "all the earth" and 133, 145
   animal sacrifices and 99
   definition of 65–66, 166
   dispensationalist claims 7, 73
   dispensationalist equivocating on "literal" 73
   of the Abrahamic covenant 71
   physical circumcision and 96–97
   the meaning of "everlasting" and 65–67
   the third temple and 105, 113
**Luther, Martin**
   Anti-Semitism of 52, 85
   on the future conversion of the Jews 52

## M

**MacArthur, John**
   ignorant of postmillenialists 50, 63
   on Israel's election 50
   on the "fig tree" 46
   on the signless, imminent Rapture 26–27
   on why Calvinists should be premillenialists 49
**Marsden, George**
   on premillenialism and Anti-Semitism 88–89
**Martyr, Peter**
   on the future conversion of the Jews 49, 54
**Moore, Thomas V.** 61
**Murray, Iain**
   2001 Shepherds' Conference and 56
   Barry Horner and 84
   John MacArthur and 63
   on the future of the Jews 53–54
**Murray, John**
   on dispensationalism 3–4
   on the future of the Jews 62–63
   on the "olive tree" and unbelief 10

## N

*Nelson Study Bible*
   on Genesis 17:8 96–97
   on the Noahic covenant 68
**New Covenant, the**
   animal sacrifices and 101
      critique of dispensational judaizing 102
   as an extension not "supersession" 82–83
   as fulfillment of OT promises 77
      Jeremiah 31:35-37 94
   circumcision and 95–97
      circumcision of the heart 98
   Ezekiel's temple and 117
   "horse and buggy" analogy 86
**New Jerusalem, the**
   Rebuilt Temple and 114–115
   the new center of worship and 115
**Noahic covenant, the** 67–69

## O

**Ogden, Arthur M.**
   on Revelation 12:6 148
***oikoumenē*** **(world)**
   as "inhabited world" 120, 136, 138
   commentaries on 122–123
      Adam Clarke 126
      B.W. Johnson 124
      John Gill 125
      John Lightfoot 127
      John S. C. Abbott and Jacob Abbott 124
      John Wesley 128
      Matthew Henry 128
      Milton Terry 129
      modern commentators misleading 123
      Philip Doddridge 125
      Thomas Scott 125
   dating the book of Revelation and 142–143
   immediate context of Matthew 24:14 134
   importance of historical context 120, 130, 149
   in Hebrews 141–142
   in Luke and Acts 137–140
   in Revelation 142–143
   in Romans 140–141

Lexicons on 121–122
Thomas Ice's failure to correctly interpret 150
used instead of *kosmos*
    in Acts 17:31 139
    in Hebrews 1:6 141
    in Hebrews 2:5 141
    in Luke 21:26 137
    in Matthew 24:14 134–135
    in Revelation 16:14 143
    in Romans 10:18 140

**oil as a prophetic sign**
dispensationalist claims
    Lindsey, Hal 161
    Spillman, James R. and Steven M. Spillman 161
    "may he [Asher] dip his foot in oil" 164–165
    Deere, Jack S. explains 164
    oil in the Bible (olive) 165
    oil in the Bible (pitch or tar) 165
    proving a point from Job 12:22 165
    "the deep that lies beneath" 162–163
    Leupold, H. C. explains 163

*olam* (forever) 69–71

**Olivet Discourse, the**
earthquakes, storms, and 154–156
Jonathan Edwards on 59
*oikoumenē* and 137
past fulfillment of 152–153
the destruction of Jerusalem and 63, 92
the "fig tree" 44–46
the worldwide gospel and 147

**Owen, John**
on *oikoumenē* 141
on the future of the Jews 55
preterism, the future conversion of Jews and 63

# P

**Parr, Elnathan** 55
**Patterson, Dr. Paige**
on the present state of Israel 47, 84
**Pentecost, J. Dwight**
on circumcision 95
on the Abrahamic covenant 65
    postponement due to Israel's rebellion 68

**Perkins, William** 55
**Pettegrew, Larry D.**
on the "fig tree" and modern Israel 46
**Preterism**
interpretation of Matthew 24 120–121
Thomas Ice attempting to refute 119–120
**promises made to Israel**
fulfilled, not postponed 17, 20–22, 91
land promises 97–98
    fulfilled, not postponed 71–75
**Protocols of the Elders of Zion**
premillennialism and Anti-Semitism 87–88
*Puritan Hope, The* 54–59

# R

**Radmacher, Earl D.**
against modern Israel as a sign of the Rapture 35
*Nelson Study Bible*
    on God's "everlasting" covenant 97
    on the Noahic Covenant 68
on *ekklēsia* (footnote) 15
on the imminent rapture (footnote) 26
**Rapture, the**
as a distinctive of dispensational premillennialism 1, 92
as following great earthquakes 151
as having and not having signs 27
as signless and imminent 25, 27, 183
    necessary for "Church Age" parenthesis 28
as the end of the "Church Age" 85
dispensationalists against date-setting 32, 40
*engus* ("near at hand") and 26
failed predictions of viii, 5, 181
Israel's 1948 nationhood and ix, 31, 35, 39
Israel's prophetic significance and 89
lack of biblical support for 93
modern signs preclude past imminency 25–26, 33–36
signs as "stage-setting" 41–43
signs of the signless 30–31
signs that come after 186, 188–189
**Rebuilt Temple, the (The Millenial Temple)**
Acts 2 silent on 83
already standing in Jesus' day 108–110
as a distinctive of dispensational premillennialism 1, 103

Daniel 9:26-27
   interpretation of 107–108
   misreading of 93
lack of biblical support for 103–104, 113
"literal interpretation" and 107
Revelation 11:1-2
   interpretation of 110–111
Romans 11 silent on 8
the reinstatement of animal sacrifices and 76
the unsupported requirement of 105
unnecessary because of Jesus' finished work 105
   dispensationalist's backward thinking 86
"Replacement Theology" (supersessionism)
   charges of Anti-Semitism 83–84
   compared to the abortion controversy 2
   definition of 81
   dispensationalist claims 81
      as "a tactical red herring" 83
   New Covenant extends not replaces 83
Rice, John R.
   Appendix B 173–190
      arguing for a signless Second Coming 183–185
      arguing that date-setting is heresy 181–182
      arguing that modern Israel is not "fig tree" 186–190
      modern Rapture signs preclude past imminency 176–178
      on the gospel preached to every creature 185–186
      on the uncertain date of the Second Coming 178–181
   critical of modern state of Israel as fulfillment of Bible prophecy 86
   critical of signs preceding the Rapture 40
   on the present state of Israel 47
Ridgeley, Thomas 56
Roman Catholic Church
   contested Tyndale's translation 168–169
*Rules to be Observed in the Translation of the [King James] Bible* 170–171
Rutherford, Samuel 55
Ryrie, Charles C.
   on "literal interpretation" 65
   on the Abrahamic covenant 69
   on the essence of dispensationalism 11, 35
   on the future Jewish Holocaust 2, 63, 91–92

# S

**Saucy, Robert L.**
   on the transformation of dispensationalism 5
   on the translation of *ekklēsia* 16, 171
*Savoy Declaration, The* **58**
*Scofield Reference Bible*
   Arno C. Gaebelein and 88
   E. Schuyler English and 28
   interpretation of "at hand" 28
   on the "Church Age" parenthesis 89
   on the "fig tree" 45
   on the reinstatement of ceremonial laws 99
   revisions of 4
   the recent invention of dispensationalism and 3, 50
**Scott, Thomas**
   on *oikoumenē* 125
**Shute, Dan**
   on the church fathers and the mass conversion of Jews 51
**Sibbes, Richard 55**
**Smith, Walter 58**
**Spargimino, Larry**
   on interpreting "near" and "shortly" 29–30
**Spurgeon, Charles H.**
   on the madness of prophetic fanaticism vii
**Stafford, William**
   on Tyndale's translation of *ekklēsia* 170
**Stanton, Gerald B.**
   on the signless rapture 25
**Stitzinger, James F. 27**
**Strandberg, Todd and Terry James**
   equivocating about Rapture signs 27

# T

**Terry, Milton**
   on interpreting "near" and "shortly" 29
   on interpreting texts within their historical context 130–131
   on *oikoumenē* 129
**Tertullian**
   *De Pudicitia* 51
*Testaments of the Twelve Patriarchs, The* **51**
**Theodore of Mopsuestia**

In Epistolam Pauli ad Romanos  51
**Toussaint, Stanley D.**
   on the fulfillment of Joel's prophecy at Pentecost  18, 90
   silent on *oikoumenē* (footnote)  124
**Tyndale, William**
   *An Answer to Sir Thomas More's Dialogue*  170
   martyred for his accurate translations  169
   translating *ekklēsia* as "congregation"  168, 170

# W

**Walvoord, John F.**
   on Israel's 1948 nationhood  5
   on Israel's dispersions and restorations  86
   on parenthetical periods  68
   on the Abrahamic covenant  71
   on the "fig tree" not being Israel  45
   on the future Jewish Holocaust  92
   on the signless Rapture's signs  36–37
   silent on *oikoumenē* (footnote)  124
**Wesley, John**
   on earthquakes  158
   on *oikoumenē*  128
***Westminster Directory for Public Worship***  57
***Westminster Larger Catechism***  49, 56–57
**Whitcomb, John C.**
   on the "Millenial Temple"  99, 116
**Wilson, Dwight**
   on premillenial ambivalence toward Anti-Semitism  86–87
**Witherington, Ben**
   against date-setting  vii
**Wycliffe Bible Translators**
   *engus* (near at hand) and  30
**Wycliffe, John**
   "church" as invisible church, not clergy  169
   translation of *ekklēsia*  167

**Other Prophecy Books by Gary DeMar**

*Last Days Madness: Obsession of the Modern Church*

*Is Jesus Coming Soon?*

*Left Behind: Separating Fact from Fiction*

*The Early Church and the End of the World*

*Why the End of the World is Not in Your Future*

*Myth, Lies, & Half-Truths*

*For information on purchasing these titles, visit:*

**www.AmericanVision.org**